50 Hikes in the Lower Hudson Valley

D0877709

50 *Hikes*

In the Lower Hudson Valley

Hikes and Walks from Westchester County to Albany County

Third Edition

DANIEL CHAZIN

NEW YORK–NEW JERSEY TRAIL CONFERENCE

THE COUNTRYMAN PRESS
Woodstock, Vermont

AN INVITATION TO THE READER
With time, access points may change, and trails,
signs, and landmarks referred to in this book may
be altered. If you find that such changes have
occurred, please let the authors and publisher
know so that corrections can be made in future
editions. Other comments and suggestions are
also welcome. Address correspondence to:
   50 Hikes Editor
   The Countryman Press
   P.O. Box 748
   Woodstock, VT 05091

Copyright © 2014 New York–New Jersey Trail
Conference

Copyright © 2002, 2008 by Stella Green and
H. Neil Zimmerman

All rights reserved. No part of this book may
be reproduced by any electronic or mechanical
means, including information storage and retriev-
al systems, without permission in writing from the
publisher, except for a reviewer, who may quote
brief passages.

Explorer's Guide 50 Hikes in the
Lower Hudson Valley

ISBN 978-1-58157-190-5

Maps by Erin Greb Cartography
© The Countryman Press
Book design by Glenn Suokko
Page composition by PerfecType, Nashville, TN

Published by The Countryman Press,
P.O. Box 748, Woodstock, VT 05091
Distributed by W. W. Norton & Company, Inc.,
500 Fifth Avenue, New York, NY 10110
Printed in the United States of America

10 9 8 7 6 5 4 3 2 1

This book is dedicated to those who work so tirelessly to protect and preserve the Hudson Valley.

Thanks go to the Harriman, Rockefeller, Osborn, Perkins, Ogden, Smiley, and Fahnestock families, who assembled, preserved, and often donated great tracts of land to the public, forming the core of our hiking areas. In recent decades, these public open spaces have been significantly augmented by land purchases and easements coordinated by Scenic Hudson and the Open Space Institute. These two organizations have helped preserve over 100,000 acres in our region. Support from the Lila Acheson and DeWitt Wallace Fund for the Hudson Highlands, established by the founders of *Reader's Digest,* also continues to ensure that our beloved Hudson Valley will long remain a prime destination for those of us who treasure and enjoy the great outdoors.

Thanks go to former New York State governor George E. Pataki. During the three terms he served as governor (1995–2007), he protected 1 million acres of land across New York State, created Sterling Forest and Schunemunk Mountain State Parks, doubled the size of Fahnestock and Minnewaska State Parks, and added more wilderness acres in the Catskill and Adirondack Forest Preserves. These achievements will surely remain a truly notable legacy.

Thanks go to the late William T. Golden, a financier, philanthropist, and science adviser to presidents of the United States, who died in October 2007 at the age of 97. In 1989, Bill purchased Black Rock Forest from Harvard University (which had been given the tract in 1949). The land now belongs to the not-for-profit Black Rock Forest Preserve, which Bill endowed. The preserve leases the forest to the Black Rock Forest Consortium, thus ensuring its continued preservation.

We also wish to thank Barbara McMartin, who spent much of her adult life working tirelessly and effectively to protect New York's outdoor legacy and co-wrote this book's predecessor, *Fifty Hikes in the Hudson Valley.*

50 Hikes in the Lower Hudson Valley at a Glance

HIKE	COUNTY
1. Mianus River Gorge	Westchester
2. Ward Pound Ridge/Leatherman's Cave	Westchester
3. Rockefeller State Park Preserve	Westchester
4. Teatown Lake Reservation	Westchester
5. Old Croton Aqueduct State Historic Park	Westchester
6. Anthony's Nose and the Camp Smith Trail	Westchester
7. Osborn Loop and Sugarloaf Hill	Putnam
8. Breakneck-Undercliff Loop	Putnam
9. Fishkill Ridge Conservation Area	Dutchess
10. East Mountain and Round Hill	Putnam
11. Jordan Pond/Perkins Trail Loop	Putnam
12. Heart of Fahnestock	Putnam
13. Dutchess County Backpack	Dutchess
14. Hook Mountain	Rockland
15. The Tors, High and Low	Rockland
16. Ramapo Torne	Rockland
17. Breakneck Mountain Loop	Rockland
18. Nurian/Appalachian Trail Loop	Orange
19. Rockhouse Loop	Rockland/Orange
20. Iron Mine Walk	Orange
21. Black Mountain	Orange
22. Anthony Wayne Loop	Rockland/Orange
23. Popolopen Torne	Orange
24. Bear Mountain Loop	Rockland/Orange
25. Sterling Ridge to the Fire Tower	Orange

E=Easy
M=Moderate
S=Strenuous
P=Possible, i.e., lean-to available
Y=Yes
Min.=Minimal
O=Optional.

DISTANCE (miles)	DIFFICULTY	RISE (feet)	TIME (hours)	VIEWS	KIDS	CAMP	X-C SKI	FALLS	SHUTTLE	NOTES
4.30	E	500	2.50		Y				Y	Closed in winter, old mine
5.20	E	700	3.00	Y	Y	Y				Historic attraction, nature center
10.40/3.80	E	varies	6:00/2:00		Y	Y				Carriage roads, lake, exhibits
4.80	M	750	3.50	Y	Y	Y				Nature center, wildflower sanctuary
5.50	E	Min.	3.00		Y	Y			Y	Level, bikes okay, museum
4.20	M	1,000	2.50	Y	Y				O	Some steep sections
5.90	M	1,000	3.50	Y	Y					Steep at start, carriage roads
6.40	S	2,000	5.50	Y						Craggy trails, views, history
7.00	S	1,700	5.00	Y						Lightly traveled area
7.30	M	1,400	4.50	Y						Less-used area, views
7.20	M/E	700	4.00							Farm fields, streamside walk, lakes
6.50/3.30	M/E	500	3.00/1.50		Y	Y				History, mining, old railbed, lakes
14.60	S	2,300	3 Days	Y		Y			Y	Three-day backpack
12.00/6/00	M/S	1,200	6.50/4.00	Y						Spectacular ridge
5.50	M	900	3.25	Y	Y					Panoramic views
4.80	M/S	1,100	4.00	Y						Deep woods, rock formations
6.90	M	900	4.00							Deep woods, interesting boulders
7.00	M	900	4.50	Y		P				Massive boulders, open slabs, mines
7.30/5.80	M	1,000/800	4.00/3.00	Y	Y					Historic mine, old cemetery
8.00	M	1,050	5.00	Y						Historic mines, varied terrain
4.50	M	900	3.00	Y		P				Open summit, varied terrain
6.00	M	1,000	4.00	Y		P				Ridge walk
4.50	M/S	1,250	3.50	Y						360° view, deep gorge, museum
4.20	M/S	1,200	3.00	Y						Many stone steps, views
7.40/5.50	M	700/400	4.50/3.00	Y	Y				O	Fire tower (one- or two-car hike alternates)

50 Hikes in the Lower Hudson Valley at a Glance

HIKE	COUNTY
26. Mount Peter to Arden on the Appalachian Trail	Orange
27. Indian Hill Loop	Orange
28. Schunemunk via High Knob	Orange
29. Schunemunk Loop	Orange
30. Mighty Storm King	Orange
31. Black Rock Forest—Northern Loop	Orange
32. Black Rock Forest—Southern Ledges	Orange
33. Shawangunk Ridge	Ulster
34. Verkeerder Kill Falls Loop	Ulster
35. Minnewaska Loop	Ulster
36. The Trapps to Gertrude's Nose	Ulster
37. Undercliff/Overcliff Carriage Roads	Ulster
38. Bonticou Crag	Ulster
39. Black Creek Preserve	Ulster
40. Shaupeneak Ridge	Ulster
41. Stissing Mountain	Dutchess
42. Ashokan High Point	Ulster
43. Table Mountain	Ulster
44. Hunter Mountain	Greene
45. Slide Mountain	Ulster
46. Huckleberry Point	Greene
47. Windham High Peak	Greene
48. South Taconic Trail	Columbia/Dutchess/Ma
49. Vroman's Nose	Schoharie
50. Indian Ladder Trail, John Boyd Thacher State Park	Albany

DISTANCE (miles)	DIFFICULTY	RISE (feet)	TIME (hours)	VIEWS	KIDS	CAMP	X-C SKI	FALLS	SHUTTLE	NOTES
12.30/ 8.70	S	2,050/ 1,450	9.00/ 6.50	Y		P		Y	Y	Cross-ridge walk
4.30	M	900	3.00	Y	Y					Historic furnace, wide stone walls
8.00	S	1,600	6.00	Y						Attractive slabs, open summit
7.80	S	1,700	5.50	Y						Puddingstone conglomerate rock, Megaliths
2.50	M	700	2.50	Y						Open summit, spectacular views
5.50	M	1,000	3.50	Y	Y					Expansive views, scenic ponds
9.00	S	1,300	6.50	Y						Varied terrain, views, historic building
6.20	M	1,350	4.50	Y			Y		Y	Cascade, interesting rock outcrops
9.60	S	1,200	6.50	Y			Y			Major falls, open slabs & summit, views
9.20	S	1,000	6.00	Y			Y			Streamside walk, open slabs, views
10.10	S	1,100	6.00	Y						Open slabs, glacial erratics, views
5.70	E	350	2.50	Y	Y		Y			Carriage roads, visitor center, cliffs
4.00	S	800	3–4	Y						Strenuous rock scramble, fields, views
2.50	E	300	1.50	Y	Y		Y			Hudson River, streamside walk
5.50	M	1,350	4.00	Y	Y		Y			Falls, lake, Hudson River view
1.70/ 4.50	M	920	1.50/ 3.00	Y	Y					Fire tower, views, lakeside walk
9.00	S	2,167	6.00	Y		P	P		Y	Streamside walk, history, views
8.00	S	2,088	5.00	Y		P	P			Typical Catskill scenery, stream, views
8.00	S	2,000	6.00	Y		P	P			Second highest Catskill peak, fire tower
6.80	S	1,800	5.00	Y						Catskill High Point 4,180 feet
4.80	M	1,250	3.00	Y			P			History, blueberry picking, views
6.80	S	1,900	5.00	Y		P				Stands of Norway spruce, views
12.00	S	1,600	8.00	Y		P				Ridge walk, tri-state monument
1.40	M	500	1.50	Y	Y					Spectacular views from cliffs
1.00	E	200	1.00	Y	Y			Y	Y	Spectacular cliffs, falls

E=Easy
M=Moderate
S=Strenuous
P=Possible, i.e., lean-to available
Y=Yes
Min.=Minimal
O=Optional.

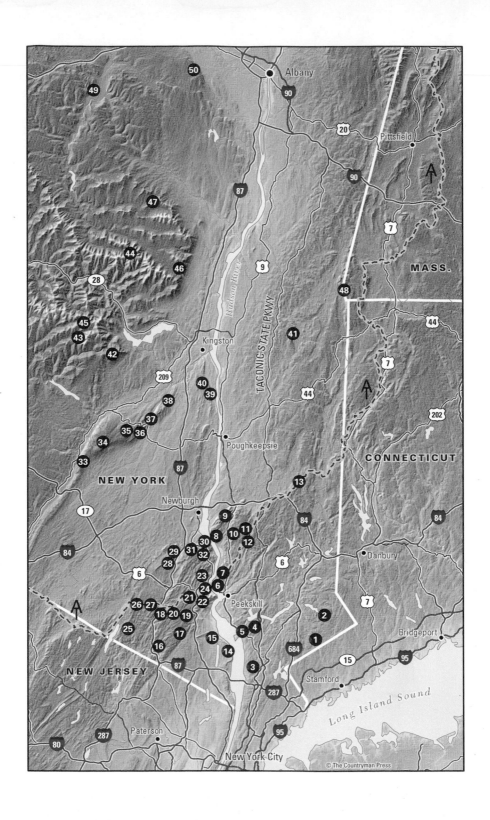

Contents

Acknowledgments

I would like to begin by acknowledging the contributions of my good friends Stella Green and H. Neil Zimmerman, the authors of the first two editions of the book. They selected the hikes to include in the book and scouted out all of the hike routes. Although many of the hike descriptions have been changed for this edition, the basic structure of the book and most of the historical and background material have been retained from the previous editions. We owe Neil and Stella a real debt of gratitude for making this book possible.

In 2012, Neil and Stella graciously donated their rights to this book to the New York–New Jersey Trail Conference (NY–NJTC). For this edition, I have undertaken to revise and update the book on behalf of the NY–NJTC. This afforded me the opportunity, over the past year, to follow some of these beautiful hikes for the first time and to rehike others.

Several other NY–NJTC members assisted me in the effort to revise and update the book. Jane Daniels revised Hike 1 (Mianus River Gorge) and Hike 6 (Anthony's Nose and the Camp Smith Trail) as well as the introductions to the Westchester County and East Hudson Highlands sections.

Jacques Van Engel revised Hike 3 (Rockefeller State Park Preserve), and Mary Dodds revised Hike 4 (Teatown Lake Reservation) and Hike 5 (Old Croton Aqueduct State Historic Park).

I also wish to thank Jane Daniels, Walt Daniels, Leigh Draper, Charlotte Fahn, Jakob Franke, Bob Fuller, Jim Haggett, John Jurasek, John Mack, Ron Rosen, and Jeff Senterman for reviewing the descriptions of various hikes and making helpful suggestions. My friends Dan Crane, Paul Cunniffe, Gershon Freund, Garrett Kroner, Greg Markowiec, Max Miller, Ariel Mozeson, and Keith Shane accompanied me on trips to check out some of the hikes in this book, for which I am grateful. I also wish to acknowledge the contributions of Tom Balcerski, Dan Balogh, Jane Daniels, Walt Daniels, Audrius Juskelis, Keith Shane, and Daniela Wagstaff—each of whom contributed one or more photos for this book.

Although the maps for each hike were prepared by The Countryman Press, the GPS tracks for each map were supplied by Jeremy Apgar, the NY–NJTC's talented cartographer.

Daniel Chazin
NY–NJTC

Introduction

The Hudson River is a 350-mile-long corridor of history and a monument to our natural heritage. For part of its length, the Hudson is an estuary—a place where seawater blends with fresh water, creating one of the most productive ecosystems on earth. This territory is the spawning ground and nursery for many species of fish, and it supports thousands of acres of tidal wetlands.

Southeastern New York State is dominated by the Hudson River, which flows past the wonders of its cities and industries. At the same time, the river touches some of the state's wilder lands, where the hiker can quickly escape the centers of civilization that dot the Hudson's banks. The wilderness at the Hudson's Adirondack headwaters needs no introduction. Some of the wildlands near the Hudson's southern cities are well known, whereas others are almost undiscovered. This guide includes a variety of day hikes that will introduce you to the best of southeastern New York's wildlands not far removed from the Hudson.

Settled by Europeans more than 350 years ago—and much earlier by Native peoples—the Hudson Valley has provided generations of Americans with rich farmland and has been a vital source of strength and inspiration for artistic expression in painting, poetry, and literature. The first visitors to the Hudson were mightily impressed by the fortresslike rocks of the Palisades, the rugged Hudson Highlands, and the mysteries of the distant blue Catskills. It is in these rocky hills and mountains bordering the Hudson that most of the hikes described in this guide take place.

The book leads you to the northern Palisades, the Ramapos, the Highlands, the isolated lump of Schunemunk, the white cliffs of the Shawangunks, and the high points of the Catskills. It reaches east to the Taconics and north to the fortress of the Helderbergs. It takes you to the tops of this series of ranges, which stand as if designed to give the best possible views of the Hudson and Mohawk Valleys.

THE HISTORY OF THE ROCKS AND MOUNTAINS

The drama of the southeastern New York landscape has a second story in the very rocks themselves. From the resistant limestone of the Helderberg Escarpment to the dissected plateau of the Catskills and the crystalline Hudson Highlands that lie beside the younger folded rocks of the Appalachians, you can see the parts of the puzzle that make up the region's geological history.

The Shawangunks are close to the Taconics in age, although their evolution is more related to that of the Catskills. Extensive sands and quartz-rich gravels were deposited in a shallow sea during the Silurian period, about 450 million years ago. Much later, the resulting sandstones and conglomerates were uplifted and differentially eroded.

The Hudson Highlands to the south are a series of granitic and metamorphic rocks. They were intruded and metamorphosed at great depth more than a billion years ago. Later, during the Taconic orogeny, the rocks were folded, faulted, and uplifted to their present form.

HIKING IN SOUTHEASTERN NEW YORK

This guide offers the hiker an excellent range of opportunities. For residents of southern New York State, the special appeal of most of these trails is their proximity to the New York City metropolitan area. The majority of the trailheads lie within two hours of the city. The area offers many more walks than are described in this book, and references to other hiking guides are given in the bibliography. Social hikers can find many walking groups that offer regularly scheduled trips to help them discover other hikes and prepare for outdoor adventures. The New York–New Jersey Trail Conference can put you in touch with many of these groups. Organizations such as the Catskill 3500 Club, the Appalachian Mountain Club, the Sierra Club, and chapters of the Adirondack Mountain Club all offer outing schedules that provide a variety of hikes. Each of these organizations—and most particularly the Trail Conference—also provides mechanisms for the hiker to return something to the land. With programs of trail maintenance, conservation, planning to prevent overuse, and education to promote wise use, these organizations help protect our wildlands.

Some of the hikes described in this book are not heavily used. Others are, but even here, early spring, winter, and late-fall trips will mix solitude with expanded vistas in ways sure to please any wilderness seeker. Many trails that are crowded on weekends are much less used on weekdays.

Almost all the lands traversed by today's trails were once settled and used by farmers, miners, loggers, and romantics. Their presence inevitably is reflected in the lore that surrounds the trails, and we explore that history as well as the natural scene. Although this guide serves as an invitation to the mountain ranges and valleys of the southern part of the state, it cannot even begin to probe the vast history that enlivens each route. For further information, consult the bibliography at the end of this book.

BEFORE YOU START

There is an enormous range of hikes in this guide, from easy strolls to strenuous climbs. The information given about distance, time, and elevation change should help you gauge the difficulty of each hike and your preparedness. Almost all hikes follow clearly marked trails.

Preparedness is key to your enjoyment, and you should be suitably equipped before you start. Knowledge should include understanding the use of map and compass to complement the information in this guide. If you are new to hiking, it is definitely a good idea to join a hiking group and learn from those with experience. The more background you have in the woods, the greater your safety as well as your enjoyment. Even if you're an experienced hiker, it is safer to hike with others. A group of four people is often considered ideal, especially if you are hiking under adverse conditions, since if someone is injured, two of the hikers can go for help while one stays with the injured person.

Carrying a cell phone for use in an emergency is a sensible precaution. However, it is often not possible to get adequate reception in backcountry areas, and nonemergency use is often annoying to others on the trail who appreciate the natural outdoor experience.

THE WEATHER

Whenever possible, wait for a sunny day, as the hiking pleasures are much greater. But even on sunny days you should be prepared for changes and extremes. It can be 20 or more degrees colder on the mountaintops of the Catskills than in the nearby Hudson Valley, and 30 degrees colder than in the city. Storms can and do appear with little warning.

The weather can often be too hot in summer for strenuous hikes. Many people prefer walking in southern New York State in late fall and early spring, but these are the most changeable times. Extremes from heat waves to snowstorms can occur—but the rewards of fewer people and expanded distant vistas in the leafless season make it worthwhile.

Walking in the winter months (and colder weather at any time of the year) is wonderful and brings its own rewards. Vistas are more easily seen when leaves are down from the trees, annoying blackflies and mosquitoes are gone, and fewer walkers are in the woods. However, the winter hiker needs to take additional precautions. Always remember to file a hike plan with a stay-at-home friend, be prepared to shorten your planned hike if necessary, and carry additional clothing and emergency supplies. In extreme cold or in windy conditions, watch your companions for signs of hypothermia and/or frostbite. Hypothermia can creep up unawares because the temperature does not need to be very low. You can become hypothermic in 50-degree weather if you become wet and are poorly prepared. Watch your companions for signs of poor reflex actions: excessive stumbling, the need for frequent rest stops, or a careless attitude toward clothing and equipment. Once uncontrollable shivering has started, it may only be a matter of minutes before the body temperature has cooled beyond the point of recovery. Immediate warmth for the affected person is the only solution.

If the snowfall is more than 8 inches deep, you may need snowshoes; if the trail is icy, crampons or other traction devices. Even if there is little or no snow in the city, places like Harriman Park could still have a foot or more of the white stuff on the ground.

PREPARATIONS

Even with the best of forecasts, you should plan for the unexpected. Possible changes in temperature may require taking extra clothing, and rain gear should always be carried. Experiment with layers of light, waterproof gear. Places to swim are noted on these hikes, so you may wish to take along a bathing suit.

Some of the trails are quite smooth, while others are very rocky. For most of these hikes, a sturdy pair of well-broken-in, over-the-ankle boots is recommended. Lightweight boots with Vibram soles give wonderful traction; if they are lined with Gore-Tex, they will also be waterproof. Wear two pairs of socks, an inner lightweight pair and a heavy outer pair. Wearing two pairs of socks helps to prevent blisters because the socks rub against one another instead of skin. Avoid cotton socks; wool or synthetic socks are much better for your feet and will stay much drier.

Carry a sturdy day pack large enough to hold your lunch, plenty of water, and a few necessities. You may wish to bring along a whistle, a waterproof case with dry matches, a knife, lip balm, and/or a space blanket (to be used in case of emergency).

Carry a map of the trail and a compass, a flashlight in case you are delayed beyond dusk, and a watch. You also need a small first-aid kit containing a few bandages, first-aid cream, and moleskin for the unexpected blister.

You may wish to take along a small bottle of insect repellent. Some hikers prefer one that contains DEET (N-diethylmetatoluamide), while others prefer a natural repellent. Black-flies will be biting in early spring, and mosquitoes later in the season.

Fill a plastic bag with toilet paper, and throw in a few moist towelettes or a liquid sanitizer to use before lunch on those dry mountaintops.

Even if you do not require prescription eyeglasses, you may wish to wear sunglasses as it's all too easy to run into an overhanging branch or twig. If you're helpless without your glasses, carry an extra pair.

You'll enjoy the hikes more if you carry binoculars and watch for birds. A small magnifying glass can add to your discoveries of nature. You may wish to carry a small, lightweight altimeter which provides a good clue to progress on a mountain. Of course, if you have a smartphone, such a device is often included as part of an app.

When you hike, you should always carry more water than you think you will need. Dehydration on summer days is a real possibility, and it can even happen on a sunny, leafless early spring or winter day. These mountains are dry much of the year, and there are few springs. It's becoming increasingly dangerous to trust open water sources because of the spread of *Giardia lamblia,* so don't drink from a stream, no matter how lovely it looks, without first purifying the water.

Remember, hiking should be fun. If you are tired or uncomfortable with the weather, turn back and complete the hike another day. Do not create a situation in which you risk your safety or that of your companions. Be sure someone knows your intended route and expected return time. Always sign in at trailhead registers where available. The unexpected can occur. Weather can change, trail markings can be obscured, you can fall, and you can get lost. But you won't be in real danger if you have anticipated the unexpected.

Timber rattlesnakes are a threatened species. Be cautious when hiking, and on no account interfere with individual snakes or their dens.

Mountain bikers and/or equestrians may be encountered in some areas. User conflicts continue to occur. Hikers often resent the silent approach from behind, the encroachment and possible trail destruction from knobby wheels. Equestrians dislike the speed at which some bikers travel the trails, which often scares horses. Cyclists must always yield the trail, but it is still a good idea for hikers to remain alert. If you wish to avoid bicycles and horses, choose a hike where they are not allowed.

Rifle hunting is allowed in the Catskills, Storm King, most of Sterling Forest, the tristate South Taconics, and some other areas described in this guide. Bow hunting is allowed in other areas, such as Fahnestock State Park. No-hunting zones include Harriman–Bear Mountain, Westchester County, and most of Minnewaska State Park Preserve. Deer season usually runs from late November into mid-December; specific dates are available from the New York State Department of Environmental Conservation. We do not recommend hiking in hunting areas during deer or bear season. However, should you decide to do so, be sure to wear a blaze-orange hat and/or vest.

LYME DISEASE

Lyme disease is caused by a tick-borne spirochete that may produce a rash, flulike symptoms, and pain in joints. If untreated it may cause chronic arthritis and nervous-system disorders. It is difficult to diagnose but treatable if diagnosed early.

The deer ticks that transmit Lyme disease are now found in the areas covered in this guidebook, and hikers should take preventive measures. There is no foolproof way to protect yourself from these very small ticks, so make sure to check yourself frequently; tuck pants into socks and boots; put insect repellent containing DEET on your pants, shoes, and socks (note that DEET does weaken elastics), and wear tightly woven and light-colored clothing (making it easier to see the ticks). Staying on the trail and avoiding tall grass is also a good preventive measure. Above all else, we strongly recommend that you shower and change clothes at the end of your hike, because this is the best time to make a complete body check. Change out of your hiking clothes to prevent any ticks that are present from attaching themselves to you. If you suspect that you may have contracted Lyme disease, contact your physician right away.

BEHAVIOR IN THE WOODS

So, now you are safe in the woods, but what about the woods themselves? The environment that may threaten you can be just as fragile as you are, and you are responsible for protecting it.

Trail erosion is becoming a serious problem in many areas. Please stay on the trail at all times to minimize damage to soils, tree roots, and vegetation. Never cut across switchbacks, and use stepping-stones whenever possible to cross wet areas of the trail. Do not pick wildflowers or dig up woodland plants.

Leave no sign of your presence. Use pit privies if available. If not, bury your personal waste at least 200 feet from water or from a trail or path. When you camp, do not bathe with soap in lakes or streams; when picnicking or camping, carry wash water and dishwater back from the shore. If you're camping, carry a stove for cooking, and do not build fires. In most parks, fires are prohibited except in designated receptacles. Respect the rights of others, and help preserve natural areas for future hikers.

The woolly adelgid has been active in the Hudson Valley for the last few years. Many hemlock trees are dying as a result of its depredations, and large stands of once-magnificent hemlocks have already succumbed in our hiking areas. The loss of hemlock groves with their deep shade changes the character of our woodlands. When deciduous hardwoods replace hemlocks, more light filters through. The forest floor dries out, and the vernal pools used by frogs and salamanders for breeding shrivel. This aphidlike insect was introduced inadvertently to the United States from Asia in 1924. Originally discovered in Oregon, the infestation has now spread to the eastern states. The insect feeds on new twig growth and can be seen at maturity between late winter and early spring at the base of individual hemlock needles when the insects cover themselves with easily seen white, cottony wax that remains attached to the branches even after the insect has left. Individual trees can sometimes be saved by spraying. A natural predator of the insect does exist, and some encouraging results are being seen in areas where the imported ladybird beetle has been introduced.

GEOCACHING

Geocaching is a high-tech treasure hunt using the Global Positioning System (GPS) to find "caches" hidden in the woods. This activity has added a new dimension to the adventure of being outdoors, and it can add an exciting dimension for the children hiking with you.

Geocaching began in the Seattle area in 2002, and it is estimated that caches now exist in every state of the United States and in more than 200 countries, with more than 15,000 active participants and many variations on the main theme. The player chooses a code name, logs on to www.geocaching.com, and enters a zip code to find a list of names and coordinates for close-by caches. Then it's up to the skill of the player to use a portable GPS unit to find the treasure. Most of the pleasure is in the hunt, but once the cache has been found, the cacher signs the log using his nom de plume and, if he wishes, takes something from the cache—replacing it with an equal or better quality item. The "find" is subsequently registered on the cache page, which keeps track of the number of "finds." New York State requires that caches be registered and a permit number assigned.

Letterboxing (www.letterboxing.com) is a similar pastime, but instead of using a GPS unit to obtain coordinates, this game uses instructions and puzzles to locate the treasure, and a rubber stamp and pad is needed to validate the find.

Other sites such as navicache.com are also available.

NOTES FOR USING THIS GUIDE

The hike description tells you how to reach the trailhead itself, but getting to the nearby highway or town is up to you. Consulting a road map will help (see the bibliography).

Summaries at the beginning of each hike list hiking distance, vertical rise, time on the trail, and United States Geological Survey (USGS) topographic map (or maps) and/or the NY–NJTC trail map for the area the hike traverses. In some cases, other maps are also listed. Unless otherwise noted, distances are for the round-trip or circuit. Where measured mileage information has not been available, distances have been estimated and are usually correct to within 10 percent.

Vertical rise refers to the total change in cumulative elevation for the hike. Where the terrain is relatively level, no numerical figure has been used. Hiking times are estimated. The times provided are designed to allow a reasonably experienced hiker to follow the route at a moderate pace, with a reasonable amount of time allowed for breaks. Faster hikers may be able to cover the route in less time, while those who are not in the best of shape or who wish to take more frequent or longer breaks will require more time to complete the hike.

All of the hikes in this book are accompanied by a map showing the route of the hike. If you don't know how to read a map, you should learn to do so before hiking. Spend time, if you can, walking with someone who does know how to read a map. The same instructions are appropriate for the use of a compass. You may not need either on the easiest of this guide's trails, but walking these routes with map and compass will allow you to become comfortable with their use so that you can extend your hikes beyond the ones described or to more difficult hikes.

Many trails are blazed with paint according to the designated trail color, either on trees adjacent to the trail or on rock underfoot, but in some locations, plastic or metal disks are nailed to trees. Two blazes, one above the other, indicate a turn in the trail, the direction of the turn being indicated by the offset of the upper blaze. Standing at one blaze, the hiker can normally expect to see the next one ahead, though where the footway is clear—such as on a woods road— blazes may be less frequent. Three blazes indicate either the beginning or the end of a trail. Some trails border on or cross private property, so please honor any NO TRESPASSING or KEEP OUT signs, leave any gates you may find along the route of your hike in the same condition as you found them, and generally be respectful of the landowner.

Keep in mind those two familiar mottos: *Take only photographs, leave only footprints* and *Carry in, carry out.* It's a good idea to bring along a small plastic bag to enable you to take out litter left by others.

LONG-DISTANCE TRAILS

Three long-distance trails traverse the Hudson Valley.

The Appalachian Trail (AT), a National Scenic Trail, passes through on its 2,185-mile journey from Georgia to Maine. Through-hikers are those completing the AT's entire length in one trip, most taking about six months on the trail and adopting trail names for the journey. Other hikers tackle the project by hiking separate sections, one or more at a time, and still others walk the trail as day hikers. The first section of the AT from the Bear Mountain Bridge to the Ramapo River south of Arden in Bear Mountain–Harriman State Parks was built by volunteers of the NY–NJTC in 1922–23. Marked with white rectangles, the AT is administered by the Appalachian Trail Conservancy, headquartered in Harpers Ferry, West Virginia. For more information, go to www.appalachiantrail.org.

The Long Path, marked with aqua blazes, begins its northward journey at the George Washington Bridge. For many years, the trail's northern terminus was at Windham in the Catskills, but the trail has now been extended as far north as the Mohawk Valley, and there are plans to extend the trail into the Adirondacks. Administered by the NY–NJTC, the Long Path is currently over 350 miles long. The Shawangunk Ridge Trail, which extends from High Point State Park in New Jersey to the northern Shawangunks, is part of the Long Path system.

Joining the other two traditional long-distance trails is the Highlands Trail, blazed with diamond-shaped teal-colored markers.

This trail, about 150 miles long, links the Delaware and Hudson Rivers. An extension east of the Hudson River to Connecticut is being contemplated. The not-yet-complete route uses established trails, with some new construction where necessary and connections made by short sections of paved road. The system links over 26 county, state, and federal parks, forests, and open spaces and is the result of cooperation among the NY–NJTC, conservation organizations, state and local governments, and local businesses.

These three trails are maintained by volunteers, as are most other trails described in this book.

OTHER HELPFUL INFORMATION

New York–New Jersey Trail Conference
    (NY–NJTC)
156 Ramapo Valley Road
Mahwah, NJ 07430
201-512-9348
www.nynjtc.org
e-mail: info@nynjtc.org

The NY–NJTC coordinates the construction and maintenance of about 2,000 miles of hiking trails, including the Appalachian Trail in New York and New Jersey, and the Long Path, which connects the metropolitan area with the Catskills and beyond. The organization publishes hiking guidebooks and maps, which may be purchased directly from the conference or from outdoors stores, with significant discounts for members on purchases made directly from the conference (see the bibliography).

About 100 hiking clubs and conservation organizations belong to the conference, along with 10,000 individual members. Applications for membership are invited, and the annual fee includes, among other things, a subscription to the *Trail Walker*. This quarterly publication features timely articles, book reviews, and trail updates.

For a list of local hiking clubs, a complete list of publications, and to order books and maps, call them or visit their website, www.nynjtc.org.

FOR THE CATSKILLS:

Department of Environmental Conservation Region 3 Headquarters
21 South Putt Corners Road
New Paltz, NY 12561-1696
845-256-3000
www.dec.ny.gov

Hiker-generated condition reports for trails in the Catskills can often be found at: http://www.vftt.org/forums/forumdisplay.php?14-New-York

Department of Environmental Conservation
Region 4—Sub Office
65561 NY 10, Suite 1
Stamford, NY 12167
607-652-7365
www.dec.ny.gov

FOR THE SHAWANGUNKS:

Mohonk Preserve Visitors Center
3197 US 44/NY 55
Gardiner, NY 12525
845-255-0919
www.mohonkpreserve.org
(A contact e-mail form is available at this site.)

The Mohonk Preserve manages this unique natural resource and supervises access to preserve lands. An admission fee is required from nonmembers.

Mohonk Mountain House
1000 Mountain Rest Road
New Paltz, NY 12561
855-883-3798
www.mohonk.com

Admission fee required except for overnight guests and Mohonk Preserve members.

OTHER:

Scenic Hudson, Inc.
One Civic Center Plaza, #200
Poughkeepsie, NY 12601
845-473-4440
e-mail: info@scenichudson.org
www.scenichudson.org

Founded in 1963, Scenic Hudson is a nonprofit environmental organization and separately incorporated land trust. They are "dedicated to protecting and enhancing the scenic, natural, historic, agricultural and recreational treasures of the majestic 315-mile-long Hudson River and its valley."

Open Space Institute
1350 Broadway, #201
New York, NY 10018
212-290-8200
www.osiny.org

Responsible for preserving many thousands of acres in the Hudson Valley.

Sam's Point Preserve
400 Sam's Point Road
Cragsmoor, NY 12420
845-647-7989

The Nature Conservancy
195 New Karner Road, #200
Albany, NY 12205
518-690-7850
www.nature.org/ourinitiatives/regions
/northamerica/unitedstates/newyork
/index.htm

Founded in 1951, The Nature Conservancy is the world's largest private, international conservation group. The organization manages and protects natural areas, and some hikes in this guide are in conservancy preserves. Threats to remaining wild places are escalating, and The Nature Conservancy is working in New York to counter and preempt these threats.

New York State Office of Parks, Recreation, and Historic Preservation
625 Broadway
Albany, NY 12207
518-474-0456
www.nysparks.com/parks

The New York State OPRHP welcomes 65 million visitors a year to its parks, historic sites, and recreation areas from Jones Beach to Niagara Falls. Regional offices, or commissions, administer the specific sites.

Taconic State Park Commission
9 Old Post Road
Staatsburg, NY 12580
845-889-4100

The Taconic State Park Commission manages the lands of the OPRHP on the east side of the Hudson. It is responsible for state parks and historic sites there, including Hudson Highlands, Taconic, and Fahnestock State Parks.

Palisades Interstate Park Commission
3007 Seven Lakes Drive
Bear Mountain, NY 10911-0427
845-786-2701

The Palisades Interstate Park Commission manages the lands of the OPRHP on the west side of the Hudson. It is responsible for state parks and historic sites there, including Nyack Beach, Hook Mountain, Rockland Lake, High Tor, Harriman, Bear Mountain, Sterling Forest, Schunemunk Mountain, Storm King, and Minnewaska State Park.

Free USGS topo maps are available online: store.usgs.gov.

I. Westchester County

Introducing Westchester

Extending some 35 miles from the New York City border north to the Hudson Highlands, Westchester is a mix of suburbs, horse farms, light industry, malls, commuting routes, corporate headquarters, and cities. Although developed, it has plenty of hiking opportunities in its wealth of natural and historic areas. Hikes are available throughout the county, ranging from short walks in small parks to longer hikes in larger parks—some of which even offer the opportunity to camp overnight. The county's park system is extensive, and there are many private preserves, municipal parks and a few state parks to round out the offerings.

In 1609, explorer Henry Hudson, sailing under the English flag, thought he had found a route to China. As he sailed up the river that would bear his name, he passed Native American villages. A hundred years later, the Native American peoples had all but disappeared, but their influence is still reflected in the names of towns, villages, rivers, and roads: Katonah was "principal hill"; Ossining, "place of stone"; Chappaqua, "rustling land"; and Kisco "muddy place."

The railroads arrived in the 1840s, and land began to be developed—some areas as estates and country retreats and others as towns and farms. At the same time, New York City began purchasing land to construct a reservoir system to provide drinking water for its residents. Later, in the early 20th century, Westchester County began acquiring land for parks. The concept of land preservation continues in the 21st century with public-private partnerships expanding public access to open space.

Hiking opportunities in Westchester County are plentiful, especially considering that the area is so close to New York City. The trails are generally not as strenuous as those located further north in the Hudson Highlands. The rolling hills feature streams, ponds, wetlands, stone walls, and rock outcrops; many woods roads built to provide access to private lands are now delightful hiking routes. Westchester County also offers a number of linear trails, some of which follow abandoned railroad rights-of-way. Others use the route of a historic aqueduct or follow parkways built for automobiles. For more information about county parks in Westchester County, go to www.parks.west chestergov.com. Those wishing to explore additional hiking opportunities in Westchester should consult *Walkable Westchester,* a comprehensive guide to over 200 parks and 600 miles of trails, published by the New York–New Jersey Trail Conference.

1

Mianus River Gorge

Total distance: 4.3 miles

Walking time: 2.5 hours

Vertical rise: 500 feet

Maps: USGS 7.5' Pound Ridge; Mianus River Gorge Preserve trail map

Trailhead GPS Coordinates: N 41° 11' 11" W 73° 37' 18"

Protection of this stretch of the Mianus River was The Nature Conservancy's first project when, in 1953, the infant organization became involved with a group of local citizens to preserve this unique area. In 1964, the Mianus River Gorge was registered as a National Natural Landmark and became the first area to be granted this designation. This preserve is now managed by an independent nonprofit organization, the Mianus River Gorge Preserve, Inc.

The Mianus River begins in Greenwich, Connecticut, and flows north through New York before reversing its direction and turning south through the gorge and on into Long Island Sound. The river is named for Chief (or Sachem) Mayano of the Wappinger tribe, whose name in the Wappinger language means "he who gathers together" and who was killed near the gorge in 1664. In 1600 the seven Wappinger tribes probably numbered about eight thousand people in thirty villages, but epidemics of smallpox and malaria and the Wappinger War of 1643–45 seriously depleted their numbers. Only a few hundred remained in the lower Hudson after 1700, and almost all were gone by 1758.

Three trails traverse the Mianus River Gorge: the Brink of Gorge Trail (red), the Fringe of Forest Trail (blue), and the Bank of River Trail (green). This hike uses the red trail for the outgoing trip, with a possible side trip on the green trail, and returns on the blue trail. The trails are well marked so that navigation is easy; the footway is mostly wide and gentle on the feet, passing quiet waterways through tranquil woods. Side trips

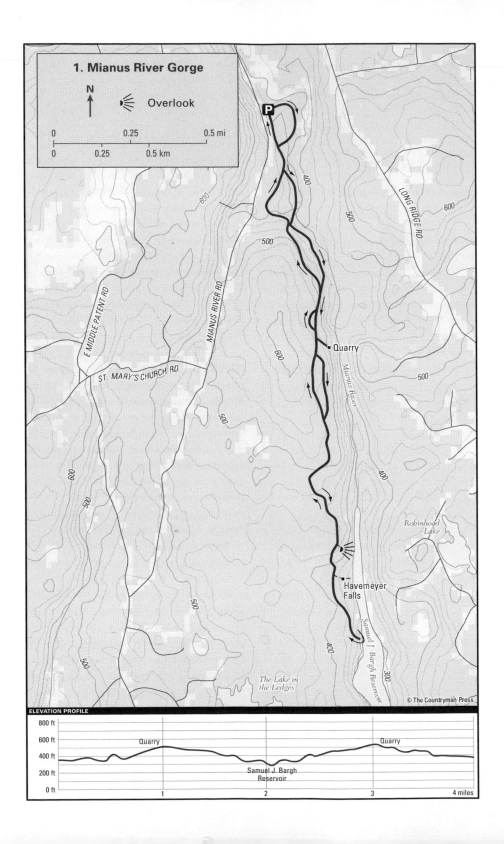

1. Mianus River Gorge

N

⋘ Overlook

| 0 | 0.25 | 0.5 mi |
| 0 | 0.25 | 0.5 km |

P

600

400

500

LONG RIDGE RD

600

E MIDDLE PATENT RD

MIANUS RIVER RD

500

500

ST. MARY'S CHURCH RD

600

Quarry

Mianus River

500

600

400

500

Robinhood
Lake

500

600

⋘

Havemeyer
Falls

500

Samuel J. Bargh Reservoir

400

300

The Lake in
the Ledges

400

© The Countryman Press

ELEVATION PROFILE

800 ft			
600 ft	Quarry		Quarry
400 ft			
200 ft		Samuel J. Bargh	
		Reservoir	
0 ft			
	1	2	3	4 miles

take the walker to an old mica mine, an over-look, a cascade, and a hemlock grove—with some trees estimated to be over 325 years old. The hardwood trees are immensely tall and straight, and the aura of peacefulness is striking throughout the gorge. Along the way, walls divide the once-farmed uplands from the steep slopes of the gorge, which are largely old-growth forest. The climbs are easy and short as the trail meanders along.

No bicycles are allowed; no dogs are allowed, even if leashed; and picnicking is permitted only in the map shelter area. Although there is no entry fee, the preserve relies on donations to continue its work, so a contribution box is provided. The preserve is open daily between April 1 and November 30 from 8:30 am to 5:00 pm, and we suggest you call 914-234-3455 beforehand to confirm that the preserve is open. Most damage occurs underfoot during freeze/thaw and mud periods, so all trails are closed for a "winter rest." For more information, go to www.mianus.org.

HOW TO GET THERE

The preserve is located in Bedford, New York. From Exit 4 on I-684, drive east on NY 172 for 1.5 miles before turning left onto NY 22 north. NY 172 and NY 22 run together for 1 mile into Bedford, where the triangular village green is reached and NY 22 leaves to the left. Bear right to stay on NY 172 (Pound Ridge Road) toward Pound Ridge and Stamford. In about 1 mile, you come to a traffic light (and gas station), where you turn right (south) onto NY 104 (Long Ridge Road). Turn right again onto Millers Mill Road (first right) after another 0.5 mile. Proceed 0.1 mile over the bridge, and immediately turn left onto Mianus Road. The entrance to the preserve is on the left, 0.6 mile farther on.

Alternatively, from Connecticut's Merritt Parkway, Exit 34, take CT 104 (Long Ridge Road) into New York State, where it becomes NY 104 for 7.7 miles. Turn left onto Millers Mill Road, and thence to the preserve on the left.

THE TRAIL

When you arrive, take time to read the material at the kiosk and pick up a trail map. Start the hike by walking to the left from the kiosk. The blazes you will follow have a red-painted circle on a light-colored wooden arrow (the blue blazes for the return trip are similar). Although the outgoing route is on the red trail, it is co-aligned with the blue trail in several locations. The start of the trail is handicapped accessible, with a bench honoring Lucy Adams, a local educator and preservationist. The trail follows the route of the Mianus River for a short distance, then turns away and dips down to the Edith Faile Footbridge, named for a conservationist. The bridge is a good example of trail work that blends into the environment. Soon, you'll reach the start of the green trail, which offers a closer look at the Mianus River. To follow this trail, turn left and continue along the river until the trail climbs a set of steps and ends at a location on the red trail named "Monte Gloria" to honor the memory of Gloria Hollister Anable, one of the five conservationists who founded the preserve in 1953.

The red trail continues ahead to the Hemlock Cathedral. Most of the hemlocks surrounding the Mianus Gorge Preserve have been infected and killed by the woolly adelgid. In an attempt to halt this destruction within the preserve in general and this impressive stand in particular, an imported ladybird beetle from Japan was released in May 2000. Most of the hemlocks are still healthy and resisting the adelgid to some degree, though a microburst has felled some trees. The preserve administration is now conducting a study to determine the

Havemeyer Falls

JANE DANIELS

assemblage of predators found in the hemlock canopy. Research will include an inventory of the introduced beetle and its overall effect. Hemlocks thrive in the cool, moist microclimate of the gorge. When hemlocks are lost, the whole environment changes. These deep-shade trees are replaced by deciduous trees, which offer considerably less shade. As a result, the moist areas, which are critical to the breeding of salamanders and frogs, dry up.

About 45 minutes into the hike, you'll arrive at the junction with the short side trail to the Hobby Hill Quarry. This one-way trail circles the quarry, which contains boulders gleaming with mica. Mica, quartz, and feldspar were mined here during the 18th century. Please honor the preserve's request not to take away any samples.

Continue ahead on the red trail which, in another mile, skirts a vernal pool and reaches a junction with a short side trail to a viewpoint over the Samuel J. Bargh Reservoir, which supplies water to several localities, including Greenwich. Bargh was the president of the Connecticut American Water Company when the reservoir and dam were constructed.

The red trail now descends to the shore of the reservoir. Just before the red trail ends, a short side trail leads to Havemeyer Falls, which is impressive after a heavy rain. Return to the co-aligned red and blue trails, and retrace your footsteps. When the trails split, in each case follow the blue blazes. At the second split with the red trail, the blue trail goes through the James and Alice de Peyster Todd Woodlands, an area donated by preserve founders.

After the third split with the red trail, the blue trail passes through fields, some of which were grazed by livestock as recently as the 1920s. Many old stone walls remain as reminders of the land's agricultural past. Constructing walls out of native stone was a practical way of using the many stones which needed to be removed in order to plant crops.

After joining and diverging from the red trail twice more, the blue trail ends at the parking area of the preserve, where the hike began.

2

Ward Pound Ridge/ Leatherman's Cave

Total distance: 5.2 miles

Walking time: 3 hours

Vertical rise: 700 feet

Maps: USGS 7.5' Pound Ridge; Westchester Parks Ward Pound Ridge Reservation trail map

Trailhead GPS Coordinates: N 41° 14' 52" W 73° 35' 40"

Covering over 4,300 acres (about 6 square miles), Ward Pound Ridge Reservation is the largest park in Westchester County. The basic tract was assembled and acquired in 1925–1926 and is named for the nearby town of Pound Ridge. Originally the Indians had a "pound" in the area where they kept live game until needed for food. The "Ward" was added later to honor William Lukens Ward, Westchester's Republican county leader from 1896 to 1933, who was instrumental in establishing the county's park system. In addition to the trails, picnic areas, and camping areas, the park is home to the Trailside Museum (914-864-7322). The park office can be reached at 914-864-7317.

HOW TO GET THERE

To get to the park, take Exit 6 off I-684 (at the merge between I-684 and the northern end of the Saw Mill River Parkway). Proceed east on NY 35 for 3.6 miles to NY 121, and turn right onto NY 121. The park entrance is almost immediately on your left. After passing the tollbooth (a per-car fee is charged on weekends, daily in the summer), turn right onto the first paved road, Michigan Road. Pass the side road to a camping area, and park at the end of the road near a circular turnaround.

THE TRAIL

Head right, across a field, to a cable gate flanked by two large white posts (trail maps are usually available at the kiosk). Almost immediately you'll reach a fork in the trail, marked with a brown number as junction

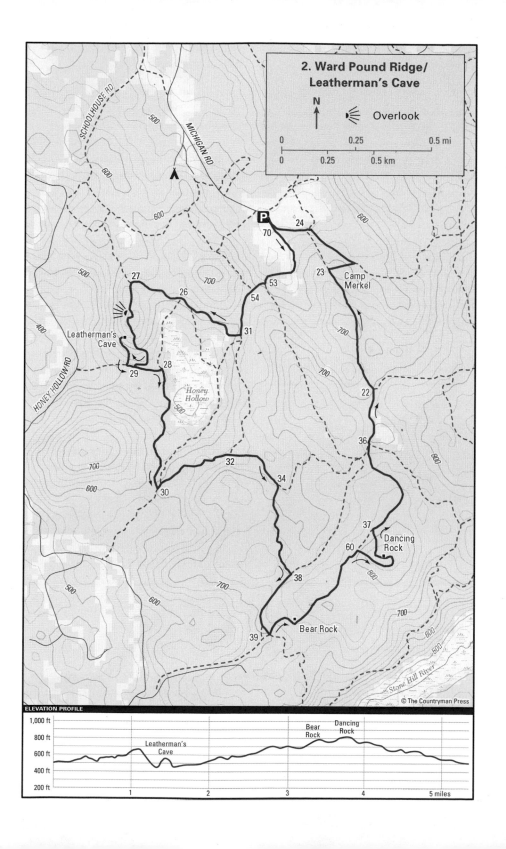

2. Ward Pound Ridge/ Leatherman's Cave

N

Overlook

0   0.25   0.5 mi

0   0.25   0.5 km

SCHOOLHOUSE RD

MICHIGAN RD

500

600

600

600

500

700

P

70

24

23

Camp Merkel

600

53

54

27

26

31

700

Leatherman's Cave

28

29

Honey Hollow

500

700

22

700

700

36

800

32

34

30

600

700

37

60

Dancing Rock

500

600

700

38

39

Bear Rock

800

700

600

500

HONEY HOLLOW RD

400

500

Stone Hill River

© The Countryman Press

ELEVATION PROFILE

1,000 ft
800 ft
600 ft
400 ft
200 ft

Leatherman's Cave

Bear Rock

Dancing Rock

1   2   3   4   5 miles

#70. (Most junctions in the park are marked with brown numbers; these numbers are referenced in this description and on the park map.) Bear right, following the metal trail markers with red and green arrows. This first section of trail is higher than the surrounding ground. Constructed by the Civilian Conservation Corps (CCC) in the 1930s, the path goes through a wetland. Most of the park was heavily farmed, and evidence of that bygone era abounds in the many stone walls and foundations.

In about five minutes, you'll reach junction #53, with a green-blazed trail continuing straight ahead. Bear right, staying with the trail marked by red and green metal blazes. Continue ahead past junction #54, and you'll soon come to junction #31. Here you should turn right onto the LL-on-white-blazed Leatherman's Loop Trail. Another five minutes brings you to junction #26. Continue straight ahead, but turn left at the following T-junction (#27) and continue to follow the LL blazes, which proceed along a narrow, winding footpath to the top of a hill, passing some interesting rock outcrops along the way. At the top, you'll come to a fine viewpoint from rock ledges just to the right of the trail. At an elevation of 665 feet, the viewpoint has an expansive western view across to the Cross River Reservoir, built in the early 1900s. On a clear day, you can see the Hudson Highlands. You are now about 30 minutes into the hike.

After your "view break," continue following the LL blazes as the trail descends,

Leatherman's Cave

DANIEL CHAZIN

turns right near a stone wall, and passes a massive rock outcrop and overhang. Ward Pound Ridge has many truly magnificent rock outcroppings, and this specimen is one of the best.

Soon—less than 10 minutes from the view—junction #29 is reached. Turn around, go back a few feet the way you came, and you'll see two small wooden signs. One points left for the short one-minute walk up to Leatherman's Cave. The cave itself is not very large—more of a rock shelter than a true cave. It's the story that makes it interesting.

Leatherman's Cave is named after a mysterious homeless man who wandered through the area from 1883 to 1889. He traveled a 365-mile circuit, stopping at the same 34 campsites on a regular schedule. His loop went from Danbury (Connecticut) to Waterbury, then to Saybrook and along the Connecticut River. Then he headed toward Long Island Sound, New Canaan, Wilton, White Plains, and back to here. He was clad in 60-pound clothes made of old leather, and mostly communicated using crude signs. People often left food for this gentle soul or invited him in for a meal. Another one of his camps is preserved on the Mattatuck Trail near County Route 6 in Connecticut.

According to one account, the Leatherman was born in Lyon, France, the son of a wealthy wool merchant—but because of economic ruin or an unhappy love affair, he left for America and soon began his treks. His photograph, a printed handout, and other information about him are available at the museum.

After your visit to the cave, return to junction #29 and turn left, following the ll blazes for two minutes to junction #28. Here, the Leatherman's Loop Trail turns left, but you should bear right and continue on

a white-blazed woods road through Honey Hollow (so named because a farmer kept bees here in the 1800s).

In another 10 minutes, you'll reach a Y-junction. Bear left, and you'll immediately reach junction #30 and the red and green trails. Take the right fork (level, not down). Soon, the trail begins to climb, but the route is wide with good footing, meandering through mature hardwoods rich with bird life and signs of settlers long since gone.

Keep your eyes open for junction signs. You'll pass junctions #32 and #34, but you're looking for junction #38, which will take 15 to 20 minutes to reach. Here you leave the green and red trails and make a sharp right turn onto a woods road with white blazes.

At the next fork, the trail bears left and crosses under a power line to reach junction #39. Turn left onto the Rocks Trail (marked with RT-on-white blazes) and climb to the Bear Rock Petroglyph (on the left side of the trail). Bear Rock is noted for its perhaps historic carving that looks like a bear's head, carved on a boulder identified as Pound Ridge leuco-granite. According to the July 1972 Bulletin of the New York State Archeological Association, 12 designs are distinguishable, measuring up to 0.5-inch deep. The investigator made out the contour of a bear, a twin deer-bear profile, and a wild turkey—with the rest being unclear. However, Jim Swager, who wrote the book Petroglyphs in America, called it "questionable" and was not willing to stake his reputation on this positively being a petroglyph.

Continue ahead on the trail. Note the vegetation change at the top of this ridge. It's a little higher, and plants must exist on direct rain with no runoff from the surrounding land. The trail recrosses the power line and, in another five minutes, comes to junction #60. Here you should turn right and follow

Along a woods road in Ward Pound Ridge

DANIEL CHAZIN

a white-blazed side trail that leads up to Dancing Rock—a large flat rock surface that was used for dancing by local farmers after the harvest. Imagine it devoid of trees and packed with rejoicing farmers. Note some of the stone constructions nearby: platforms and fire rings, probably over a hundred years old. Notice, too, the moss along the access trail—some of the most brilliant green vegetation you'll ever see.

Proceed ahead along the white-blazed side trail, which loops around and descends to end at the Rocks Trail (junction #37). Turn right and continue along the Rocks Trail, which now descends steadily. In about 10 minutes, you'll reach the next (unnumbered) junction, where the red trail joins from the left. Just ahead, you'll come to junction #36.

Continue straight ahead on the Rocks Trail (do not turn right). After crossing a stream, you'll climb to junction #22. Here, the Rocks Trail turns right, but you should turn left and continue on the yellow trail, which heads downhill.

In another 10 minutes, you'll reach junction #23, the former site of the park's main CCC camp. Known as Camp Merkel, it was in operation from 1933 to 1941, when America's entry into World War II ended the CCC program. Turn right at this junction onto an unmarked trail, passing the steps and foundations that are all the remains of CCC camp "CO210 Camp SP Katona." The CCC camp may be gone, but the work remains for us to enjoy: trails, bridges, shelters, and even the Trailside Museum.

Just past the CCC camp, you'll reach a T-junction. Turn left onto the red and yellow trails, soon passing through an open field and curving to the left. Just ahead, you'll come to the cable gate and parking lot where the hike began.

OPTIONS

To complete the day, consider a trip to the nearby John Jay Homestead State Historic Site, home of the first chief justice of the United States. Follow NY 35 west (toward I-684) for about 3.5 miles, then turn left (south) onto NY 22 for 1.6 miles to the entrance on the left (400 Jay Street, Katonah, NY 10536). There is no admission charge for the grounds and a self-guided walk, but the one-hour house tour (seasonal) has a modest fee (914-232-5651; www.johnjay homestead.org).

3

Rockefeller State Park Preserve

Total distance: 10.4 miles (3.8-mile alternate)

Walking time: 6 hours (2-hour alternate)

Vertical rise: 900 feet

Maps: USGS 7.5' White Plains; Rockefeller State Park Preserve brochure map

Trailhead GPS Coordinates: N 41° 06' 42" W 73° 50' 14"

Rockefeller State Park Preserve was created in 1983 when the Rockefeller family deeded 715 acres to New York along with an endowment fund for its upkeep. Subsequent donations have increased the preserve's size to over 1,400 acres. A beautiful visitors center, opened in 1994, contains exhibits on the historical and natural features of the park. A pleasant place for a walk or a stroll, the preserve is open for public use during daylight hours. The office phone is 914-762-0209.

Attracted by the commanding views of the Hudson Valley, oil magnate and philanthropist John D. Rockefeller Sr. began buying land in the Pocantico Hills area in 1893. His estate would eventually reach 4,000 acres. A 40-room Georgian mansion, "Kykuit" (Dutch for "lookout"), was built as the family home. During the 1900s, the Rockefellers restored much of the land to a natural state. An earthen dam created Swan Lake in 1932, and to this day some family land is still used for growing corn and breeding cattle.

The Rockefellers built 55 miles of carriage roads during the 1920s and 1930s. Designed to highlight the beauty of the area, they have been traditionally (but informally) open for public use. The carriageways, as they are now often called, are used by walkers and equestrians alike, though bicycles are not allowed. Much of the hike is in the park proper, where all the junctions are well marked with concrete or fiberglass posts. Triangular arrows on the posts indicate the shortest route back to the parking area. However, some portions of the hike use

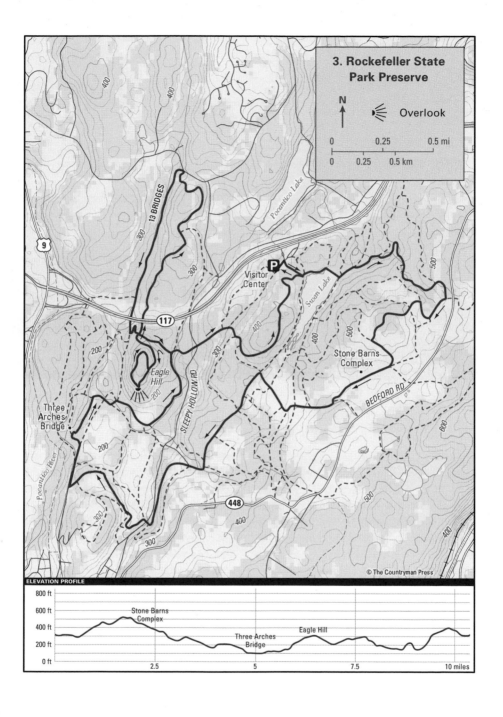

3. Rockefeller State Park Preserve

N

Overlook

| 0 | 0.25 | 0.5 mi |
| 0 | 0.25 | 0.5 km |

Pocantico Lake

13 BRIDGES

400

400

300

300

300

9

117

500

Swan Lake

Visitor Center

P

400

400

500

Stone Barns Complex

Eagle Hill

200

200

SLEEPY HOLLOW RD

BEDFORD RD

Three Arches Bridge

200

600

Pocantico River

300

448

400

500

300

400

300

© The Countryman Press

ELEVATION PROFILE

| 800 ft |
| 600 ft |
| 400 ft |
| 200 ft |
| 0 ft |

Stone Barns Complex

Three Arches Bridge

Eagle Hill

2.5 5 7.5 10 miles

Along a carriage road in Rockefeller State Park Preserve   AUDRIUS JUSKELIS

carriageways on the adjacent property of the Greenrock Corporation. There are no signs at the intersections in Greenrock, and we recommend that you bring along a copy of the map available online at www.friendsrock .org. As the carriageways are smooth and have been well maintained, any good walking shoe or sneaker will suffice.

HOW TO GET THERE

To get to the park, take the New York State Thruway (I-87) to Exit 9 (at the eastern end of the Tappan Zee Bridge). Proceed north on US 9 through Tarrytown and Sleepy Hollow for 3 miles to a junction with NY 117. Turn right onto NY 117 for 1.4 miles to the park entrance. In season, there is a parking fee.

THE TRAIL

The hike begins at the tollbooth. From the parking lot, cross the road, pass the visitors center, and continue to Swan Lake. Here, you should turn left onto the Brothers Path, which runs along the northern shore of Swan Lake. Keep bearing right until you cross the earthen dam and the outlet of the lake on stepping-stones. Turn left here onto the Old Railroad Bed. You are now walking on the right-of-way of the former Putnam Division of the New York Central Railroad, built in 1881. When John D. Rockefeller Jr. wanted to expand his estate around 1930, he financed the cost of relocating the line to bypass his estate. The former rail line is now a delightful hiking trail.

Continue ahead on the Old Railroad Bed for only about 500 feet and turn right onto the Brook Trail. You'll follow this trail uphill for the next 0.8 mile, paralleling a cascading brook and crossing it several times. After passing a junction with David's Loop on the left, you'll come to a breached dam. The Brook Trail briefly curves away from the brook but soon returns to it. Then, to the right, a side trail crosses two bridges and soon rejoins the main trail. After crossing another bridge, you'll see a drained cistern on the left, with a large solitary rock that was never removed. The Brook Trail now passes the other end of David's Loop on the left and heads slightly downhill to reach a T-junction with the Ridge Trail. You have now hiked for 1.4 miles.

Turn right onto the Ridge Trail and enter an area of farmland managed by Greenrock Corporation. Turn left at the second junction you reach, and continue heading uphill, soon paralleling an old stone wall on the left. When you reach a junction with a red farmhouse on the right, turn left onto a gravel road with stone walls on both sides. Soon, the trail levels off, and the Hudson River comes into view. This is one of the two spots on this hike from which the Hudson River can be seen.

The trail now heads downhill, curves to the right, and reaches a T-junction with a paved road. Here you turn right. The impressive mansion in front of you is known as the Stone Barns. It features a cafeteria with an outside patio, where drinks and snacks are available.

From the Stone Barns, proceed along the paved road downhill toward the greenhouses. Opposite the small parking area for the greenhouses (on the left side of the road), proceed ahead on the carriageway, with a vertical metal pole on each side and a caution sign on the right. In another 500 feet, turn right at a T-junction and soon begin to descend. Continue straight ahead when a side trail leaves to the right and another trail crosses. Just beyond, the carriageway bends sharply to the left; immediately thereafter, bear right onto another carriageway with an open concrete storage area on the left. Continue ahead and proceed downhill to a junction at the bottom of the valley with the Farm Meadow Trail. You have now hiked for 3.1 miles.

If you've had enough hiking for the day, turn right onto the Farm Meadow Trail, continue to Swan Lake, and proceed ahead with the lake on your right. At the end of the lake, turn left to return to the visitors center parking lot. If you choose this option, your hike will have been about 3.8 miles long.

To continue along the route of the hike, turn left onto the Farm Meadow Trail, which soon leaves park property and continues through lands managed by the Greenrock Corporation. Several side trails leave to the left and to the right, but you should continue straight ahead to the crest of a hill, with a red barn on your right. The trail now descends, crosses a brook, and reaches a T-junction with another carriageway (a wire fence is just beyond). Turn right and follow the carriageway downhill, curving gently to the left. Soon, you'll begin to parallel the paved Sleepy Hollow Road. At the next intersection, turn right and cross beneath the paved road on a stone-arch underpass. You've now walked 4.3 miles.

If you wish to cut the hike short at this point, turn right on the other side of the underpass and, in 350 feet, bear right at the fork. You are now walking parallel to a tiny but picturesque brook. Continue to parallel the brook, crossing it several times, until the brook ends at the Pocantico River. Cross the river and turn right onto the Pocantico River Trail. Continue to follow the Pocantico River Trail, which parallels the river, until you reach a pedestrian footbridge over the river. Turn right and continue ahead on the Old Sleepy Hollow Road Trail, which soon crosses the paved Sleepy Hollow Road, and continue ahead to the parking area. The total length of your hike would be 6.0 miles.

To continue along the route of the hike, turn left on the other side of the underpass and head uphill. The road soon curves to the right. Keep right at the first fork and continue with an old wooden fence on your left and views of the countryside below. Bear left at the next junction and continue downhill, then bear right at the following intersection and continue until you reach a T-junction. Turn right and head downhill, with the Old Croton

Aqueduct running parallel to you on the left. Continue ahead, bearing left at each intersection, until you reach a marked triangular intersection—where you turn right.

Before making this turn, however, continue straight ahead to the bridge right in front of you which crosses the Pocantico River. This bridge, known as the Three Arches Bridge, is generally considered to be the finest stone bridge built by the Rockefellers.

Return to the previous intersection and continue on the Pocantico River Trail, which parallels the river below you on the left. Counting the Three Arches Bridge as the first crossing, continue on the Pocantico River Trail until you come to the fourth bridge. Here you turn left and cross the river. On the other side of the bridge, you'll reach a concrete

Three Arches Bridge

DANIEL CHAZIN

Westchester County

signpost marking the junction of the Pocantico River Trail with the Gory Brook Road Trail. Turn right to stay on the Pocantico River Trail. The river should now be on your right, and the route will soon take you through open fields. You'll pass two more junctions (where side trails cross the river on bridges). The trail now bends left and comes nearer to the river. Soon, it passes by a smooth-topped stone wall, with cascades in the river that are especially lovely if the water level is high. When you reach a junction with the Eagle Hill Trail, you will have hiked 6.2 miles.

If you've had enough hiking by now, bear right at the junction and cross the pedestrian bridge over the Pocantico River on your right. Continue ahead on the Old Sleepy Hollow Road Trail, which crosses paved Sleepy Hollow Road and continues ahead to the parking lot. This hike would cover, in total, just under 7.0 miles.

To continue along the route of the hike, turn left onto the Eagle Hill Trail. After a short climb, you'll reach a junction with the Eagle Hill Summit Trail. Turn left and head uphill. When you reach a fork (the start of a loop), bear left, and you'll soon reach a viewpoint, with the Kykuit mansion of the Rockefeller estate visible on the opposite hill. Just beyond, you'll come to a stone bench on your right, from which the Hudson River can be seen. Continue ahead to complete the loop, then bear left and descend to the Eagle Hill Trail. You've now hiked 7.6 miles.

To return to the parking lot from here, turn right onto the Eagle Hill Trail, retrace your steps to the Pocantico River Trail, then cross the pedestrian bridge over the Pocantico River and continue ahead on the Old Sleepy Hollow Road Trail to the parking lot. You will have hiked a total of 8.5 miles.

But to continue along the route of the hike, proceed ahead, crossing a steel bridge over NY 117. One might wonder why such a substantial limited-access road was built here, as it is certainly out of character for the area. Interestingly, this section of highway was part of a major controversy in the mid-1960s. NY 117 was to be upgraded to connect with the planned Hudson River Expressway, I-487. A major interchange was to be built on landfill in the river. By the time the plans for I-487 were abandoned, this upgraded section of NY 117 had already been constructed.

On the other side of NY 117, proceed ahead along the 2-mile-long 13 Bridges Loop. There are a few junctions, but this trail is well signed and easy to follow. The 13 bridges, of standard design, are primarily on the last part of the loop as it crosses and recrosses meandering Gory Brook. This part of the preserve, somewhat distant from the parking area, is less traveled and usually quite peaceful. But it was not always so. Gory Brook was named for a Revolutionary War skirmish that left the stream red with the blood of British troops.

After crossing under NY 117, the 13 Bridges Loop ends. Turn left and head uphill on the Eagle Hill Trail, follow it back to the Pocantico River Trail, and cross the footbridge over the river. Continue on the Old Sleepy Hollow Road Trail and cross the paved Sleepy Hollow Road. In another 0.2 mile, you'll reach a junction with the Ash Tree Loop. Turn right, and at the next junction turn left onto the Overlook Trail, which meanders high above Swan Lake, offering beautiful views over the lake. When you reach a five-way junction with a signboard, a sharp left will take you back to the visitors center. The complete hike is 11.6 miles long.

4

Teatown Lake Reservation

Total distance: 4.8 miles

Walking time: 3.5 hours

Vertical rise: 750 feet

Maps: USGS 7.5' Ossining; Teatown Lake Reservation map; NY–NJTC Teatown-Kitchawan t rail map (available online at www.nynjtc.org /map/teatownkitchawan-trail-map)

Trailhead GPS Coordinates: N 41° 12' 40.5" W 73° 49' 38.5"

The 1,000-acre Teatown Lake Reservation, Westchester County's largest private nature preserve, has much to interest visitors. In addition to approximately 15 miles of marked hiking trails, Teatown has three lakes, a scenic gorge, cascading streams, hardwood swamps, mixed forests, meadows, and laurel groves. Teatown Lake was created in 1923 when Gerard Swope Sr., president of the General Electric Company, built a dam on Bailey Brook. The preserve was established in 1963 when 190 acres surrounding the lake were donated by the Swope family. Teatown Lake Reservation is a nonprofit organization that depends on contributions to support its educational and land preservation efforts.

The Teatown Nature Center (open daily from 9:00 am to 5:00 pm except certain holidays) has a small shop focused on nature items, educational exhibits, and rotating art exhibits. The center and an outdoor enclosed area house birds of prey, reptiles, amphibians, and mammals. Many have been rescued and most are native to the area.

One special attraction of Teatown is the 2-acre Wildflower Island, home to over two hundred native and endangered species of wildflowers. It is reached by crossing a bridge from Wildflower Woods, a fenced-in, deer-free area, which (when complete) will feature native plants, trees, shrubs, and wildflowers. Guided tours of Wildflower Island given by experienced volunteer guides are offered from mid-April through September. To preregister, call 914-762-2912, ext. 110. A nominal fee is charged.

Teatown Lake

DANIEL CHAZIN

The hike described here includes the Croft, Hidden Valley, Overlook, Hilltop, Teatown-Kitchawan, Briarcliff-Peekskill, and Lakeside Trails. Both the Hidden Valley Trail and the Overlook Trail are loops, and one or both of these loops can be omitted if you would like a shorter hike.

HOW TO GET THERE

To reach the preserve from the Taconic State Parkway, exit at NY 134 for Ossining, proceed west for 0.3 mile, and turn right onto Spring Valley Road—a winding country road. In 0.7 mile, turn left at the fork (at the sign for the preserve), then turn right into the preserve after another 0.2 mile.

Alternatively, from US 9, turn right onto NY 133 in Ossining (left if approaching from the north) and in 0.2 mile turn left onto NY 134. In 3.9 miles, turn left onto Spring Valley Road, then left again for the preserve at the fork mentioned above.

If the main parking lot is full, overflow parking is available nearby on Blinn Road. Turn left from the main parking lot, then turn left at the next intersection onto Blinn Road and continue to the parking area on the left side of the road.

THE TRAIL

After visiting the nature center (where a trail map is available for a small fee), cross

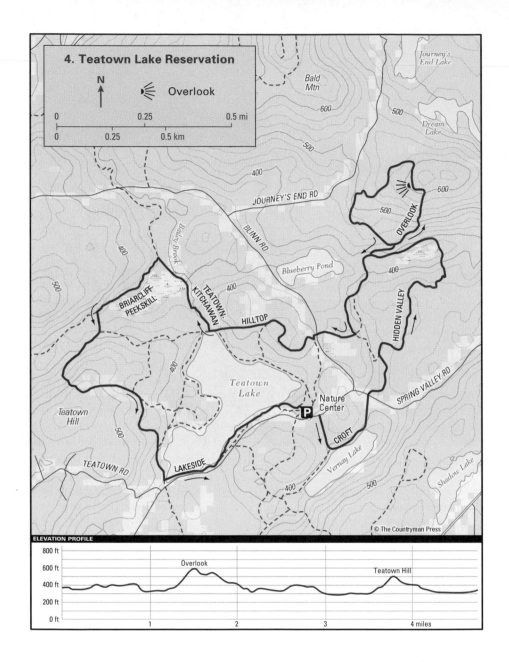

4. Teatown Lake Reservation

ELEVATION PROFILE

Spring Valley Road, go through an opening in a stone wall, and pass a kiosk to the left and a stone-lined pond to the right. Continue ahead on the yellow-blazed Croft Trail, which descends toward Vernay Lake on a woods road. Near the base of the descent, the trail bears left, leaving the road, and makes the final descent to the lake on stone steps. Just ahead is a concrete dock—the site of the former Croft boathouse—that affords panoramic views of this pristine lake. The orange-blazed Back 40 Trail begins on the right, but you should turn left to continue on the yellow-blazed trail, which follows a narrow footpath along the lakeshore. At the end of the lake, the trail turns left and begins to climb on a footpath. After crossing a grassy field, the Croft Trail ends at a gate in a stone wall along Spring Valley Road.

Turn right and follow the road for 50 feet, then turn left onto a black-blazed connector trail, which climbs to a stone wall at the crest of the rise and then descends. Near the base of the descent, you'll reach a T-junction. The black-blazed trail ends here, and you should turn right (uphill) onto the red-blazed Hidden Valley Trail. The trail now passes interesting rock outcrops and a vernal pond on the left and goes through mountain laurel thickets.

Soon, the trail bears left and descends into Hidden Valley, first gradually, and then more steeply. At the base of the steep descent, the trail begins to parallel a stream. The trail crosses a boardwalk over a wetland (with abundant skunk cabbage), then turns sharply left and follows a path between the wetland on the left and a rocky slope on the right. Soon, you'll reach a junction with the yellow-blazed Overlook Trail.

Turn right and follow the yellow-blazed Overlook Trail, which climbs steeply to reach a T-junction at a small pond, with a private home visible across the pond. Turn right to follow the Overlook Trail loop in a counterclockwise direction. Soon, the trail crosses a bridge over a gorge and climbs alongside it (with ropes and wooden posts provided to assist hikers). At the top of the climb, turn right and proceed to a rocky area with a view over Hidden Valley. The trail continues to climb, steeply at times, and passes through gaps in several rock walls before ascending rock steps to the trail's highest point, with

views of Hidden Valley and the Hudson Highlands in the distance.

The Overlook Trail now begins a winding descent. Watch for a sharp left turn leading to a wet section of trail. Immediately after passing a large rock formation on the left, bear right to reach an open grassy area. The trail now descends, with houses visible to the right. Soon after passing a line of old telephone poles, the trail bears left and descends to a paved road. It turns left and follows the road for 50 feet, then turns right and reenters the woods. The trail continues to descend, with wooden steps provided in places, and soon reaches the small pond encountered at the start of the loop. Turn right, and retrace your steps downhill to the junction of the Overlook and Hidden Valley Trails.

Turn right onto the red-blazed Hidden Valley Trail, which almost immediately reaches a stone wall and turns left to cross a wooden bridge. The trail now begins to climb out of the valley. After reaching the top of the climb, the pink-blazed Pine Grove Trail begins on the left. Continue on the red-blazed Hidden Valley Trail, which passes through stands of invasive barberry and wineberry bushes before reaching an open area, with a picnic table uphill on the left. Here, the pink-blazed Pine Grove Trail ends on the left, but you should turn right (following the sign to the nature center) to continue along the red-blazed Hidden Valley Trail, which crosses a boardwalk over a wet area and continues along a dirt road to paved Blinn Road, where it passes through a gate in a red fence.

Cross the road and follow the trail as it turns left and climbs slightly to reach a junction with the orange-blazed Hilltop Trail. Turn right onto the Hilltop Trail, and proceed over a hill, with plastic disks used for orienteering visible along the trail. You'll pass the start of the black-blazed Hilltop Shortcut, which leads left to the boathouse on Teatown Lake, but continue ahead on the orange-blazed Hilltop Trail.

At the base of a short descent, the Hilltop Trail ends at a junction with the co-aligned blue-blazed Lakeside Trail and the purple-blazed Teatown-Kitchawan Trail. Continue straight ahead, with the dam of Teatown Lake on your left. Just before crossing Bailey Brook (the outlet of the lake), turn right, leaving the Lakeside Trail and continuing to follow the purple-blazed Teatown-Kitchawan Trail. You'll pass an outdoor classroom on the right and cross a bridge over the brook, with a bench nearby—a good place to take a break.

Soon, the trail crosses Griffin Swamp on a boardwalk. At the end of the swamp, you'll reach a junction. The purple-blazed Teatown-Kitchawan Trail proceeds ahead, but you should turn left onto the green-diamond-blazed Briarcliff-Peekskill Trailway.

In a short distance, you'll cross another section of Griffin Swamp on boardwalks and a bridge. Just before the longest section of boardwalk, the white-blazed Cliffdale/Teatown Trail joins. Turn left to continue on the Briarcliff-Peekskill Trailway, now following white and green-diamond blazes. After a short uphill stretch, you'll come to a Y-junction. Here, the Cliffdale/Teatown Trail leaves to the left. You should bear right and continue to follow the green-diamond-blazed Briarcliff-Peekskill Trailway, which heads uphill through a mountain laurel thicket.

Soon, you'll reach a clearing for a power line. The climb by the side of the power line is steep and rocky, and at the top of the first ascent, a detour to the left of the trail leads to the summit of Teatown Hill. Unfortunately, a power line tower has been placed at the summit. There is a broad north-facing view from the base of the tower, but it is marred by the power lines that traverse the countryside.

The trail now begins to descend. A black-blazed shortcut trail begins on the left, but you should bear right and continue along the green-diamond-blazed Briarcliff-Peekskill Trailway, which passes under one of the power line towers and then moves away from the power line. Passing between a rock outcrop on the left and a stream on the right, the trail now descends toward Teatown Lake. Just after crossing a bridge, the Briarcliff-Peekskill Trailway turns to parallel a stone wall, and at a gap in this wall it reaches a junction with the blue-blazed Lakeside Trail.

The Lakeside Trail circles the lake. If you wish to take the longer route back to the nature center, you can turn left, but to follow the route of this hike, bear right, now following the co-aligned Briarcliff-Peekskill Trailway and Lakeside Trail. The trails head south, toward Spring Valley Road, but just before reaching the road, follow the Lakeside Trail as it turns left onto the floating Bergmann Boardwalk, which offers views across the lake and into the shallow areas where turtles can sometimes be seen. After crossing the boardwalk, the trail closely follows the shore of the lake (except for a short section where it climbs and descends on stone steps). Benches are provided at intervals along the trail.

Before reaching a wooden bridge (with additional benches and interpretive signs), you'll pass through a wooden gate into Wildflower Woods, which is protected from deer by a chain-link fence that extends into the lake and across to Wildflower Island. You'll then pass the gatehouse entry to the bridge leading to Wildflower Island. There are several short side trails in this area, but you should follow the main Lakeside Trail across another bridge and pass through another gate. Here, you should turn right and proceed uphill to return to the nature center.

5

Old Croton Aqueduct State Historic Park

Total distance: 5.5 miles

Walking time: 3 hours

Vertical rise: Minimal

Maps: USGS 7.5' Ossining; a detailed map in color containing historical comments on the aqueduct and nearby features of interest can be purchased from Friends of the Old Croton Aqueduct, Inc., www.aqueduct.org

Trailhead GPS Coordinates:
N 41° 13' 41" W 73° 51' 25.5"

Originally known as Old Croton Trailway State Park, the Old Croton Aqueduct State Historic Park extends a total distance of 26.2 miles but covers only a portion of the 41-mile aqueduct route that once carried water into New York City. Its acquisition in 1968 by New York State enabled one of the great engineering feats of the 19th century to be converted into a linear park. Construction of the aqueduct and the Croton Reservoir and dam began in 1837 and was carried out largely by Irish immigrant labor. It seems incredible that this gravity-fed tube maintains its steady gradient of 13 inches per mile over its entire length, modeled on principles used by the Romans.

Water first flowed through the tube in 1842, and the aqueduct continued to supply New York City until 1955. Plentiful water encouraged the growth of the city, but increased demands by new industries and the need for flush toilets and baths rendered the old aqueduct inadequate to supply the city's fast-growing population. Construction of the New Croton Aqueduct, three times the size and a few miles to the east, began in 1885, and the new aqueduct was put into service in 1890. The northernmost 3-mile section of the Old Croton Aqueduct was brought back into service in 1987 to supply the town of Ossining with water.

This hike begins at the New Croton Dam above Croton Gorge Park and ends in Ossining, close to the unique double arch across the Sing Sing Kill. The water conduit is usually only a few feet under the surface. As a result, no buildings could be

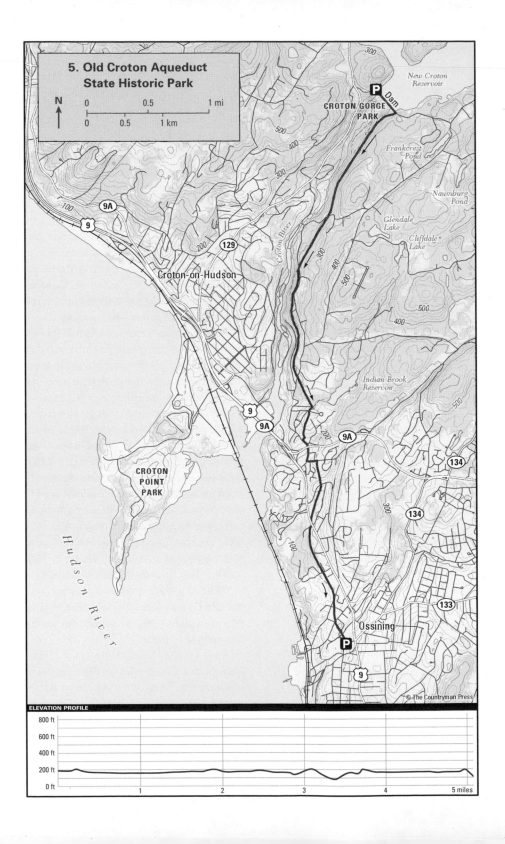

5. Old Croton Aqueduct
State Historic Park

N

0		0.5		1 mi
0	0.5		1 km	

New Croton
Reservoir

P
CROTON GORGE
PARK

Dam

300

500

400

Frankcrest
Pond

Naumburg
Pond

300

Glendale
Lake

Cliffdale
Lake

9A

9

100

200

Croton River

129

300

400

500

Croton-on-Hudson

500

400

300

200

Indian Brook
Reservoir

100

500

9

9A

9A

134

CROTON
POINT
PARK

134

300

Hudson River

100

133

Ossining

P

9

© The Countryman Press

ELEVATION PROFILE

800 ft					
600 ft					
400 ft					
200 ft					
0 ft					
	1	2	3	4	5 miles

constructed over the masonry tunnel, thus making this unobstructed path ideal for nonmotorized recreation. The flat, grassy mound, often with a dirt path in the center, is easy to follow, sometimes passing close to homes and often over streams running from left to right down to the river. Mountain bikes are permitted on the trail, and dogs must be leashed. Please be considerate as you walk by backyards. Most of the route is unmarked, though round yellow-disk markers may be seen periodically, and care must be taken when the trail crosses or uses public streets. The traveler is alerted at the northernmost road crossings by single metal bar gates with concrete posts. The aqueduct at first parallels the Croton River, east of the Hudson. Along the way the route passes several attractive stone towers called ventilators. Their purpose—before the introduction of chlorination—was to freshen the water.

HOW TO GET THERE

A car shuttle is needed unless you wish to retrace your steps. Park one car where your hike will end in Ossining at the Ossining Heritage Area Visitors Center at 95 Broadway, just west of the junction of US 9 and NY 133 in Ossining. The two-hour parking rule is usually not enforced on weekends, though as a safeguard you should confirm this fact at the visitors center. There are restrooms here and a museum (914-941-3189) with exhibits relating to the construction of the aqueduct. The facility is located in the Village of Ossining Community Center and is usually open from 9:00 am to 9:45 pm, daily except Sunday.

Use a second car to reach the beginning of the hike by turning left out of the community center parking lot, and make an immediate right onto US 9 at the light (only right turns are permitted here). Almost immediately turn right again onto Main Street, and quickly bear left onto Church Street (do not go down the hill on the right into town), then left (north) again at the traffic light back onto US 9. Proceed north on US 9 for just over 3 miles, and immediately after the open water crossing, exit on NY 129. Turn right at the bottom of the ramp, then turn left onto Riverside Avenue at the T-junction. Continue for 0.5 mile, and then bear right, continuing on NY 129 at the Croton Diner. Continue in a northeasterly direction for 2.3 miles, and watch for, but do not turn into, an entry road on the right that leads down to the Croton Gorge Park.

The first right after the park entry is Croton Dam Road, the access road for the dam. The road and dam have been closed to vehicular traffic (except emergency vehicles) since 1999, but parking is permitted at the entrance to the road and across the street on Batten Road. Although parking is also available in Croton Gorge Park, a parking fee is charged on weekends and holidays from May to December.

The aqueduct is also reachable by train via the Metro-North Railroad's Hudson Line, which parallels the aqueduct from Yonkers to Ossining. For train information, call 1-800-638-7646 or go to www.mta.info. For bus information, call Westchester County's Beeline Bus System at 914-682-2020.

THE TRAIL

After parking, walk around the sawhorse barriers which block vehicle access to Croton Dam Road. The green-blazed Briarcliff-Peekskill Trailway, a 12-mile trail through Westchester County, comes down a steep hill and joins the road from the left. Soon you reach the dam. Take time to admire the New Croton Dam, also known as the Cornell Dam, and to look right (down into Croton Gorge Park) and left (across the Croton Reservoir). More than 200 feet high, the dam was completed in 1907 and resulted in the original dam being submerged under a greatly enlarged reservoir.

On the far side of the dam, you'll walk around concrete vehicle barricades. The Briarcliff-Peekskill Trailway continues straight ahead, but you should turn right onto a white stone road just past a "high voltage" area behind a chain-link fence. Soon, the road splits. The right fork continues down to Croton Gorge Park, but you should bear left, passing a sign OLD CROTON AQUEDUCT STATE HISTORIC PARK. The tube is now immediately below.

After passing between concrete posts that once supported a metal bar blocking the route to vehicles, the first ventilator comes into view. The path soon becomes sandy, passing beneath power lines. A garage and stone house appear to the right. Between them are stairs which lead to trails that head down to Croton Gorge Park. The trail is now wide, with evidence of an old stone wall up to the left and glimpses through the trees of the river below and the ridge on the opposite side of the river. Soon, you pass through a rock cut—one of only three such rock cuts along the aqueduct in Westchester County.

Quaker Bridge Road East, reached in about 1 mile along the aqueduct, is the first road crossing. Continue straight across and around another gate to arrive at the second ventilator. For the most part, these ventilators were placed roughly 1 mile apart. After crossing Quaker Bridge Road, the aqueduct parallels that road, which is above on the left. The river, which runs rapidly at this point, is down a steep hill on the right. Next, the Croton Gorge Unique Area is reached, marked by a Department of Environmental Conservation sign. Here, the trail overlooks the gorge, passing a large tulip tree with exposed roots. An old trail leads down to the river along the south side of the gorge.

After passing a spectacular view down the Croton River to the point where it flows into the Hudson River, you'll parallel an old wall on the left and reach the third ventilator. A short distance beyond, you'll recross Quaker Bridge Road.

After walking on an embankment—a narrow ridge with steep slopes on both sides—you'll reach the end of the section of the aqueduct that carries water to Ossining and pass a small building on the left that houses a pump to move the water up to the town's water treatment plant. Immediately ahead is the campus of General Electric's John F. Welch Leadership Development Center.

Ventilator along the Old Croton Aqueduct

DANIEL CHAZIN

New Croton Dam

DANIEL CHAZIN

Turn right onto the paved road and watch for a green post, between the entrance to the General Electric campus and Fowler Avenue, with OCA carved into its side. Turn left here onto a footpath that skirts the campus, with a chain-link fence on your left. Continue to follow the fence as it turns left, right, and left again, eventually emerging onto paved Shady Lane Farm Road.

Turn right onto this road, head down to Old Albany Post Road, and turn left—immediately crossing under a bridge carrying NY 9A. On the west side of Old Albany Post Road, there are two historic buildings—the former Crotonville one-room schoolhouse and a church. The old schoolhouse is now the Parker Bale American Legion Post #1597. Just beyond, you'll notice a face carved into a tree stump, and then you'll come to the old church, which is now the home of a fraternal organization. The inscription on the building—F.O.E. Ossining Aerie 1545—stands for "Fraternal Order of the Eagles"; the number 1545 is assigned to Ossining; and an aerie is the nest of a raptor. Below appears the date: A.D. 1897.

Continue for another two blocks, turn left onto Ogden Road, and head straight uphill almost to the crest of the road. Another green OCA post appears next to house #9. Looking left, behind the OCA post, the aqueduct route appears to continue north. However, in a short distance it ends at NY 9A, which cannot be crossed. You should turn right onto the southbound aqueduct. The brown building on the left bears a trail marker and is now in use as a maintenance barn. Look down to the left to see a stream

Old Croton Aqueduct State Historic Park 51

that is neatly channeled into a culvert. By now, you have walked almost 4 miles.

You now approach the fourth ventilator. Just beyond, you climb on a rough, steep path. At the top, you cross Piping Rock Road and proceed steeply down the other side to a delightful grassy section, partially along an embankment, that is mowed by the property owners adjacent to the trail. Users of the trail owe these volunteers a debt of gratitude.

In a short distance, you'll reach US 9, passing a sign on the left: OLD CROTON AQUE-DUCT. Cross this busy road using the pedestrian crossing, walk down a paved driveway toward a chain-link fence, and turn left (between three wooden posts) onto a footpath. Soon, you will pass through the grounds of the Kane Mansion, a Gothic Revival mansion built around 1843. As of this writing, the former office building adjacent to the Kane Mansion has been demolished and major construction of a luxury housing complex is underway. Current plans include restoration of the Kane Mansion and the maintenance of the aqueduct route as part of the complex. The trail remains open during construction. Continue across the lawn to Beach Road. At almost 5 miles into the hike, you reach a large rectangular stone building. The tube is visible if you look through the gate on the river side.

Pass a fire station of the village of Ossining on the right, and cross Snowden Avenue. Walk up the four cement steps at the left of the sidewalk, and continue on grass to a wooden barricade. Cross two streets, Van Wyck and North Malcolm, through gaps in the protective wooden posts, and walk up the paved path with a children's playground on the left. Admire the gorgeous maple tree whose roots penetrate the tube 40 feet down, and walk down the shallow stone steps to the right of this venerable giant. Cross Ann Street to approach the Waste Weir, built in 1882.

This weir was constructed to allow the flow of water through the tube to be controlled when inspection or maintenance was required further south in the tube. A huge solid-cast-iron gate was dropped, diverting the water into the Sing Sing Kill. This weir chamber was one of a series that made it possible to drain the entire aqueduct. The mechanism was also used to spill off, or "waste," water in times of flood. Old images indicate that when the aqueduct was in full operation in the early days, inspections were carried out inside the tube by engineers in boats—not an enviable occupation.

Cross the bridge over the Sing Sing Kill, and walk down to the viewing platform to see the double-arch bridge over the Sing Sing Kill. These bridges are one of the most prominent features of the Old Croton Aqueduct. The upper bridge, known as the Aqueduct Bridge, was completed in 1839 and passes over the lower bridge, the Broadway Bridge. The lower bridge was originally made of wood and was rebuilt with stone in the 1860s. You may wish to visit the museum at the Ossining Heritage Area Visitors Center before returning to your car.

6

Anthony's Nose and the Camp Smith Trail

Total distance: 4.2 miles

Walking time: 2.5 hours

Vertical rise: 1,000 feet

Maps: USGS 7.5' Peekskill; NY–NJTC East Hudson Trails #101

Trailhead GPS Coordinates:
N 41° 19' 19" W 73° 58' 33.5"

The Camp Smith Trail has many views of the Hudson River, the best of which is from Anthony's Nose in the northwest corner of Westchester County. This beautiful trail was "a long time a-coming." Camp Smith, a unit of the New York National Guard, was acquired by the state from 1885 through the mid-1920s. Public entry was officially prohibited, but hikers would climb via the Appalachian Trail (AT) to Anthony's Nose, which offers a fabulous view of the Hudson River.

In 1992, efforts by the Greenway Conservancy of Hudson River Valley resulted in Camp Smith granting permission to build a 3.7-mile trail through its property, from the toll house at the eastern end of the Bear Mountain Bridge approach road to the bridge itself. Constructed by volunteers from the New York–New Jersey Trail Conference, with the assistance of the New York National Guard's Challenge Program for high-school dropouts, the trail was completed in 1995. The trail route (including a 50-foot strip of land extending east of the trail and the land between the trail and the Hudson River) is now part of Hudson Highlands State Park.

This hike, as described, requires two cars. If you have only one car, possible out-and-back hikes are described in the Options section at the end of this description.

HOW TO GET THERE

Leave one car on US 6 at the tollhouse, 2.6 miles east of the Bear Mountain Bridge (or 0.7 mile west of the Camp Smith entrance). Then drive toward the bridge (but don't cross it) and turn right onto NY 9D. Park

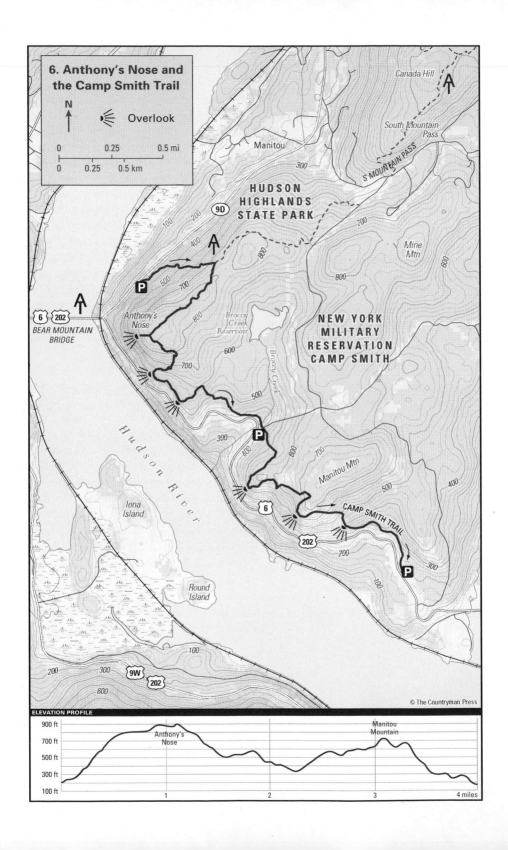

6. Anthony's Nose and the Camp Smith Trail

N

☀ Overlook

| 0 | 0.25 | 0.5 mi |
| 0 | 0.25 | 0.5 km |

Canada Hill

South Mountain Pass

S MOUNTAIN PASS

Manitou

300

HUDSON HIGHLANDS STATE PARK

9D

700

Mine Mtn

600

100

200

400

500

700

800

P

Anthony's Nose

Brocey Creek Reservoir

600

800

NEW YORK MILITARY RESERVATION CAMP SMITH

6 202

BEAR MOUNTAIN BRIDGE

700

Brocey Creek

500

300

400

P

600

700

Manitou Mtn

500

400

Hudson River

300

6

CAMP SMITH TRAIL

Iona Island

200

202

300

P

100

Round Island

100

200 300

9W 202

600

© The Countryman Press

ELEVATION PROFILE

900 ft		Anthony's Nose		Manitou Mountain	
700 ft					
500 ft					
300 ft					
100 ft					
	1	2	3	4 miles	

along the shoulder of NY 9D, just north of the bridge. If no parking can be found along the narrow shoulder, consider an out-and-back hike from one of the two US 6 parking areas noted below. Alternatively, you could park at the Bear Mountain Inn on the other side of the river (fee charged) and add the distance of 1.3 miles from the inn to the trailhead across the bridge to your day's hike.

THE TRAIL

The 2-by-6-inch white-blazed Appalachian Trail (AT) leaves NY 9D just north of the sign for the Westchester-Putnam county line. Follow the AT as it climbs unrelentingly uphill. After about half an hour of hiking and 500 feet of elevation gain, you'll reach a wide woods road 0.6 mile from the start. The AT turns left along the road, but you instead

should turn right and follow the 2-by-6-inch blue blazes. The trail continues uphill along the rocky, wide woods road, but much less steeply (in places, the trail is actually flat). In another 15 minutes, you'll reach a second trail junction. Turn right and head toward the almost bald rock face of Anthony's Nose.

The expansive 270-degree view from Anthony's Nose often attracts a crowd. It is an excellent place to watch raptors, including the peregrine falcons that nest on the Bear Mountain Bridge. To your left (southwest), across the river, Bald, Dunderberg, and Timp Mountains in Harriman State Park dominate. Directly across the river is the Bear Mountain Inn complex, including Hessian Lake, the ice skating rink, and the carousel. The Perkins Memorial Tower on Bear Mountain is in front of you, and you may catch the glint of cars

Popolopen Gorge from Anthony's Nose

JANE DANIELS

on the Perkins Memorial Drive that leads to the top of the mountain. The bald, rocky summit of Popolopen Torne is just beyond the Bear Mountain Bridge. Fort Montgomery is to the right of the bridge, with the United States Military Academy at West Point just barely visible to the north. On the east side of the river are Canada and Sugarloaf Hills. In the summer, you'll probably notice pleasure boats on the river (but, with any luck, not the loud whine of Jet Skis). There are rail lines on both sides of the river, and trains pass by frequently (Metro-North and Amtrak passenger trains use the tracks on the east side of the river; CSX freight trains use the tracks on the west side).

So who was this Anthony with his magnificent nose? His identity is the subject of much folklore and speculation, but no one really knows. Early maps called it Saint Anthony's Nose. Washington Irving spun his own humorous tale in the early 1800s. One version of the tale is that when Henry Hudson sailed up the river later to be named for him, he had an Italian cook aboard named Anthony who, it was said, had previously lived with local Indians. When Henry Hudson spotted the cliffs, he asked aloud, "What's that?!" One of his crew immediately responded, "Don't know, sir, but you should ask Anthony. Anthony knows." One thing is sure: It was named long before the time of Revolutionary War General "Mad Anthony" Wayne.

Now return to the marked trail and look for a small cairn and the 2-by-4-inch blue blazes (smaller than those you've seen previously) of the Camp Smith Trail. A short scramble brings you up to a rock outcrop with a U.S. Geological Survey benchmark that marks the summit of Anthony's Nose. There is another great view from here, this one to the south. The footpath now becomes narrower and begins to descend, passing through a field of sweet ferns. Be sure to follow the blue blazes. After a descent of about 250 feet, you'll reach a rock outcrop with a view over Iona Island.

The trail continues downhill, passing another viewpoint at the edge of the cliff, and then turns inland. Occasionally, you'll hear the noise of traffic on the nearby but unseen highway cut into the cliff below you. After crossing a small stream and a gully, the trail joins a woods road. At an hour-plus into the hike, the trail crosses Broccy Creek and reaches the midpoint parking area (known as the "U-Bend"), with spaces for six to eight cars. You have now descended about 550 vertical feet from the summit.

Leaving the parking area, the Camp Smith Trail begins another ascent and reaches a viewpoint, 2.3 miles from the start. Turning away from the river, you head downhill, cross a flat area, and reach a massive jumble of rocks. The trail ascends this steep section on switchbacks built by a volunteer trail crew. This trail section was carefully designed to minimize erosion and make the trail safe and enjoyable. At the top, you'll turn toward the river and then away from it as you continue to head uphill. Soon, you'll reach a sweeping viewpoint across the Hudson River, with the dominant building downriver a cogeneration plant at Charles Point. On the opposite shore, farther downstream, the sharp outline of Hook Mountain (Hike 14) protrudes into the river.

After nearly two hours of hiking, you'll reach the "Two Pines" viewpoint, marked by two pitch pines near the edge. A third pine tree is now large enough that the name of the viewpoint might have to be changed to "Three Pines." Take time to enjoy the view, which encompasses rail lines on both sides of the Hudson, the wetlands of Iona Island (a noted bird habitat), and the domes of the Indian Point nuclear power facility.

Iona Island from Anthony's Nose   WALT DANIELS

It should take you about 30 to 45 minutes to cover the final 1 mile of the hike. After heading away from the river, you'll pass a view to the south from the top of a large sloping rock face and then turn toward the river and the last view on the hike, also to the south. At the base of a descent on stone steps, the noise from the road may tease you into thinking you are at the end of the hike, but there is one more ascent.

After about two and a half hours of walking, you'll come to the end of the Camp Smith Trail at the tollhouse. This stone structure was built to collect tolls from westbound motorists when the Bear Mountain Bridge and the approach road were first opened in 1924. Operated privately by the Harriman family, the tollhouse was abandoned when the state acquired the bridge in 1940. In the early 1990s, it was threatened with demolition, and the opening of the Camp Smith Trail helped galvanize support to preserve this historic structure. It was restored as a visitors center in 2002 and features a small gift shop that is open weekends in season. There is a portable toilet available, and parking has been provided to encourage use of the trail.

OPTIONS

For a shorter two-car hike, parking is also available at a U-bend on US 6, 2.1 miles west of the Camp Smith entry or 1.1 miles east of the bridge. You also might want to consider doing the hike in the opposite direction (starting at the tollhouse and ending on NY 9D). Hiking in this direction has the advantage that the views become more impressive as you head north, ending at the most spectacular one.

Should you have only one car available, start from any one of the three parking areas noted above, and hike up and back to Anthony's Nose. From NY 9D it's a 2-mile round-trip. From the tollhouse it's a 6.2-mile round-trip, with the opportunity to savor the many views twice. From the U-bend it's a 2.4-mile round-trip, with an elevation gain of 600 to 700 feet.

II. The East Hudson Highlands

Introduction to the East Hudson Area

State parks on the east side of the Hudson River are managed by the Taconic Park Commission, a state agency with offices in Staatsburg. From the precipitous cliffs of Breakneck Ridge to the more gentle uplands of Fahnestock, the wide hiking choices available offer wonderful recreational opportunities.

FAHNESTOCK STATE PARK

Astride the Taconic State Parkway, this 14,000-acre park offers lakes and rolling terrain. In the summer, the park offers swimming, boating, and picnicking. In the winter, a cross-country ski center, known as Winter Park, operates from the swimming area. The park also has many miles of trails that can take you far from the crowds that regularly enjoy the more developed facilities. Although not as mountainous as parkland closer to the Hudson, the varied terrain makes for peaceful excursions into the woodlands. Bow hunting is allowed in season, and some trails are open to mountain bikes and horses.

The park has its roots in the 1929 gift of Dr. Ernest Fahnestock in memory of his brother, Clarence. It was significantly expanded in the 1960s and the 1990s.

Much of the land that now forms the park was purchased by Adolphe Philipse in 1691 and established as the Philipse Grant six years later by King William III. The vast and rugged wilderness surrounding the interior range of hills could not be farmed and thus never had many settlers. Only the 8-mile-long vein of iron ore that follows the ridgeline of the hills to the south managed to attract settlers—and then not until after 1800. Even the early miners regarded these dark woods with foreboding; because they have not been logged for many years, the woods probably look now very much as they did then.

The mines in the park once provided iron ore to the West Point Foundry at Cold Spring, where the ore was turned into Parrott artillery for the Union Army. The bed of the railroad built in 1862 to carry the ore from the mines is now a hiking trail.

Thanks to the purchase of 4,400 acres in 1991 and 1995 by the Open Space Institute, the park was able to significantly expand its trail system. In 1996 the New York–New Jersey Trail Conference opened a 22-mile network of trails in what was then known as the Hubbard-Perkins Conservation Area, including two trails that connected to the adjacent Fahnestock State Park.

The park is adjacent to NY 301; the office phone is 845-225-7207.

HUDSON HIGHLANDS STATE PARK

"Eastward a high chain of mountains whose sides were covered with woods up to no more than half of their height. The summits, however, were quite barren; for I suppose nothing would grow there on account of the great degree of heat, dryness, and the violence of the wind to which that part was exposed." Thus, the Swedish botanist Peter Kalm observed the Hudson Highlands on the east side of the Hudson River in 1749. One highlight of his trip was his discovery and the first botanical description of the American mountain laurel, *Kalmia latifolia*, a shrub that grows on every slope from the Ramapos to the Shawangunks and whose blooms make walking here and everywhere in southern New York in late May and early June so special.

Hudson Highlands State Park, managed by the Fahnestock superintendent, consists of nearly 4,000 acres along the Hudson River in Westchester, Putnam, and southern Dutchess Counties. Both Hudson Highlands State Park and Fahnestock State Park are traversed by the Appalachian Trail.

South of Garrison is the 1,000-acre Osborn Preserve. Here, old carriage trails provide for relaxed walking.

But the most impressive section of the park straddles the Putnam-Dutchess border north of NY 301 and protects a wonderful and rugged area. Bull Hill, the aptly named Breakneck Ridge, and the impressive Sugarloaf Mountain (not to be confused with the nearby Sugarloaf Hill, located further south) rise steeply above the Hudson and provide numerous challenging climbs and spectacular views.

Behind these peaks, the 1,000-acre Fishkill Ridge Conservation Area was acquired by Scenic Hudson beginning in 1992. This preserve, managed as part of Hudson Highlands State Park, connects with watershed lands owned by the city of Beacon. Standing as the northern gateway to the Highlands, the area's rocky outcrops offer panoramic views of the Hudson River and the Catskill Mountains. Bow hunting is allowed in season.

7

Osborn Loop and Sugarloaf Hill

Total distance: 5.9 miles

Walking time: 3.5 hours

Vertical rise: 1,000 feet

Maps: USGS 7.5' Peekskill; NY–NJTC East Hudson Trails #101

Trailhead GPS Coordinates: N 41° 21' 02" W 73° 55' 34.5"

The Hudson Valley is rich in Revolutionary War history. The Beverly Robinson House, built by the Philipse family in 1758 on part of the Philipse Patent near Sugarloaf South, was confiscated and used as headquarters by Generals Israel Putnam and Samuel Holden Parsons in 1778 and 1779. In 1780, the house was used by General Benedict Arnold as his headquarters, and it was used as a military hospital during Arnold's command of West Point. Aboard the British ship *Vulture*, loyalist Beverly Robinson planned with Benedict Arnold and Major John Andre to deliver West Point to the British. When Arnold learned that Andre had been captured and that the discovery of his treason was imminent, he fled from the house down a path to the river and then downriver on the *Vulture*; General Washington arrived only an hour or so later.

The Osborn Preserve, a 1,000-acre section of Hudson Highlands State Park, was established when William Henry Osborn II donated the land around Sugarloaf Hill in 1974. His grandfather, president of the Illinois Central Railroad, had assembled the property for a summer home in the 1880s. The charming home, just north on Castle Rock, remains private. In the early 1980s, the National Park Service purchased surrounding property on the ridge to reroute the Appalachian Trail (AT) onto protected land. Many of the preserve's trails are easy-to-follow carriageways and old roads and are suitable for novice hikers.

This moderate hike, with one steep ascent at the start, is largely on old carriage

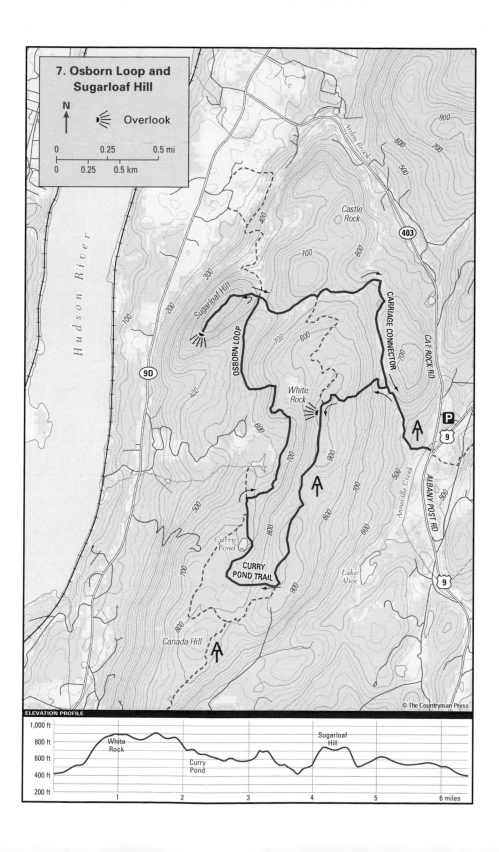

© The Countryman Press

7. Osborn Loop and Sugarloaf Hill

N

Overlook

0   0.25   0.5 mi
0   0.25   0.5 km

Hudson River

Arden Brook

Castle Rock

403

800

500

700

600

500

9D

300

200

100

400

Sugarloaf Hill

OSBORN LOOP

700

800

CARRIAGE CONNECTOR

CAT ROCK RD

700

White Rock

P

9

ALBANY POST RD

600

700

800

500

Annsville Creek

500

9

Curry Pond

CURRY POND TRAIL

800

Lake Alice

700

500

800

Canada Hill

ELEVATION PROFILE

1,000 ft
800 ft
600 ft
400 ft
200 ft

White Rock

Curry Pond

Sugarloaf Hill

1   2   3   4   5   6 miles

Along the Osborn Loop Trail

DANIEL CHAZIN

roads, and occasionally equestrians are encountered. The highlight is a climb of Sugarloaf Hill—a name derived from the cone shape in which sugar was sold in colonial times.

HOW TO GET THERE

The hike begins on the AT crossing of US 9 at its junction with NY 403 in Graymoor, Putnam County. This junction—easily located on a road map—is 3.8 miles north of the major junction of US 9, US 202, and US 6 in Peekskill. Parking is available along Cross Road, which connects NY 403 with US 9, about 0.1 mile north of the trail crossing at the junction (there is abundant poison ivy in this area, so be careful when getting out of your car).

THE TRAIL

From the junction of US 9 and NY 403, head west on the AT, crossing a field on puncheons (wooden planks used to cross wet areas) and going through a gap in a stone wall. Soon the trail turns right and ascends gradually on an old carriage road. In 0.5 mile, after crossing a stream, follow the white blazes as they turn uphill and begin a steeper climb on a footpath. (Ahead, the carriage road is the route of the yellow-blazed Carriage Connector Trail, which will be your return route.) Near the top of the hill, turn sharply left, as the blue-blazed Osborn Loop Trail leaves to the right. You now join another carriage road, this one being relatively level. You have now hiked just less than 1 mile and have gained about 500 feet in elevation. In about three minutes, you'll come to a junction with a blue-blazed trail on the right that leads in about 100 feet to a limited viewpoint over the Hudson River.

Continue south along the AT for another 0.75 mile to a junction with the Curry Pond Trail. The junction is well marked, but you could pass it if you're not alert. Don't be confused by some yellow paint blazes which you may see before the junction; they mark an old boundary line. Turn right onto the yellow-blazed Curry Pond Trail, which heads generally downhill through mountain laurel stands and thick forests while passing interesting rock outcrops.

After crossing its inlet stream, the trail reaches Curry Pond. Your impression will depend on the recent weather; it can be just a big swamp during low water, but small wildlife abounds at this peaceful and seldom-visited spot. Another five minutes of walking brings you to the end of the Curry Pond Trail at a junction with the Osborn Loop Trail. Turn right and follow the Osborn Loop Trail, which soon turns right, leaving the carriage road. It crosses several small streams, bears left, and climbs along an old stone wall. At the top of the climb, it bears right, with views to the left through the trees over the Hudson River 700 feet below.

The Osborn Loop Trail now begins a switchback descent of 150 vertical feet before resuming its northerly course. After a while you'll start to see the outline of Sugarloaf Hill in front of you through the trees. You'll descend to cross a small stream, then climb to an intersection with the red-blazed Sugarloaf Trail at the height of the land.

You'll return to this intersection, but for now turn left and follow the red-blazed trail, which ascends about 220 vertical feet to the summit of Sugarloaf Hill. The trail climbs steeply, follows the crest of the narrow ridge, and then descends slightly to reach one of the best viewpoints over the Hudson River: Anthony's Nose, Bear Mountain, and Dunderberg Mountain frame the Bear Mountain Bridge. This is a good spot for a break. You should be able to spot the interesting patch of prickly pear cactus on the warmer south-facing slope.

Bear Mountain Bridge from Sugarloaf Hill   DAN BALOGH

After enjoying the spectacular views from the summit of Sugarloaf Hill, retrace your steps to the intersection with the Osborn Loop Trail. Continue straight ahead, following the blue-blazed Osborn Loop Trail along a wide carriage road. Soon you'll pass a large gazebo, rebuilt in the late 1990s by equestrian users of the area. After passing a small pond with a stone dam on the right, the blue-blazed Osborn Loop Trail makes a sharp right turn, but you should continue ahead on the carriage road, now following the yellow blazes of the Carriage Connector Trail. The trail soon turns sharply right and levels off, making walking easy.

When the Carriage Connector Trail ends at a junction with the white-blazed AT, continue ahead along the carriage road, now following the white blazes. Retrace your steps along the AT until you reach the intersection of NY 403 and US 9, then turn left and continue to Cross Road, where you parked your car.

8

Breakneck-Undercliff Loop

Total distance: 6.4 miles

Walking time: 5.5 hours

Vertical rise: 2,000 feet

*Maps: USGS 7.5' West Point;
NY–NJTC East Hudson Trails #102*

*Trailhead GPS Coordinates:
N 41° 25' 36" W 73° 57' 56"*

The Hudson Highlands State Park had its inception in 1938, when 177 acres was donated as a gift to the state by the Hudson River Conservation Society. Land acquisition continued and resulted in the creation of one of the most spectacular hiking venues in the state, with acreage extending to approximately 3,800 acres. Here the Hudson River becomes narrow and winding as it curls between Breakneck Point and Storm King, with towering cliffs on both sides. The construction in 1916 of the Storm King Highway (now NY 218) around the steep slopes of Storm King Mountain on the west side of the river and the tunnel blasted through bedrock in 1912 to carry the waters of the Catskill Aqueduct 1,100 feet beneath the river were remarkable engineering feats. The handsome Bear Mountain Bridge was conceived in 1922 and opened in 1924, but in spite of its technological success, the suspension bridge (then privately owned) was a financial failure at first.

Climbing the Breakneck Ridge Trail is probably one of the most popular hiking adventures in the Hudson Highlands because of the strenuous effort and extreme exposure encountered while scrambling up the very steep face. However, the hike described does not use this trail, which is overused and can be dangerous in certain weather conditions. The route of this hike takes the walker on a newer hiking trail constructed by volunteers from the New York–New Jersey Trail Conference in 1997, which has comparable views. The hike uses part of the Washburn, Undercliff, Breakneck Ridge, Notch,

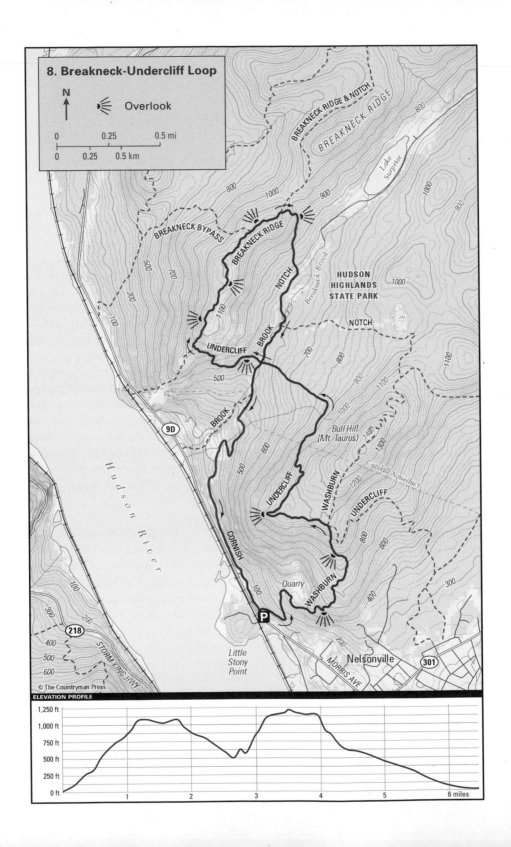

8. Breakneck-Undercliff Loop

N

Overlook

| 0 | 0.25 | 0.5 mi |
| 0 | 0.25 | 0.5 km |

BREAKNECK RIDGE & NOTCH

BREAKNECK RIDGE

Lake Surprise

800

1000

900

BREAKNECK BYPASS

BREAKNECK RIDGE

NOTCH

HUDSON HIGHLANDS STATE PARK

Breakneck Brook

1000

800

700

500

300

100

1100

UNDERCLIFF

BROOK

500

NOTCH

700

800

900

1100

BROOK

600

1000

1300

Bull Hill (Mt. Taurus)

1400

Catskill Aqueduct

9D

500

UNDERCLIFF

WASHBURN

1200

UNDERCLIFF

800

600

Hudson River

CORNISH

100

Quarry

WASHBURN

300

400

100

218

300

200

400

500

600

STORM KING HWY

P

Little Stony Point

WASHBURN

200

MORRIS AVE

Nelsonville

301

© The Countryman Press

ELEVATION PROFILE

| | 1 | 2 | 3 | 4 | 5 | 6 miles |

1,250 ft
1,000 ft
750 ft
500 ft
250 ft
0 ft

Storm King Mountain from Breakneck Ridge AUDRIUS JUSKELIS

and Cornish Trails. The going is moderately strenuous, with two sections of boulder scrambling on the Undercliff Trail, so be sure to allow sufficient time to enjoy the outing.

HOW TO GET THERE
Drive 0.6 mile north on NY 9D from its junction with NY 301 in the village of Cold Spring to a small parking lot on the east side of the road. Another small parking lot is available on the west side of NY 9D, where a bridge gives access over the railroad tracks onto Little Stony Point, where there are a few hiking trails. These trailheads can also be reached from the north by driving south on NY 9D approximately 2 miles from the Breakneck Ridge railroad tunnel.

For hikers without a car, the east side of the Hudson River can be reached using Metro-North's Hudson Line, which offers hourly service from Grand Central Terminal in New York City to the Cold Spring station. The walk from the train station to the Washburn Trailhead is 0.8 mile. Turn left at Fair Street, across the street from the village hall, and turn left again when this street ends at NY 9D. This main road is busy, but the trailhead is just ahead on the east side of the road. For more information on train schedules call Metro-North, 1-800-638-7646, or go to www.mta.info.

THE TRAIL
From the northern end of the parking area, proceed north on the white-blazed Washburn Trail. In 100 feet, you'll reach a junction with the blue-blazed Cornish Trail, which continues straight ahead. The Cornish Trail

will be your return route, but for now bear right and continue to follow the Washburn Trail uphill along an old road once used to access a quarry.

In 0.5 mile, you'll reach the site of the quarry, which was opened in 1931 by the Hudson River Stone Corporation and closed in 1967. It is now growing in with grasses and small trees, though remnants of an old circular road on the quarry floor are still visible. Just before reaching the quarry, the white blazes lead sharply right and skirt around the south end of the quarry rim. On the way, you'll see old pieces of iron piping and cables that remain as evidence of the quarrying operation.

The trail resumes its climb, leaving the eroded quarry road and going up over a hump on the ridge to the right. Soon, you'll reach a panoramic viewpoint over the Hudson River. You now continue uphill, and after climbing another 400 vertical feet, you'll come to another viewpoint. The village of Cold Spring and Constitution Island to the south—along with West Point, Butter Hill, and Storm King across the river (with its gash for the highway)—make up the panorama. During the Revolutionary War, the Hudson River was chained from Constitution Island to West Point to deter the British advance. The heavy iron chain laid in 1778 was never breached. The trail continues to climb steeply and soon reaches a junction with the yellow-blazed Undercliff Trail at about 1,000 feet in elevation. You've now hiked for 1.4 miles.

Turn left onto the Undercliff Trail, which soon emerges on a rock slab overlooking the quarry on the left. At the right-hand end of this viewpoint, the trail meanders around a large glacial erratic—the first of several in the area.

The first opportunity to see Breakneck Ridge comes after 45 minutes on the Undercliff Trail. Upon reaching the far end of

the shoulder, the trail emerges on a rock outcrop with a sweeping view to the north. Breakneck Ridge, with its highway and railroad tunnels, is the ragged ridge to the north; Storm King is directly across the river. In clear weather, the view includes the Shawangunks and the Catskills.

The Undercliff Trail now turns sharply right and begins to head in a northeast direction. After crossing a stream, it descends on switchbacks to reach the stone foundations of a woods road that was never completed. The trail turns right and proceeds along the road, which soon acquires a dirt-and-gravel surface, crossing a stream on a one-log bridge. After bending to the left, the trail resumes its steady descent, soon beginning to parallel a stream.

A short distance beyond, the Undercliff Trail turns right, crosses the stream, and reaches a wide woods road—the route of the red-blazed Brook Trail. You'll be returning on the Brook Trail, but the hike continues along the yellow-blazed Undercliff Trail. (If you'd like to cut the hike short, turn left onto the Brook Trail, then bear left onto the blue-blazed Cornish Trail and continue down to NY 9D.)

The Undercliff Trail now briefly turns left onto the woods road, then turns right, crosses Breakneck Brook on a bridge, and soon reaches the most rugged and exciting part of the hike. Follow yellow blazes up a boulder field to the base of a cliff wall, and just as it looks as if the trail leads over the cliff edge in front, make a left turn downhill away from the cliff wall. Turn right to begin a switchback climb around and through large boulders, passing under cliffs on the way to the notch. Approximately 30 minutes walking from the bridge over the Breakneck Brook brings you to the end of the Undercliff Trail. Turn right on the white-blazed Breakneck Ridge Trail.

The Breakneck Ridge Trail follows an undulating footpath along the ridge, which takes you up and down over several false summits. The Hudson River and the Newburgh-Beacon Bridge are visible to the left when the leaves are off the trees, and on your right you'll be able to look down on Lake Surprise and its camp. Along the way, watch for an attractive wetland filled with cattails on the right.

When you reach a junction with the red-blazed Breakneck Bypass Trail, which begins on the left at a large boulder, continue ahead on the white-blazed Breakneck Ridge Trail. A short distance beyond, the trail climbs to a small rocky knob. This is the end of the climbing for the hike; the rest of the way is downhill.

After leaving this high point, watch carefully for the junction with the blue-blazed Notch Trail halfway down a steep, rocky descent. Turn right onto the Notch Trail (if you start to follow both white and blue blazes, you've gone too far). The trail descends steeply along the side of the hill, then turns right onto a woods road and levels off.

Soon, you'll pass a dam and several derelict buildings. These ruins are the remnants of a dairy farm once operated by the Cornish family as a gentleman's farm. The Notch Trail bears left and passes these ruins. A short distance beyond, the Notch Trail turns sharply left, but you should continue ahead (parallel to Breakneck Brook), now following the red-blazed Brook Trail.

In 0.25 mile, you'll come to the wooden bridge on the Undercliff Trail that you crossed earlier on the hike, but you should proceed straight ahead, continuing to follow

View of Hudson River and Crow's Nest Mountain from the Washburn Trail   DANIEL CHAZIN

the red blazes of the Brook Trail. Breakneck Brook is on the right, and more remnants from the past—a small concrete building and a dam—line its course.

A short distance beyond, you'll reach a fork. Bear left and continue on the blue-blazed Cornish Trail, which soon crosses the route of the Catskill Aqueduct. The trail follows an old road down to NY 9D, swinging first right and then left, and passing a cement-and-stone water tank and the ruins of the mansion of the estate of Edward G. Cornish, chairman of the board of the National Lead Company, who lived here during the 1920s. The mansion was destroyed by fire in 1956.

The road, now paved, continues to descend toward the river. Down to the right, the Metro-North railroad tracks and NY 9D can be seen. Turn sharply left just before the concrete pillars at NY 9D and continue along the Cornish Trail, which now follows a footpath, for another five minutes back to your car.

9

Fishkill Ridge Conservation Area

Total distance: 7.0 miles

Walking time: 5 hours

Vertical rise: 1,700 feet

Maps: USGS 7.5' West Point; USGS 7.5' Wappingers Falls; NY–NJTC East Hudson Trails #102

Trailhead GPS Coordinates: N 41° 29' 17.5" W 73° 54' 31"

The Fishkill Ridge Conservation Area was purchased in 1992 and 1993 by the Scenic Hudson Land Trust (845-473-4440, ext. 270) with funding from the Lila Acheson and DeWitt Wallace Fund, which was established by the founders of Reader's Digest. A free map with brief trail descriptions is available online at www.scenichudson.org.

Standing as the northern gateway to the famed Hudson Highlands, the area's rocky outcrops offer panoramic views of the Hudson River and the Catskill Mountains. Turkey vultures, eagles, hawks, and falcons soar high above the cliffs of this rugged 1,000-plus-acre site. This "lollipop-loop" hike includes a steep climb up (and back down), but the loop itself is moderate. Hunting is not allowed, but the start of the hike is near a private shooting preserve. Extra caution should be taken during big-game hunting season, usually mid-November through mid-December (see www.dec.ny.gov/out door/hunting.html). Because of the steepness of the climb, this hike is also best saved for cooler days.

HOW TO GET THERE
To reach the trailhead in North Highland, proceed north on US 9 from its junction with NY 301 for 3.3 miles. Turn left onto Old Albany Post Road, a semicircle loop with two connections to US 9 some 0.4 mile apart. If you reach the signed Putnam-Dutchess County border, you've gone 0.1 mile past the second connection. If coming from the north, use Exit 13 of I-84 and proceed south on US 9 for 2.6 miles to the junction on your right,

---

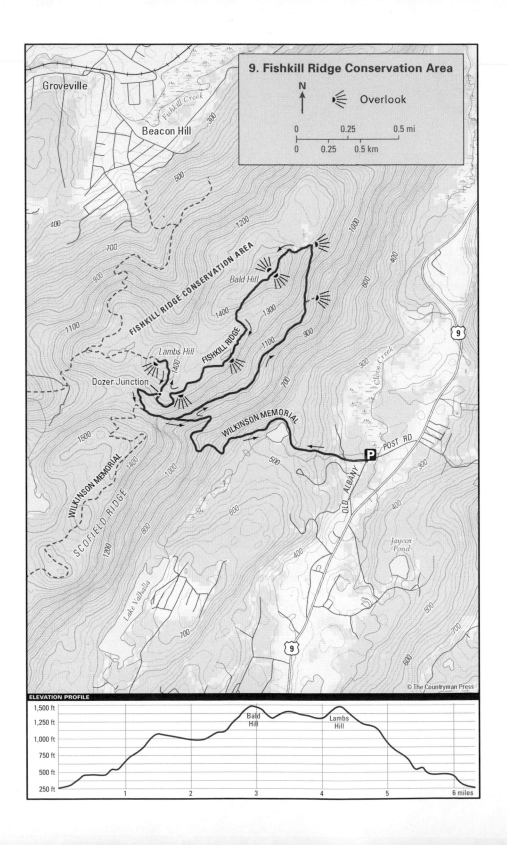

9. Fishkill Ridge Conservation Area

N

Overlook

| 0 | 0.25 | 0.5 mi |
| 0 | 0.25 | 0.5 km |

Groveville

Fishkill Creek

Beacon Hill

300

500

400

700

900

1100

1200

1000

400

800

600

FISHKILL RIDGE CONSERVATION AREA

Bald Hill

1400

1300

FISHKILL RIDGE

1100

Lambs Hill

900

700

1400

Dozer Junction

WILKINSON MEMORIAL

300

Clove Creek

9

1500

1400

WILKINSON MEMORIAL

WILKINSON MEMORIAL

500

OLD ALBANY

POST RD

P

300

400

SCOFIELD RIDGE

1000

800

1200

600

400

Jaycox Pond

Lake Valhalla

700

600

500

700

9

600

© The Countryman Press

ELEVATION PROFILE

1,500 ft			Bald		Lambs	
1,250 ft			Hill		Hill	
1,000 ft						
750 ft						
500 ft						
250 ft	1	2	3	4	5	6 miles

0.1 mile past the signed Putnam-Dutchess border.

Proceed along Old Albany Post Road, looking for shoulder parking. Some good spots are located near a bridge a short distance north of the trailhead. The trail itself starts at a junction with Reservoir Lane (private, no parking but OK to walk).

THE TRAIL

Walk to the junction with Reservoir Lane where the yellow-blazed Wilkinson Memorial Trail, named after a dedicated trail worker, begins. Walk up the dirt road, passing around a metal gate. Soon afterward, the trail turns sharply left into the woods and begins a moderate climb.

In 10 minutes the climb eases off as the trail passes a dam and circles an unnamed pond that straddles the Putnam-Dutchess border. From here, there is a good view up to Hell's Hollow, the rugged gap between the ridges.

Soon the serious 600-foot climb begins. Half of this climb is on woods roads with switchbacks moderating the ascent, but other sections just go up—straight up.

As the Wilkinson Memorial Trail nears the ridgetop at almost 1,100 feet, it turns left onto a woods road. Here, the white-blazed Fishkill Ridge Trail begins on the right. The loop, which you will follow in a counterclockwise direction, begins here. You will return to this point before heading down the mountain. Turn right, leaving the Wilkinson Memorial Trail, and begin to follow the white-blazed Fishkill Ridge Trail.

The Fishkill Ridge Trail, on a woods road, loses a little elevation in the beginning and then starts to climb—first gradually, then more steeply. As the trail climbs steeply through an eroded section, pay careful attention to the blazes—you will soon reach a sharp left turn, which is easily missed. If the grade

moderates and you see no blazes, check to be sure you have not missed this turn.

You're at 1,200 feet elevation as the trail makes this left turn and climbs to the open summit of Bald Hill at 1,500 feet, about 45 minutes to an hour along the Fishkill Ridge Trail. The summit provides expansive views to the east, but as the trail begins to descend, there is an even better view from a rock outcrop just off the trail to the left. This overlook is a good place for a break.

Far to the south, an unusual view of a bend in the Hudson makes it look more like a large lake. The grassy area on the mountaintop ahead is Glynwood Farm in Fahnestock State Park. The skyline of New York City as well as the tops of the George Washington Bridge towers can be seen on a clear day.

About 15 more minutes along the trail is another fine 360-degree view that includes an unsightly quarry. As you continue walking, you'll pass more viewpoints, including Lake Valhalla to the south.

The trail then dips toward Hell's Hollow—you'll assume you're about to descend. However, steep drop-offs preclude a direct course. Instead, the trail bends right, climbs, and makes a short descent to a woods road.

Known by hikers as "Dozer Junction," this spot is the start of a blue-blazed connecting trail. As for the name, "Dozer Junction": To your left, down the woods road just a few yards, is the wreck of an old bulldozer. Hop on up. The backdrop makes for a fine photo, especially if one of you climbs into the driver's seat.

You'll soon return to this spot, but for now proceed across the road and continue to follow the white-blazed trail for a 10-minute, 120-foot climb to the summit of Lambs Hill (elevation 1,500 feet). The short climb is worth the effort, especially if you go a few yards beyond the summit, where the views really open up. Below, the Hudson

Dozer Junction

DANIEL CHAZIN

stretches out in all its magnificence. The Newburgh-Beacon Bridge is to the northwest, with the Mid-Hudson Bridge at Poughkeepsie visible further up the river, and the high peaks of the Catskills on the horizon to the west. North and South Beacon Mountains, with their ubiquitous transmission towers and a reservoir between them, are just to the southwest.

Look to the right of North Beacon Mountain and across the Hudson. On the far horizon, you may see a tower on top of a rise. That's New Jersey's High Point Monument, more than 40 miles away.

Retrace your steps to Dozer Junction, turn right, and head downhill on the blue-blazed woods road past the bulldozer. Soon, you'll pass some iron ruins. Just beyond (but before a big washout cuts across the woods road), the blue trail turns sharply left and heads downhill toward the gap between two peaks. After only a minute (at a low point), the trail reaches a T-junction with another woods road. Turn left here, head slightly uphill, and bear left at a fork. In less than a minute you'll see the yellow blazes of the Wilkinson Memorial Trail. Continue straight ahead (not uphill), now following the yellow-blazed trail.

Parts of this section of the Wilkinson Memorial Trail are on woods roads, parts on a narrow footpath. One stretch even goes under a dramatic rock outcrop. After just 10 minutes or so you'll spot the three white blazes of the Fishkill Ridge Trail where you began the loop earlier in the hike.

Turn right, continuing to follow the yellow-blazed Wilkinson Memorial Trail, which heads steeply downhill. You're now retracing your steps, following the yellow blazes all the way back to Old Albany Post Road, where you left your car.

10

East Mountain and Round Hill

Total distance: 7.3 miles

Walking time: 4.5 hours

Vertical rise: 1,400 feet

Maps: USGS 7.5' Oscawana Lake; NY–NJTC East Hudson Trails #103

Trailhead GPS Coordinates: N 41° 26' 36" W 73° 54' 54"

This hike follows less-used trails in the northwest corner of Fahnestock State Park in Putnam County. The old rock walls seen on your hike are remnants from when the land was cleared for farming. The area was also once used for iron mining, and roads and railroads were constructed to transport the iron ore and farm produce to the Hudson River and elsewhere. The route of this hike is mostly through hardwoods with limited views, includes some moderate climbing, and ends with a pleasant walk by the side of an attractive stream. When you are in need of a low-key, quiet saunter, this circuit is the one to take.

HOW TO GET THERE
From the intersection of NY 301 and US 9 just east of Cold Spring, proceed north on US 9 for 0.2 mile, then turn right onto a paved road at a brown sign for the "Hubbard Lodge." Bear left at the fork, continue past a house on the left, and park along the right side of the road.

THE TRAIL
Walk back along the paved road to a junction with a grassy road on the left. Turn left on the grassy road and, almost immediately, you'll reach a gate. A triple-white blaze on the gate marks the start of the white-blazed School Mountain Road, and the blue-blazed Fahnestock Trail joins just ahead.

Follow both blue markers and white markers along School Mountain Road—a multiuse woods road that makes for easy walking in a tranquil setting. In the next few minutes, the road twice crosses Clove Creek on

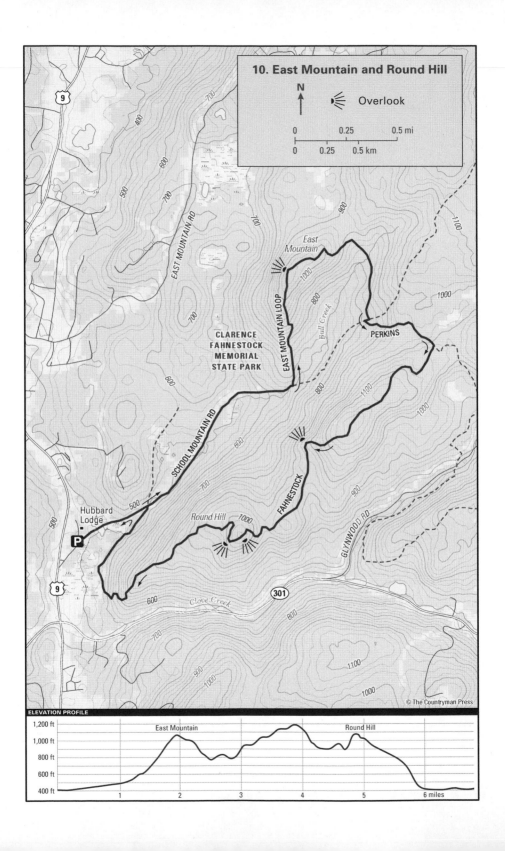

10. East Mountain and Round Hill

N

Overlook

0   0.25   0.5 mi

0   0.25   0.5 km

East Mountain

EAST MOUNTAIN LOOP

Bull Creek

PERKINS

CLARENCE
FAHNESTOCK
MEMORIAL
STATE PARK

EAST MOUNTAIN RD

SCHOOL MOUNTAIN RD

Hubbard
Lodge

P

Round Hill

FAHNESTOCK

GLYNWOOD RD

Clove Creek

301

9

9

© The Countryman Press

ELEVATION PROFILE

1,200 ft		East Mountain		Round Hill	
1,000 ft					
800 ft					
600 ft					
400 ft					

1   2   3   4   5   6 miles

steel-plate bridges. In about 10 minutes, you'll notice two stone pillars on the left flanking a woods road that leads to the site of the old Hubbard mansion. There used to be another steel-plate bridge here, but it was destroyed by Hurricane Irene in August 2011, and you have to cross the creek on two I beams. On the other side of the creek, the Fahnestock Trail—marked with blue disks—leaves to the right. At the end of the hike, you return to this junction before retracing your steps on School Mountain Road.

Continue ahead on the white-blazed School Mountain Road, crossing two more steel-plate bridges. After a while, you'll begin a steady ascent between old rock walls. After crossing a wooden footbridge, you'll notice a triple-red blaze on the left which marks the start of the East Mountain Loop. Bear left onto the East Mountain Loop, leaving School Mountain Road, which heads to the right.

Recross the stream on another wooden footbridge and follow the red blazes uphill along a woods road, paralleling an old rock wall on your right. The footpath crosses another wall, then snakes upward to the summit of East Mountain and a view of Fishkill Ridge—a good place to rest for a while.

The East Mountain Loop now descends until it crosses a seasonal watercourse and turns immediately right to continue its downward trend on a woods road. Walk for approximately 10 minutes on this woods road to reach the end of the East Mountain Loop, confirmed by three markers on a tree to the right. Traversing this loop will probably take the best part of an hour before you reach School Mountain Road (marked

Fishkill Ridge from East Mountain

DAN BALOGH

East Mountain and Round Hill

Abandoned farmhouse along School Mountain Road DAN BALOGH

by an abandoned building on the left). Continue by turning right onto School Mountain Road, and you'll almost immediately cross a stream on rocks. On the left, you will see a triple-yellow blaze that marks the start of the Perkins Trail. If you wish to cut the hike short, continue ahead on School Mountain Road to your car, but if you wish to continue, turn left onto the yellow-blazed Perkins Trail. The trail climbs, sometimes on rocks, alongside a cascading stream, until after about 15 minutes it arrives at the junction of the blue-blazed Fahnestock Trail. Here you are probably a little more than two hours into the hike. Turn right onto the Fahnestock Trail, now following only blue blazes.

The Fahnestock Trail proceeds to climb, then descends into a low-lying area before undulating along the ridge and beginning the ascent of Round Hill. The first viewpoint to the southwest on a clear day offers a view of the Bear Mountain Bridge; the second, a view to the west. The area is dotted with many beautifully shaped red cedars. All the climbing is now finished, so you may wish to tarry awhile before starting downhill. The trail jogs along on the ridge before recommencing its descent. Very soon now you begin to hear traffic on US 9, and in fact you'll get a view of the junction with NY 301.

At the base of the descent, the trail turns right onto a woods road. Walk for about 10 minutes along a stream containing many moss-covered rocks until you reach School Mountain Road at the junction noted earlier. Cross the I beam bridge over the stream, turn left, and walk back to your car along School Mountain Road.

11

Jordan Pond/ Perkins Trail Loop

Total distance: 7.2 miles

Walking time: 4 hours

Vertical rise: 700 feet

Maps: USGS 7.5' West Point; USGS 7.5' Oscawana Lake; NY–NJTC East Hudson Trails #103

Trailhead GPS Coordinates: N 41° 26' 36.5" W 73° 51' 36"

The hike described passes through preserved farmlands that may remind you of walking in southern England. The section that runs along the cascading Clove Creek is particularly beautiful, and visiting this area in June when the mountain laurel blooms is especially rewarding. Most of the trails are rocky and interrupted by small streams that are usually dry in summer. This hike uses portions of the Charcoal Burners Trail, the Fahnestock Trail, the Perkins Trail, and the Cabot Trail.

HOW TO GET THERE

From the junction of NY 9D and NY 301 in Cold Spring, proceed east on NY 301. In 4.5 miles, Dennytown Road begins on the right. Continue for another 0.6 mile on NY 301 and look carefully for a trail crossing, marked by a brown wand on the south side of the road and a sign for the Charcoal Burners Trail on the north side of the road (there is also a faded white cross on a rock on the north side of the road, about 50 feet beyond the trail crossing). Park along the shoulder of the road near the trail crossing. If coming from the east, the distance to the trailhead from the junction of NY 301 with the Taconic State Parkway is 2.9 miles.

THE TRAIL

Cross to the north side of the road and proceed north on the red-blazed Charcoal Burners Trail (named for the men who felled trees in the area during the 19th century and carefully burned them to make charcoal). The trail briefly parallels the road, then bears

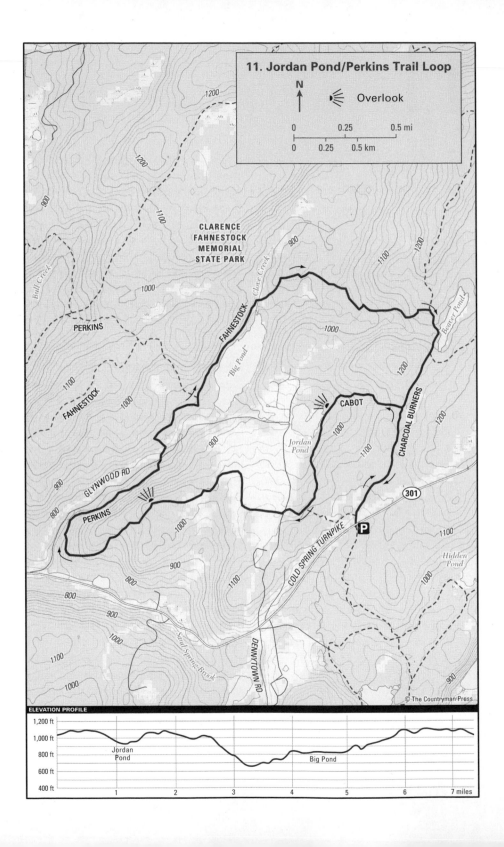

11. Jordan Pond/Perkins Trail Loop

N

Overlook

| 0 | 0.25 | 0.5 mi |
| 0 | 0.25 | 0.5 km |

CLARENCE
FAHNESTOCK
MEMORIAL
STATE PARK

1200

1200

900

1100

1200

1000

Bull Creek

900

PERKINS

FAHNESTOCK

1100

1000

FAHNESTOCK

800

900

GLYNWOOD RD

PERKINS

1000

900

1100

1000

800

900

1000

1100

1000

1200

900

1000

1100

Clove Creek

FAHNESTOCK

"Big Pond"

Jordan Pond

900

1100

CABOT

1000

1100

CHARCOAL BURNERS

1200

Beaver Pond

P

COLD SPRING TURNPIKE

301

1100

Hidden Pond

1000

900

DENNYTOWN RD

Sand Spring Brook

© The Countryman Press

ELEVATION PROFILE

1,200 ft							
1,000 ft							
800 ft	Jordan Pond				Big Pond		
600 ft							
400 ft	1	2	3	4	5	6	7 miles

Field along the Perkins Trail

DANIEL CHAZIN

left and heads into the woods. Soon, you'll reach the eastern end of the yellow-blazed Perkins Trail (named for the former owners of this land), but you should continue ahead on the red-blazed Charcoal Burners Trail. The relatively level trail passes through thickets of mountain laurel, with an understory of blueberry bushes.

In 0.7 mile, a cairn and a triple-white blaze mark the start of the Cabot Trail. Turn left and follow the Cabot Trail, which descends gradually, reaching Jordan Pond in 0.5 mile. After crossing the inlet of the pond, a short side trail leads down to the water. Here, a bench has been placed on a rock slab overlooking the pond—a great spot to take a break.

Continue ahead on the white-blazed Cabot Trail, which soon goes by a large rock outcrop and begins to ascend. After passing between old stone walls, the trail emerges onto a clearing—with lovely fir trees on the right, a woodpile, and an old gate. Here, the yellow-blazed Perkins Trail comes in from the left. The Cabot Trail ends here, and you should continue ahead on the yellow-blazed trail, briefly following a wide, grassy road. Watch carefully for a double-blaze, which marks a right turn.

Just beyond, you'll come to an unlocked gate—the first of several you'll encounter in this portion of the hike. This section of the trail crosses private property and several active fields. Please stay on the trail and leave each gate in the same position (locked or unlocked) that you found it. Follow the trail as it turns left on a dirt road for about 200 feet, then turns right and reaches a wooden gate (before coming to a road that goes off to the right). After passing through this gate, you'll emerge alongside an open field that attracts many butterflies, insects, and birds.

Jordan Pond

DANIEL CHAZIN

Continue ahead, passing between a fence on the right and an old stone wall on the left, with views to the right over the ridge to the north. Soon, you'll pass a large horse barn on the left.

After following a path between two fences, the trail turns right and follows along the right side of another large field. As you reach the crest of the hill, views appear over a large lake below. After descending for a short distance, bear left on a farm road (indicated by two ruts) that crosses the field (on the right, a double-yellow blaze on a fence post indicates the turn, but the blazes might be obscured by vegetation). Continue along the farm road, which passes another gate and crosses a third field. There are relatively few blazes along this section of the trail, and you will have to look carefully to find them. Enter the woods at the end of the field, bear right at the next fork, and emerge onto a fourth field. Here, the trail bears right, skirting the perimeter of the field, then continues along the road, soon reentering the woods at a gap in a stone wall.

After reaching a limited viewpoint to the north and west from a rock outcrop, the trail begins a steady descent through mountain laurel thickets. Soon, you'll hear the sounds of traffic, as the trail comes close to NY 301. Near the base of the descent, the trail swings sharply to the right, heads away from the busy road, and begins to parallel the cascading Clove Creek. For 0.5 mile, the trail runs for a splendid stretch along this attractive stream. The trail then bears left, crosses the stream on a wooden bridge, crosses the private Glynwood Road (a little-used dirt road), and climbs rather steeply to a grassy woods road.

A red-blazed trail begins on the left, but you should turn right to continue along the yellow-blazed Perkins Trail, which follows this grassy road. Soon, you'll come to a T-junction, where the yellow-blazed trail turns

left. In another 150 feet, it reaches a junction with the blue-blazed Fahnestock Trail. The Perkins Trail turns left here, but you should bear right—leaving the Perkins Trail, and following the blue blazes of the Fahnestock Trail. A short distance ahead, you'll pass a large pond to the right, visible through the trees. Although the pond is unnamed, it is known to local residents as the "Big Pond."

Just beyond the northern end of the pond, the trail bears right, crosses the pond's inlet on a moss-covered cement bridge, and begins a steady climb. At the crest of the rise, the trail turns right, leaving the woods road, and heads into the woods on a footpath. It descends a switchback, climbs a rock outcrop, and continues to ascend more gently through mountain laurel. Eventually, it turns right onto a woods road. The trail briefly turns left onto another woods road, then turns right and continues on a footpath through dense barberry bushes.

After a moderate climb, the blue-blazed Fahnestock Trail turns right onto a wide, grassy woods road. A short distance beyond, the red-blazed Charcoal Burners Trail joins from the left. Continue ahead, now following both blue and red blazes, and descend to Beaver Pond. The trail briefly follows the shore of this scenic pond, offering a panoramic view of it.

The trail now turns right, descends to cross the outlet of the pond on a concrete bridge below the dam, then climbs through highbush blueberry bushes and dense mountain laurel thickets to reach another junction, where the two trails diverge. The blue-blazed Fahnestock Trail leaves to the left, but you should continue ahead, now following only the red-blazed Charcoal Burners Trail. You'll pass the start of the white-blazed Cabot Trail on the right and retrace your steps on the red-blazed trail to NY 301, where the hike began.

12

Heart of Fahnestock

Total distance: 6.5 miles (3.3-mile alternate)

Walking time: 3 hours (1.5-hour alternate)

Vertical rise: 500 feet

Maps: USGS 7.5' Oscawana Lake; NY–NJTC East Hudson Trails #103

Trailhead GPS Coordinates: N 41° 27' 18.5" W 73° 50' 02"

This pleasant woods walk passes peaceful lakes and lush swamps, and even uses a Civil War–era railroad bed. As you walk along, picture the rural communities that once dominated this region. Old stone walls, foundations, historic mine pits, and woods roads are all that remain of the active history of this now quiet area.

HOW TO GET THERE

To reach the parking area on NY 301, take the Taconic State Parkway to the exit for NY 301 West (Cold Spring). Proceed west on NY 301 for 1.3 miles to a parking area on the north side of the road, on a small peninsula jutting into Canopus Lake. If this lot is full, a second parking area is located a short distance farther west, at the Appalachian Trail (AT) crossing. A free brochure map of Fahnestock State Park can be downloaded at www.nynjtc.org/view/maps.

THE TRAIL

Walk over to the other side of NY 301, and head west along the shoulder for a very short distance. You may notice, on the guardrail, a triple-blue blaze, which marks the start of the Three Lakes Trail. Climb over the guardrail and scramble down to the trail. Most of the trails in Fahnestock State Park are marked with the blue plastic disks of the Taconic Park Commission, but you may also notice some older paint blazes.

The Three Lakes Trail crosses an old paved road (known as the Philipstown Turnpike) that parallels NY 301 and heads into the woods, following a woods road. Rock

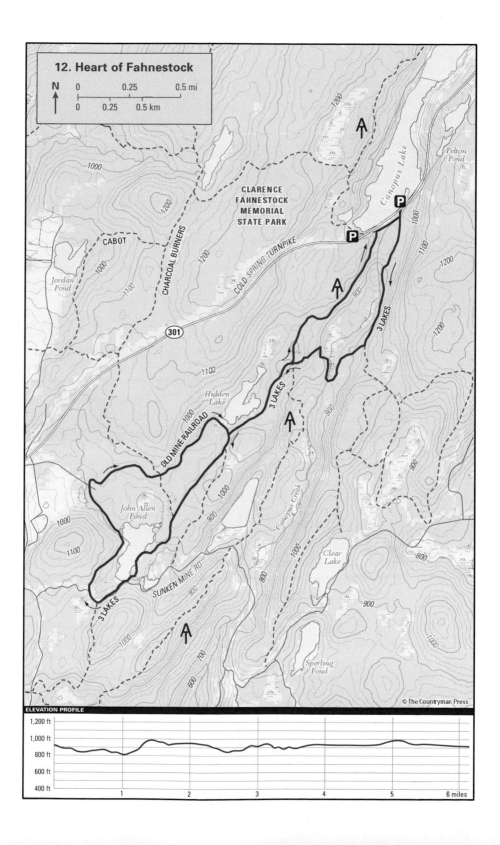

12. Heart of Fahnestock

N

0   0.25   0.5 mi

0   0.25   0.5 km

CLARENCE
FAHNESTOCK
MEMORIAL
STATE PARK

Canopus Lake

Pelton
Pond

P

P

CABOT

CHARCOAL BURNERS

Jordan
Pond

301

COLD SPRING TURNPIKE

3 LAKES

3 LAKES

Hidden
Lake

OLD MINE RAILROAD

3 LAKES

John Allen
Pond

Canopus Creek

Clear
Lake

SUNKEN MINE RD

Sperling
Pond

© The Countryman Press

ELEVATION PROFILE

1,200 ft

1,000 ft

800 ft

600 ft

400 ft

1   2   3   4   5   6 miles

John Allen Pond

DANIEL CHAZIN

cuts and piles of stone (called tailings) are dramatic evidence of mining activity from the late 1700s through the late 1800s. The first mine you pass—identifiable only by its tailing pit—belonged to Richard Hopper, who opened it in 1820. The mine remained a small operation until the Civil War, when the heirs sold the mineral rights to Paul S. Forbes, the builder of the railway. The mining operations were abandoned after the panic of 1873, and the surrounding land was acquired by Dr. Clarence Fahnestock in 1915 after a series of intervening land sales.

In about 0.5 mile, the route passes a lovely marsh with an extensive stand of phragmites that rustle in the wind. There are many birds here, heard but often unseen. Soon the woods open up, and old stone walls offer evidence of long-gone settlements.

Remember, you are following the blue blazes, not just the obvious footway. There are several points on this hike when the marked trail abruptly leaves a woods road and turns onto a narrower footpath.

One such point comes about 0.75 mile into the hike as the blue trail turns right, leaving the woods road. If you notice green markers, you've passed the turn and are heading toward the Durland (formerly Clear Lake) Scout Reservation. Continue on the blue-blazed Three Lakes Trail, which passes fields of hay-scented fern and heads down to charming Canopus Creek (the outlet of Canopus Lake). A small, picturesque gorge just upstream is worth a short detour for a peek. The trail crosses the creek on large rock slabs and heads slightly north. It then turns sharply left and climbs through an impressive forest, certainly one of the more handsome second-growth forests in southern New York.

Soon the white-blazed AT crosses, but you should continue ahead on the blue-blazed Three Lakes Trail. You'll now pass through dense mountain laurel thickets. In a short distance, you'll approach the shore of Hidden Lake. A short unmarked trail on the right leads to the dam, which offers fine views. You may wish to take a short detour out to the dam, then return to the Three Lakes Trail.

For those wanting a shorter hike (so far, you've walked 1.8 miles), follow the blue blazes back the way you came to the junction with the white-blazed AT. Turn left at the junction and follow the AT for 0.9 mile back to NY 301, then turn right and follow the road to your car, a short distance away.

For those who wish to complete a longer hike, continue south on the Three Lakes Trail, which almost immediately reaches a junction with the yellow-blazed Old Mine Railroad Trail (which begins on the right). This will be your return route, but for now continue ahead on the blue-blazed Three Lakes Trail, which soon leaves the woods road it has been following and continues on a footpath.

About 0.5 mile from the lake, you'll pass the southern terminus of the red-blazed Charcoal Burners Trail in the midst of a laurel grove. A short distance beyond, the trail passes the stone foundations of several buildings from John Allen's homestead. It then turns right and begins to follow an old mine railbed. Soon, it leaves the railbed and crosses a stream on rocks (to the right, the stone abutments of the mine railway are visible, but the bridge is gone).

The trail now arrives at the shore of beautiful John Allen Pond. It parallels the lakeshore for a short distance, reenters the woods, then crosses the outlet of the pond on rocks just below an old stone dam (now breached). It now climbs to the dirt Sunken Mine Road (also known as Sunk Mine Road). Turn right onto the road, passing the southern end of John Allen Pond on the right. In about 0.2 mile, the blue-blazed Three Lakes Trail leaves the road on the left, but you should continue ahead on the road. In another 500 feet, as the road bends to the left, the yellow-blazed Old Mine Railroad Trail begins on the right. Turn right and follow this wide trail, which gradually descends toward John Allen Pond. After approaching the pond, the trail crosses a small stream on rocks.

Note how well the trail is constructed and elevated. No, volunteers did not build this trail. They just used the features that give the trail its name—literally, an old mine-railroad bed.

During the Civil War, a narrow-gauge railroad was built to serve the iron mines in the area. However, the development of open-pit mines in the Midwest in the late 1800s brought these operations to an early end. Starting a new life, much of the railbed was opened as a hiking trail in 1994, but in the early 2000s the northern section was closed as a result of constant beaver-caused flooding.

A few more minutes along, the marked trail makes a sharp right. Follow the blazed route, avoiding the woods road that branches left and leads to private land.

About 0.3 mile beyond John Allen Pond, follow the Old Mine Railroad Trail as it turns right, leaving the old railroad bed. Then, in another 0.3 mile, you'll cross the red-blazed

Stone abutment of the Old Mine Railroad   DANIEL CHAZIN

Charcoal Burners Trail. Just beyond, look for a large glacial erratic. Doesn't it appear that two trees are supporting the rock?

Continue ahead on the yellow-blazed Old Mine Railroad Trail. Just before reaching Hidden Lake, the trail turns right and crosses the outlet of the lake below the dam on stepping-stones. A short distance beyond, the Old Mine Railroad Trail ends at the blue-blazed Three Lakes Trail. You were here earlier in the hike.

Turn left and proceed north on the Three Lakes Trail for 0.5 mile to the junction with the white-blazed AT, then turn left onto the AT and follow its white blazes along an old railbed. Here, the elevated rock roadway is sometimes 15 feet above the surrounding land. The path continues through a rock cut and overlooks the marsh you passed near the start of the hike.

Soon you'll begin to hear the sounds of the traffic on NY 301. Follow the AT up to the highway, and turn right to reach your car—or turn right onto a distinct woods road paralleling the highway that takes you back to the hike's starting point.

13

Dutchess County Backpack

Total distance: 14.6 miles

Walking time: 2 to 3 days

Vertical rise: 2,300 feet

Maps: USGS 7.5' Poughquag; 7.5' Pawling; Guide to the Appalachian Trail in New York–New Jersey, Map #1

Trailhead GPS Coordinates: N 41° 32' 25.5" W 73° 43' 59"

First proposed in 1921, the Appalachian Trail (AT) extends from Maine to Georgia—a distance of over 2,185 miles, crossing 14 states along the way—and is the result of the tireless efforts of many thousands of volunteers and decades of advocacy and work.

The first section was built by the New York–New Jersey Trail Conference (NY–NJTC) on Bear Mountain in 1923, but there was little additional progress for several years. Serious efforts resumed in 1925 with the formation of the Appalachian Trail Conference (ATC) (now known as the Appalachian Trail Conservancy) to coordinate efforts. The Civilian Conservation Corps (CCC) completed the last section on a ridge in Maine in 1937.

The original AT route did not last for long. After World War II, highways, housing, and other developments encroached on the trail, forcing many sections onto highways. As the situation became more serious, the hiking community turned to Congress and President Lyndon Johnson for assistance. The result was the enactment of the National Trails System Act in 1968, with the AT and the Pacific Crest Trail being the first trails designated under this legislation. After President Jimmy Carter signed the Appalachian Trail Amendments to the act in 1978, true protection efforts finally began. About $90 million was appropriated to acquire a corridor for the trail where it was not already in a public park or forest. Today, fewer than 6 miles are still unprotected—scattered over five states (but mostly in one location in central Virginia).

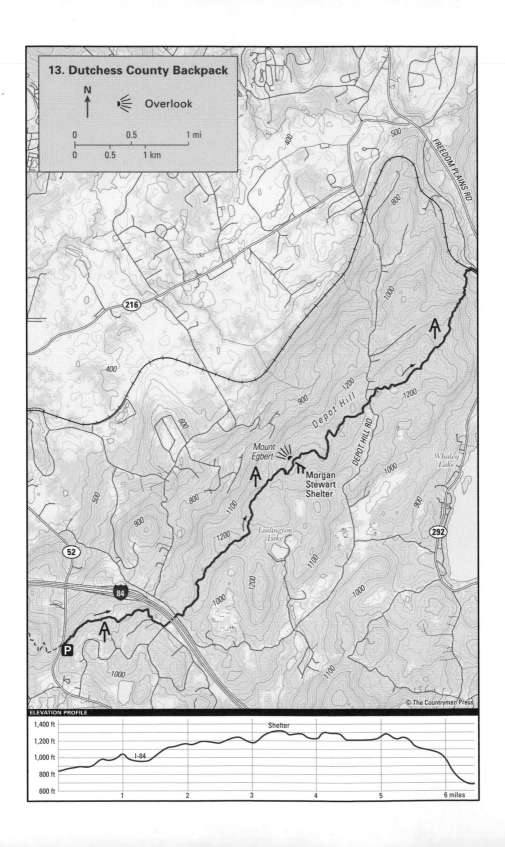

13. Dutchess County Backpack

N

Overlook

0   0.5   1 mi

0   0.5   1 km

216

400

500

FREEDOM PLAINS RD

800

1000

1200

Depot Hill

900

1200

DEPOT HILL RD

Mount
Egbert

Morgan
Stewart
Shelter

Whaley
Lake

1000

900

292

Ludington
Lake

1100

52

1200

1000

84

1000

1100

P

1000

© The Countryman Press

ELEVATION PROFILE

1,400 ft				Shelter		
1,200 ft						
1,000 ft	I-84					
800 ft						
600 ft						
	1	2	3	4	5	6 miles

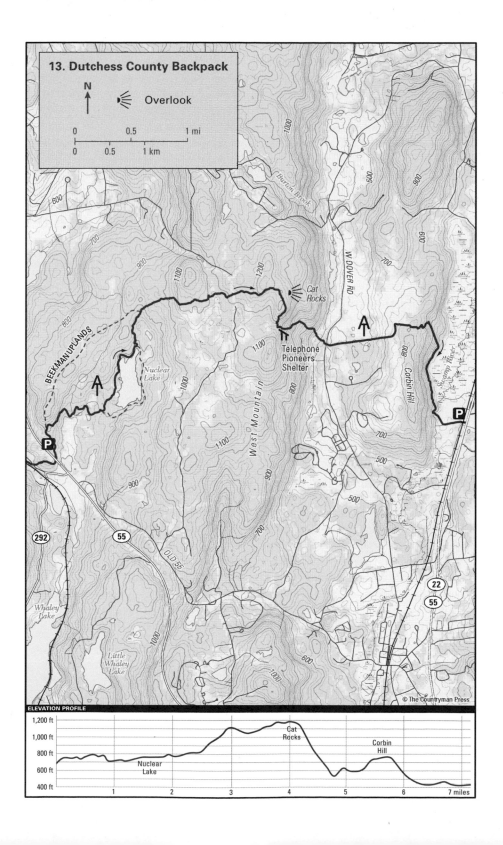

13. Dutchess County Backpack

N

Overlook

0   0.5   1 mi
0   0.5   1 km

Burton Brook

W DOVER RD

Cat Rocks

Telephone
Pioneers
Shelter

BEEKMAN UPLANDS

*Nuclear
Lake*

West Mountain

Corbin
Hill

Swamp River

P

P

P

292

55

OLD 55

*Whaley
Lake*

*Little
Whaley
Lake*

22

55

© The Countryman Press

ELEVATION PROFILE

1,200 ft
1,000 ft
800 ft
600 ft
400 ft

Cat
Rocks

Corbin
Hill

Nuclear
Lake

1   2   3   4   5   6   7 miles

Under a unique agreement, the ATC has been entrusted by the National Park Service with the primary responsibility for maintaining the footpath and associated facilities (mostly shelters). The 88.5 miles that lie in New York State are maintained by volunteers of the NY–NJTC and some of their member clubs. At some 4,000 acres, the AT corridor here constitutes Dutchess County's largest park.

This two-night "family" backpack consists of a short 4-mile hike to the first lean-to, a moderate 7.6-mile day to the next lean-to, and a short 3 miles out on the final day. It can be started on Friday afternoon and end early on Sunday. The full distance can also be done as a vigorous day hike. For a longer backpack, see Options at the end of this hike.

Backpacking requires preparation. If you are not experienced, get advice from a back-packing basics book or a good specialized outdoor store. In addition to normal day-hike equipment, you'll need at least a good sleeping bag and pad, food, a cooking pot or two, dishes, utensils, backpacking stove, matches or lighter, flashlight, and a tent (in case the lean-to is full). The more you take, the heavier your pack. Take what you need and *only* what you need (easier said than done). Many outdoor-equipment stores offer backpack equipment checklists; these are also available on the Internet. AT guidelines require overnight groups to be no larger than 10 people. Be aware of seasonal con-ditions; during dry periods, the streams that ordinarily provide water for the lean-tos may not be flowing.

HOW TO GET THERE

The end point is on NY 22, 2.4 miles north of the center of the village of Pawling and 1.8 miles north of the Trinity-Pawling School footbridge. Parking is permitted in a small parking area at the trail crossing, just west of NY 22. Additional parking is available in a designated parking area on the east side of NY 22, about 0.1 mile north of the trail crossing. NY 22, a major thoroughfare, is accessible from Exit 20 of I-84 and Exit 10 of I-684. If you have two cars available, spot one at the end, and then drive to the start. Otherwise, you'll have to arrange with a friend for a pickup or drop-off.

It's worth noting that the AT station on Metro-North's Upper Harlem Line (also known as the Wassaic Branch) is located at the end of the hike. You could take a train home from this station, although trains stop here only on weekends and holidays. If you end your hike on a weekday, you'll have to head south about 2.5 miles to the Pawling station (which has rail service every two hours or so). For schedule information, call 212-532-4900 or go to www.mta.info.

To get from NY 22 parking to the hike's start on NY 52 (see below), take NY 22 south about 3 miles to NY 55, then turn right onto NY 55 for 7 miles to its junction with NY 216 in Poughquag. Turn left onto NY 216 for another 7 miles to NY 52. Turn left again onto NY 52 for about 2 miles (going under I-84) to the parking area (on the left, near the crest of the hill). If you come to Leetown Road, you've gone 0.4 mile too far. If you don't need to shuttle a car, you can reach the start of the hike by taking I-84 to Exit 16. Proceed north on the Taconic State Parkway for less than 1.5 miles to NY 52. Turn right (east) onto NY 52 and continue for just under 4 miles. After passing under I-84, proceed uphill to a small AT parking area on the left side of the highway.

THE TRAIL

Day One

Distance: 4 miles
Walking time: 1.5 hours
Vertical rise: 800 feet

The East Hudson Highlands

From the parking area off NY 52 (800 feet elevation), proceed through the boulders on a blue-blazed connector trail, soon intersecting the AT. Do not turn right, but continue straight ahead on the AT, blazed with 2-by-6-inch white rectangles, and proceed uphill to a kiosk. In about 10 minutes, you'll cross an old stone wall (one of many in this area) and a seasonal stream. The trail undulates and skirts a grassy field with young saplings. Portions of this field are cleared as part of an open-area management plan to increase natural diversity. The views to the north and northwest are of the Catskills and Shawangunks.

Soon the roar of traffic on I-84 fills the air as the trail ascends a small hill and bears left down to the paved Old Stormville Mountain Road. Turn right a short distance to Mountain Top Road, where a left turn takes you over I-84 to Grape Hollow Road (very limited parking). You've now covered about 1.5 miles of walking. The trail immediately reenters the woods, heads down an embankment on stone steps, and begins a moderate ascent of the ridges leading to Mount Egbert (1,329 feet). Soon, you'll pass a small pond (a swamp in dry seasons) and some nice rock outcrops. A short distance beyond, you'll pass a blue-blazed access trail on the left that leads to a cul-de-sac in the town of Beekman. (You may also see some yellow blazes which are used to mark property boundaries, and also to blaze a side trail that skirts the perimeter of Girl Scout Camp Ludington.) The trail passes over the crests

Boardwalk across the Great Swamp

DANIEL CHAZIN

of small hills, crosses seasonal streams, meanders through patches of mountain laurel, and comes to an attractive rock cut before ascending the first ledges of Mount Egbert, with its fine views. In another 0.25 mile, after cresting the summit, you'll reach the Morgan Stewart Memorial Shelter (75 feet to the right of the trail).

The shelter—named for a deceased trail worker—was built in 1984 by local volunteers with $2,500 in funds donated by IBM. This raised-floor, three-sided lean-to accommodates six; it's first-come, first-served, so you should bring a small tent—especially on weekends or in summer—in case it's fully occupied. There's a fireplace, a privy 200 feet to the side, and a water pump downhill about 400 feet. The round concrete ruin near the shelter is the remains of a cistern that served a farmhouse that once stood nearby.

All backcountry water should be boiled, chemically treated, or filtered before use. Many backpackers find filtering to be the best method, as the filtered water has no unpleasant taste and is cool and refreshing. To avoid having your food taken by bears or other smaller animals, make sure you bring a rope to hang your food high from a tree branch.

Day Two
Distance: 7.6 miles
Walking time: 5 hours
Vertical rise: 1,000 feet
Leaving the shelter, the AT undulates through the woods. There are no views except near the start, and the terrain is generally gently down. You cross the gravel Depot Hill Road in about 20 minutes. Depot Hill is a state reforestation area. The area has been naturally regenerated from farmland abandoned in the early 1900s. Selected timber harvests are done periodically.

About an hour from the start, you'll pass a large balanced boulder and reach a viewpoint overlooking Whaley Lake. You now begin a 700-foot descent ending with a crossing of railroad tracks (the yellow paint markers are the boundary of the railroad right-of-way). Note the stand of Japanese knotweed (the stems resemble bamboo) on the far side of the tracks. Continuing down an embankment, the trail crosses an outlet stream of Whaley Lake on a bridge and continues up to cross Old NY 55. Bear right across the road and through some boulders, and reenter the woods.

Soon the trail crosses NY 55 (parking is available uphill to the left) and enters the Nuclear Lake area. This property, which was acquired by the National Park Service in 1979, derives its name from the previous owner, United Nuclear Corporation, which conducted nuclear fuel processing research here until the early 1970s. The buildings have been removed, the area cleaned, and the lake declared safe for unrestricted use.

After passing a blue-blazed trail to a parking area, another blue-blazed trail is reached. This route was used by the AT before the 1998 opening of Nuclear Lake for public use and is still maintained as an alternative trail, known as the Beekman Uplands Loop. Stay on the AT, which skirts along the side of a hill through mixed hardwoods and hemlocks, continuing for more than 1 mile before crossing the Nuclear Lake outlet stream three times. After paralleling the stream for a short distance, you'll pass the trailhead of a yellow-blazed side trail that loops around the eastern side of the lake, but stay on the white-blazed AT, which passes through a rock crevice, goes through an area with dense mountain laurel thickets, and continues to the lake. Completely surrounded by public land, Nuclear Lake is most often a peaceful area—a great place to stop and

Dover Oak

DANIEL CHAZIN

explore. The lake is large. At-your-own-risk swimming is OK . . . and it's only 3 more miles to the shelter. (Be aware, however, that there is evidence of beaver activity in the lake, and the water may contain giardia cysts.)

The walk along the lake takes 10 to 15 minutes. At the northern end of the lake, you'll encounter the north end of the yellow-blazed side trail that loops around the lake, and in another 0.5 mile you'll reach the second junction with the blue bypass trail. The route, which has been undulating, now begins a steady ascent to a stone wall, then levels off on a 1,200-foot-high ridgetop and begins a descent, crossing a swampy area on puncheons. When you cross an old dirt road (Penny Road), you have hiked nearly 7 miles from the Morgan Stewart Shelter.

In the next 0.5 mile, the trail passes a swamp and ascends to the summit of West Mountain. There are only limited views from the summit, but a short distance beyond you'll notice a side trail on the left that leads to Cat Rocks—a panoramic east-facing viewpoint from an open rock outcrop. Down below, you can see West Dover Road, with fields beyond. The AT crosses this road and follows along the edge of these fields.

Return to the AT and continue along the trail, which now descends to a junction with a blue-blazed side trail that leads right to the Telephone Pioneers Shelter. The shelter accommodates six. There's a privy, and water is available seasonally from a stream at the trail junction. Built in 1988, the shelter was funded by the White Plains Chapter of the Telephone Pioneers of America, whose members also helped build it.

Day Three

Distance: 3.1 miles
Walking time: Less than 2 hours
Vertical rise: 500 feet

The hike out is fairly short and mostly downhill. It begins by paralleling the stream, with the descent sometimes steep. After about 0.5 mile, the AT descends over jagged rock outcrops, with some lovely cedars. It crosses a wet area on rocks and puncheons before climbing to West Dover Road (County Route 20), where limited parking is available.

Cross the road, passing a huge white oak to the left of the trail. Known as the Dover Oak, this oak is estimated to be about three hundred years old, has a circumference of over 20 feet, and is the largest blazed tree along the entire AT from Maine to Georgia. The trail now begins to climb. It cuts across a field, crosses a wet area on puncheons and a bridge, and climbs alongside some more fields, with woods on the right. The puncheons can be slippery—take your time. Some of the fences in the area are electrified, so use caution. A relocation of the trail in this area is being considered, and you should take care to follow the white blazes.

About an hour from the shelter, the trail reenters the woods and soon begins to descend Corbin Hill, passing through gaps in several stone walls. At the base of the descent, it crosses the Swamp River on a wooden bridge and continues across the Great Swamp, a large wetland, on a 1,600-foot-long handicapped-accessible boardwalk. The bridge and the boardwalk were constructed between 2009 and 2012 by volunteers, with the assistance of the Mid-Atlantic Trail Crew of the Appalachian Trail Conservancy. At the end of the boardwalk, you'll cross the Metro-North railroad tracks at the AT station. NY 22 and the parking area where you left your car are just beyond.

OPTIONS

Day one can be lengthened by about 5 miles by beginning near the AT crossing of the Taconic State Parkway near Miller Hill Road. No parking is available on the Taconic State Parkway, but limited parking is available along Hortontown Road (0.3 mile west of the parkway). Miller Hill Road crosses the Taconic State Parkway about 1 mile north of the Dutchess-Putnam County line and about 2 miles south of its intersection with I-84 (Exit 16). The trail in this area traverses a side of Hosner Mountain and crosses the multiple summits of Stormville Mountain. This option adds about 1,100 feet of elevation gain. There are numerous fine views.

There are several other options to shorten the route. Midhike parking areas are mentioned in the text.

III. Rockland County and Harriman Park

Introduction to the Ramapos: Harriman–Bear Mountain State Parks and Rockland County

The Ramapo Mountains extend from northern New Jersey into Rockland and Orange Counties. Their eroded slopes have risen above nearby seas for nearly 600 million years, making them among the oldest landmasses on the continent. These mountains are part of the Reading Prong, which extends from Reading, Pennsylvania, to the Hudson Highlands and north to the Green Mountains of Vermont. This Precambrian formation is the result of periods of intense folding and metamorphism of sediments deposited more than a billion years ago and of intrusions of magma that occurred several times in the Precambrian era. Although these forces leave a complicated picture for the geologist, later events, like the Ice Ages, are much clearer. The striations and polished rocks and the ubiquitous glacial erratics are obvious to the hiker on any walk through the Ramapos.

Whether the name "Ramapo" derives from a Native American name for the potholes that mark the Ramapo River or whether it comes from a Leni-Lenape word that means "place of slanting rock" is not known. The latter is certainly more descriptive, for the views of uplifted faces of various metamorphosed layers are also a part of each hike.

HARRIMAN AND BEAR MOUNTAIN STATE PARKS

Bear Mountain and Harriman State Parks span most of the Ramapos in New York State. Their origins are unusual. In 1908 the state proposed building a prison at Bear Mountain. Among the many who protested this desecration of beautiful and historic lands was Mary Harriman, widow of the railroad tycoon Edward Harriman, who offered to give the Palisades Interstate Park Commission (PIPC) 10,000 acres, the nucleus of the modern parks. In return, it was agreed that the commission's jurisdiction would be extended north along the Hudson, and plans for the prison would be dropped. Subsequent gifts and purchases have expanded the park to its present 52,000 acres and allowed for scenic parkways and the building of dams to create or enlarge the numerous bodies of water that dot the park.

PIPC (often pronounced "pip see"), under the leadership of its president, George W. Perkins, and chief engineer, Major William A. Welch, fostered much development. Lakes were formed, and roads and children's camps were built. During 1910 and 1911 a dock for steamboat excursions and a railway station were built, and the park officially opened for public use in the summer of 1913. By 1914 it was estimated that more than 1 million people a year visited the park.

The Bear Mountain Inn was completed in 1915. It was constructed with huge boulders and chestnut logs, and at that time guests paid $4.50 per day for a room and three meals. Upstairs, the magnificent fireplace was constructed with stones from old walls.

Although officially separate, the two contiguous parks are jointly administered and offer today's hikers more than 225 miles of marked trails. The present foot-trail system within the parks was the vision of early "trampers" belonging to nascent walking clubs in New York City. During the summer of 1920, Major Welch, working with others, formed a permanent federation of hiking clubs known as the Palisades Interstate Park Trail Conference—the roots of the present New York–New Jersey Trail Conference (NY–NJTC). Their first venture, the building of the Tuxedo–Jones Point Trail (later known as the Ramapo-Dunderberg Trail), enabled trampers to catch the ferry to New Jersey and the railway to Tuxedo on a Saturday afternoon, spend one night in the woods, and emerge in time to catch a train back to the city on Sunday evening. The first section of the Appalachian Trail, which now extends more than 2,185 miles from Georgia to Maine, was opened from Arden to Bear Mountain in 1923.

By 1930 new trail building had largely come to an end, but quite soon trail wars broke out between competing outdoor clubs. Hiking groups accused one another of establishing their own trails and, worse, of painting out blazes put on trees by rivals. In addition, individuals began to paint routes for their own use. Kerson Nurian was one of these culprits (Hike 18). It was at this time that trail maintenance standards were established under the guidance of the NY–NJTC. No new trail cutting was permitted without reference to the group, and the willy-nilly proliferation of new trails ceased.

Today Harriman and Bear Mountain State Parks are the most popular hiking destination for city residents because several bus routes and a rail line connect with numerous trailheads. These parks often attract throngs of people who enjoy the activities in the more developed areas. However, escaping the big crowds is not hard if you are prepared to walk.

Most hikes in Harriman and Bear Mountain State Parks involve loops that include segments of various trails. Sites of old mines, cemeteries, and other signs of human habitation can often be found, and maps and guidebooks educate the walker. Much detailed history, specifically keyed to the trail system, can be found in *Harriman Trails: A Guide and History* by William J. Myles and Daniel Chazin.

Parking is permitted only in designated areas; no one is allowed to build fires or disturb flora and fauna. Overnight backcountry camping is permitted only at designated shelters.

OTHER STATE PARKS

From the New York–New Jersey border north to Haverstraw, a string of smaller parks is administered by PIPC and provide a route for the Long Path. Tallman Mountain, Clausland Mountain (a county park), Blauvelt, Hook Mountain (Hike 14), the highly developed Rockland Lake, and High Tor (Hike 15) provide for a variety of walking and hiking as well as more developed recreation, including swimming and golf. Descriptions of each are provided in the *New York Walk Book*.

14

Hook Mountain

Total distance: 12 miles (6-mile alternate)

Walking time: 6.5 hours (4-hour alternate)

Vertical rise: 1,200 feet

Maps: USGS 7.5' Haverstraw; USGS 7.5' Nyack; NY–NJTC Hudson Palisades Trails #110 and #111

Trailhead GPS Coordinates: N 41° 07' 14.5" W 73° 54' 41"

The towering cliffs of the Hook have awed travelers to southern New York State for centuries. Henry Hudson and the sailors who followed took note of this impressive headland as they made their way up the Hudson River. The cliffs created by the abandoned quarries further etch the skyline into sheer red-brown walls that appear to continue the Palisades. Whether walking to the high point in spring or fall to watch the hawk migration or bicycling along the paths that hug the shores, you'll find much to enjoy in the parklands administered by the Palisades Interstate Park Commission that stretch from Nyack to Haverstraw on the Hudson's western shore.

The Long Path takes the high route from Nyack across the Hook and the hills called the Seven Sisters. You can make a 12-mile loop hike by first following the Long Path along the hills and then returning on the bike path along the shore of the Hudson, enjoying the best views of woods and water. If you want a shorter hike, you can do a 6-mile loop by leaving the Long Path at Landing Road in Rockland Lake State Park and heading down to the bike path to return to Nyack Beach.

HOW TO GET THERE

The hike begins at Nyack Beach State Park in Nyack, where a seasonal parking fee may be charged. To get there, take US 9W north to Nyack. Two blocks north of its intersection with NY 59 (Main Street), turn right onto High Avenue. Continue for one block and turn left onto North Midland Avenue.

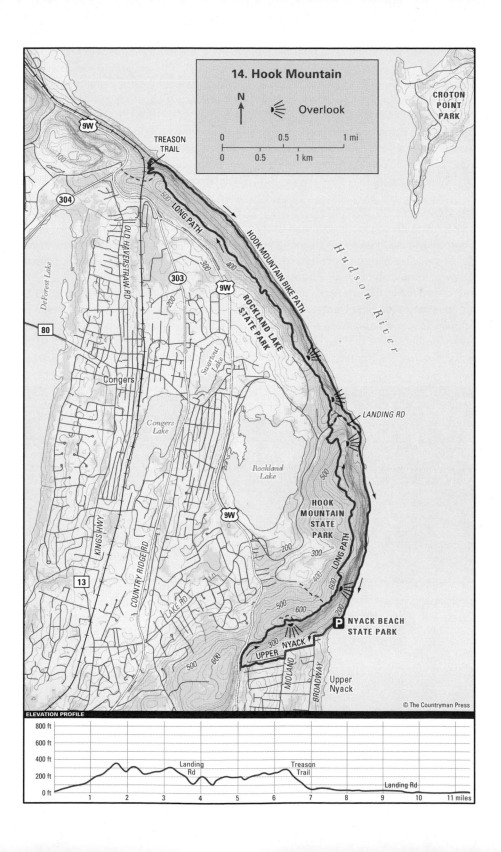

14. Hook Mountain

N

☀ Overlook

0   0.5   1 mi

0   0.5   1 km

CROTON POINT PARK

9W

TREASON TRAIL

100

304

LONG PATH

500

400

300

HOOK MOUNTAIN BIKE PATH

303

9W

200

ROCKLAND LAKE STATE PARK

Hudson River

DeForest Lake

80

Congers

Swartout Lake

Congers Lake

Rockland Lake

LANDING RD

500

HOOK MOUNTAIN STATE PARK

9W

300

200

LONG PATH

400

600

200

KINGS HWY

COUNTRY RIDGE RD

LAKE RD

13

500

600

500

600

300

NYACK

UPPER

MIDLAND

BROADWAY

Upper Nyack

P NYACK BEACH STATE PARK

© The Countryman Press

ELEVATION PROFILE

800 ft
600 ft
400 ft
200 ft
0 ft

Landing Rd

Treason Trail

Landing Rd

1   2   3   4   5   6   7   8   9   10   11 miles

After about 1 mile, continue straight ahead as the main road curves to the left. Follow Midland Avenue through the village of Upper Nyack until the road ends at the entrance to the Marydell Faith and Life Center, then turn right onto Larchdale Avenue. At the next intersection, turn left onto Broadway and follow it into Nyack Beach State Park. Continue ahead to the parking area.

THE TRAIL

Walk back to the tollbooth, and on a utility pole you'll see the three blazes denoting the start of the white-blazed Upper Nyack Trail. Follow this trail, which begins by running along paved roads. It heads south on Broadway, then turns right onto Larchdale Avenue and follows it to its end. Note the cliffs on your right—that's the top of the Hook, where you're headed. At the end of Larchdale

Avenue, the trail turns left onto Midland Avenue and in 300 feet (after passing a private road on the right) turns right, this time into the woods. As you climb, you'll begin to hear the sounds of traffic on the busy US 9W just above you. About 0.75 mile from your car, the Upper Nyack Trail ends at a junction with the aqua-blazed Long Path. Turn right, and head north on the Long Path, which follows the (thankfully) never-completed Tweed Boulevard, part of an 1870s scheme by cohorts of the infamous Boss Tweed to build a road from Nyack across Hook Mountain to Rockland Lake—complete with a hotel on the summit.

In about half an hour, you'll reach the top of the Hook, with views toward New York City and north to Rockland Lake. Beyond the quarry lies the massif of Dunderberg that ends in the Timp. Farther north and on the

Cemetery along the Long Path   DANIEL CHAZIN

other side of the river lies the ragged contour of Breakneck Ridge leading up toward South Beacon Mountain. The Hudson River, wide here at Tappan Bay, is pinched to the north by Croton Point. Farther north it opens out into its widest segment at Haverstraw Bay before becoming choked into the narrows of the Hudson Highlands.

You are standing on the 736-foot peak of the Verdrietege, or tedious headland—so-called by early Dutch sailors who struggled to sail upwind around it. But the landscape at your feet is not what the Dutch sailors saw, and the history of that landscape accounts for a good portion of the preservation movement that resulted in the parks now lining the Hudson's shores.

The Palisades' traprock diabase, which is volcanic in origin, surfaces here through the base of Triassic sandstone and shale. Quarries along the river to the south were active in the 19th century, and the columnar cliffs of the Hook were quarried extensively in the 1870s and 1880s with the introduction of dynamite and heavy earthmoving equipment. The basalt columns were crushed for traprock for macadam roads and, later in the 1890s, for concrete for New York City buildings. Angered at first only by the ear-shattering explosions heard up and down both sides of the river, residents of both New York and New Jersey began to speak out against the quarries. It was not until 1894 that a well-organized group opposed the visual desecration of the cliffs caused by the quarrying.

Finally in 1900, after several years of legislative debate fueled by the argument that "preservation would largely benefit those who enjoyed the view from the New York side of the Hudson," a study commission report was accepted. It called for a permanent interstate park commission and the acquisition of land along the Palisades for recreational purposes. With both private and public funds, the acquisition program progressed from acquiring lands from the top of the cliff face to the river to adding cliff-top lands north to Nyack. The Hook was still threatened until the Palisades Interstate Park was extended northward in 1906. By 1915, the entire Hook was acquired by the Palisades Interstate Park Commission.

The trail continues straight ahead, descending from the summit and following the narrow and sinuous ridge of the mountain, with more views over the river to the south and east. In another 0.3 mile, at the base of a descent, a yellow-blazed trail leaves to the left. Continue ahead on the Long Path, which now begins to climb again. A short distance ahead, you'll reach a series of panoramic viewpoints to the right of the trail, with Nyack Beach State Park visible directly below.

After continuing along the ridge for a few more minutes, the trail turns sharply left and begins a steady descent. Soon, it reaches a switchback in an old road and joins the road as the road curves to the right. The Long Path follows the road as it descends gently along the western side of the ridge, then levels off.

At one point, the river is again visible through the trees on the right. Just beyond, the road bears left and ascends gently. You'll be amazed at the amount of rock work that was used to support this road! After reaching the crest of the rise, the road begins to descend, passing an interesting wide stone wall on the left. The road climbs a knoll, then begins a steady descent.

When you reach a sharp switchback turn to the left, you'll notice a well-defined side trail that leads off to the right. Follow this trail uphill to another viewpoint—undoubtedly one of the best views of the day—with Croton Point jutting out into the river and Ossining visible across the river. This is a good place

Croton Point from Hook Mountain

DANIEL CHAZIN

to observe the clues to the second major industry of the region's past—clues that are much less obvious than those of the quarries. At the shore below are the remains of old docks, the successors to Slaughter's Landing, a settlement begun in 1711 by John Slaughter from Rockland Lake. An ice business was started at Rockland Lake in 1831 when Moses G. Leonard impressed New York City hoteliers with the cleanliness and purity of the lake's ice. In 1855, the business became the Knickerbocker Ice Company, the largest in New York, employing as many as one thousand men. Ice was cut from the lake and stored for shipment south

to New York City. It was moved from the lake via an endless conveyor cable to the landings, where three pairs of tracks led across the docks whose ruins are now guarded by an old lighthouse. Loads of 400 tons were carried south on barges.

Return to the Long Path and follow it as it curves sharply to the left and descends on a rocky, eroded section of the road. The trail soon turns right, leaving the old road, and continues on a footpath, passing a stone foundation on the left. After descending very steeply on a rocky footpath, the trail bears right, skirting old moss-covered concrete foundations, and reaches paved Landing

Hill Road. If you want to shorten the hike, turn right on the paved road and follow it downhill, passing a stone cabin (a private residence). A short distance ahead, you'll reach a junction with the Hook Mountain Bike Path, which joins from the left. Paint markings on a rock at the junction indicate that the distance from here to Nyack Beach State Park is 1.5 miles. Proceed ahead and follow the bike path south for 1.5 miles back to your car.

For those who wish to traverse the full length of the ridge, the Long Path continues across the road and into the woods, soon passing an early 19th-century cemetery. Beyond the cemetery, the climb steepens. As the grade moderates and the trail bends to the left, there is an unobstructed viewpoint over the Hudson River to the right of the trail. Just beyond, you'll be amazed to see Dutchman's breeches blooming in spring only a short distance from the prickly pear cactus that seems to enjoy this dry location. The trail continues on the west side of the ridge, emerging to a series of more or less obscure views, depending on the season. At one spot you look down on red-brown cliffs and pine seedlings that are filling in a second quarry.

The trail descends, turns left past a filtration plant, and heads up the next ridge bordered by vine-covered stone walls. For a short time, the trail follows the park boundary. Just beyond, a side trail on the right leads to a lookout atop a third quarry, with spectacular views. A series of gentle ups and downs ends in a sharp, short drop into a hemlock-filled valley. Immediately you emerge with views to the north and northwest. The next downhill leads off the ridge.

The way out of the small valley is viewless, its taller trees making the segment feel like a remote woodland trail where the roller-coaster effect of the ridge continues for a delightful 45-minute walk. One summit yields views of narrow DeForest Lake. As the trail turns sharply east and heads steeply down toward the river, almost above the railroad tunnel, you feel suspended above the water. The hemlock-covered bank parallels the shore 400 feet above it. As the trail descends along the ridge, keep an eye open for the white-blazed Treason Trail (if you reach a major power line, you've gone too far). This trail provides a connector to the bike path, avoiding a walk into Haverstraw. You have walked about 3 miles from Landing Road, and your trek from the Hook across the hills of the Seven Sisters—and surely twice that number of small knobs and crests—has taken about four and a half hours.

Now follow the white trail as it switchbacks down the steep hillside toward the river. In about 10 minutes, it brings you to the shore bike path at a three-sided old stone structure that was probably used to store explosives when the quarrying was active. The newer ruin was an administrative structure for Haverstraw beach, where swimming was allowed. Just to the north is Treason Rock (for which the Treason Trail is named). Here, Major John Andre supposedly met the traitor Benedict Arnold. Turn right and follow the wide path south.

Bicyclists, joggers, and strollers will join you for the return, but the lack of privacy does not detract from the pleasant route. The mostly level 4.8 miles back to Nyack State Park are easily walked in two hours, unless you stop to examine the quarries en route.

15

The Tors, High and Low

Total distance: 5.5 miles

Walking time: 3.25 hours

Vertical rise: 900 feet

Maps: USGS 7.5' Haverstraw, NY–NJTC Hudson Palisades Trails #112

Trailhead GPS Coordinates: N 41° 10' 35" W 73° 57' 43.5"

High Tor is one of Rockland County's most conspicuous landmarks. Rising 800 feet above the Hudson River, with a broad view of the surrounding area, the peak of High Tor has served as both signal and sentinel. During the Revolutionary War, beacons were placed on the mountain to alert the Americans of a possible British attack. In Celtic lore, "high tor" is a place in which to commune with the gods, "tor" being a gateway.

The Maxwell Anderson play *High Tor* (1937) signaled the beginning of a campaign to protect the mountain from quarrying. The end result was the acquisition and transfer to the Palisades Interstate Park Commission (PIPC) of 564 acres in 1943. In 1995, Scenic Hudson purchased a 54-acre former vineyard on the south face of the mountain, which has since been transferred to PIPC.

HOW TO GET THERE

From Exit 11 of the Palisades Interstate Parkway, proceed east on County Route 80 (New Hempstead Road) for 1.4 miles to a T-junction with Main Street in New City. Turn right, and then turn quickly left at the light, continuing east on County Route 80 to a junction with NY 304. Turn left (north) onto NY 304, and continue for 3 miles to its end at an intersection with US 9W. Turn left onto US 9W and, in 1 mile, turn sharply left onto Old NY 304 (County Route 90). Park in the grassy area at the junction with Ridge Road (County Route 23).

View from High Tor

DANIEL CHAZIN

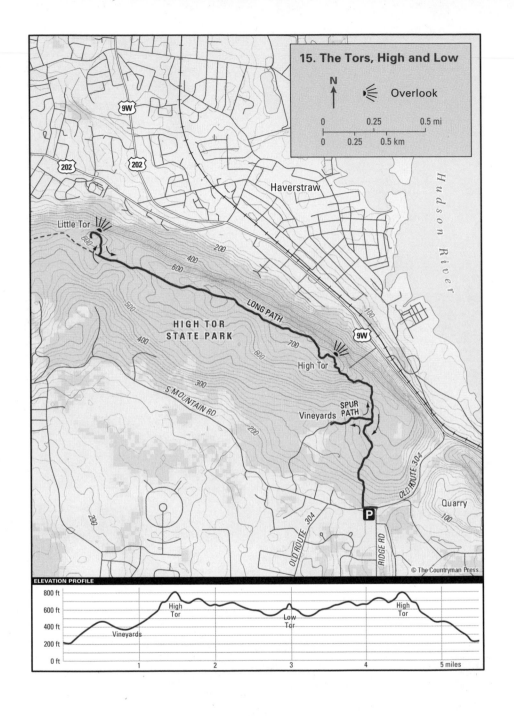

15. The Tors, High and Low

N

Overlook

| 0 | 0.25 | 0.5 mi |
| 0 | 0.25 | 0.5 km |

9W

202

202

Haverstraw

Hudson River

Little Tor

600

LONG PATH

400

200

600

100

HIGH TOR
STATE PARK

500

400

300

700

600

9W

High Tor

S MOUNTAIN RD

200

SPUR
PATH

Vineyards

200

OLD ROUTE 304

RIDGE RD

P

Quarry

100

OLD ROUTE 304

200

© The Countryman Press

ELEVATION PROFILE

800 ft

600 ft

High
Tor

Low
Tor

High
Tor

400 ft

Vineyards

200 ft

0 ft

1   2   3   4   5 miles

THE TRAIL

Hike west along the road (the direction you were driving) for a short distance, passing four utility poles on your side of the road. The route is marked with the aqua blazes of the Long Path, which turns into the woods opposite house number 330.

You are now following a narrow footpath, which soon begins to climb—steeply in places. A few sections are quite rocky, evidence of quarrying that still continues nearby. The land in this section is owned by the Tilcon Company and used with their permission. After 15 minutes of hiking, a large trail sign is reached, indicating a 0.2-mile side trail that leads gently down to The Youmans–Van Orden House and High Tor Vineyards. Follow the white-blazed Spur Path down to a peaceful pond, where a sign explains the history of the area.

Return to the main trail and make a left, continuing for another 10 minutes of uphill hiking. The trail crests the ridge and makes a sharp left turn. Now begins the ascent to High Tor itself.

Although the summit is only 832 feet high, the 360-degree view is truly superb. DeForest Lake (a reservoir), the skyline of New York City, and even part of Newark are visible to the south. The two round domes to the north are reactors of the Indian Point nuclear power plant. To the northwest are the rolling summits of Harriman State Park. Forested areas of Rockland County and northern New Jersey spread out to the west.

DeForest Lake from High Tor

DANIEL CHAZIN

The Tors, High and Low

Below you is Haverstraw, with its active waterfront. The long curved mountain along the shore of the Hudson River is Hook Mountain, another PIPC-protected park (see Hike 14). The old footing at your feet is the remains of an airplane signal beacon.

Linger if you wish, but the hike is not over. Carry on to Little Tor (aka Low Tor) by continuing on the Long Path as it heads downhill, away from the river. The short descent is steep and very rocky. The marked route now follows a fire road as it runs just below the crest of the ridge. There are numerous opportunities to take a short bushwhack up to the crest for a fine view.

After about 30 minutes, a gravel road crosses the trail. To the right, a white-blazed side trail leads up to Little Tor and its fine view. Haverstraw is some 700 feet below. You're more likely to have company here because it's just a short 1-mile walk to Central Highway, which crosses the ridge to the west.

Hike back the way you came. You may wish to take another break on High Tor.

16

Ramapo Torne

Total distance: 4.8 miles

Walking time: 4 hours

Vertical rise: 1,100 feet

Maps: USGS 7.5' Sloatsburg; NY–NJTC Harriman–Bear Mountain Trails #118

Trailhead GPS Coordinates: N 41° 10' 26" W 74° 10' 07.5"

The southern end of Harriman State Park, accessed from the Reeves Meadow parking area off Seven Lakes Drive, is one of the most popular areas in the park. But a large majority of the visitors head up toward Pine Meadow Lake. This hike, which follows a less-used route, can take you away from the crowds and provide you with a feeling of remoteness. The many ups and downs will ensure a rewarding workout, and you'll be afforded plenty of fine views. Unless you're hiking on a weekday, be sure to start this hike early, as the Reeves Meadow parking area is often full by 9 am on weekends.

HOW TO GET THERE

Take the New York Thruway (I-87) to Exit 15A and proceed north on NY 17 for 2.7 miles, through and past the village of Sloatsburg, to a traffic light. Turn right onto Seven Lakes Drive and continue for 1.5 miles into the park. This loop hike starts at the parking area adjacent to the Reeves Meadow Visitors Center (open seasonally on weekends). Overflow parking is available across the road or along the shoulder (pay careful attention to the signs that prohibit parking in some areas).

THE TRAIL

From the parking area, proceed into a field on the southwest side of the visitors center, where a brown post indicates the route of the Pine Meadow Trail—marked with a red dot on a white background. Turn right and follow the Pine Meadow Trail, heading southwest (back toward NY 17). In about 0.25 mile, you'll come to a junction with the

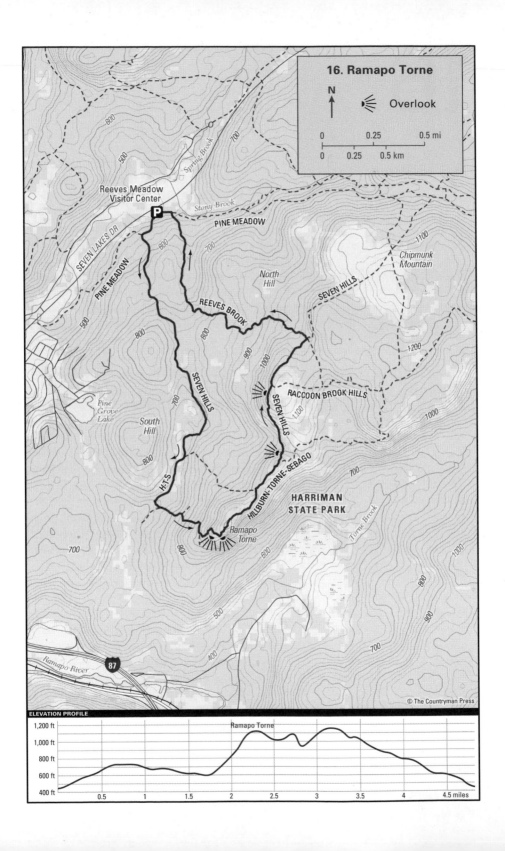

16. Ramapo Torne

N ↑

≋ Overlook

| 0 | 0.25 | 0.5 mi |
| 0 | 0.25 | 0.5 km |

Reeves Meadow
Visitor Center
P

PINE MEADOW

SEVEN LAKES DR

PINE MEADOW

Spring Brook

Stony Brook

800

700

500

REEVES BROOK

North
Hill

SEVEN HILLS

Chipmunk
Mountain

1100

1200

600

700

800

900

1000

1100

RACCOON BROOK HILLS

SEVEN HILLS

1000

Pine
Grove
Lake

South
Hill

SEVEN HILLS

700

800

H-T-S

HILLBURN-TORNE-SEBAGO

700

HARRIMAN
STATE PARK

Torne Brook

1000

Ramapo
Torne

600

800

700

500

400

87

Ramapo River

800

900

700

© The Countryman Press

ELEVATION PROFILE

Ramapo Torne

| 1,200 ft |
| 1,000 ft |
| 800 ft |
| 600 ft |
| 400 ft |

0.5   1   1.5   2   2.5   3   3.5   4   4.5 miles

Landfill in Torne Valley

blue-on-white-blazed Seven Hills Trail. Turn left onto the Seven Hills Trail, which starts a long uphill climb of varying pitches.

The trail meanders through the woods, following several woods roads for part of the way. Remember to follow the blazes, which can sometimes unexpectedly diverge from a more obvious route that you might expect to follow.

About 1.5 miles from the start, you'll reach a T-junction with a woods road. Here, the Seven Hills Trail turns sharply left, but you should turn right, now following the orange blazes of the Hillburn-Torne-Sebago (HTS) Trail, which begins here. This is the former route of the "Old Red" Trail—an informal route up the Ramapo Torne which became an official trail in the spring of 2007.

The HTS Trail follows a level woods road for about 0.3 mile, then turns left at a cairn, crosses a stream, and climbs rather steeply on a woods road. After gaining about 300 feet in elevation, the trail turns sharply left and climbs very steeply over rocks, emerging at a viewpoint to the southwest. It bears left and soon climbs some more to a rock ledge, just below the summit of Ramapo Torne.

Here, on a clear day, you can look south to the New York City skyline, west across the almost unbroken Sterling Forest State Park lands, and even north toward the Shawangunks and the Catskills. Below lies the unattractive Torne Valley, a former landfill, which now features electric power lines and a substation. To the south, the tall black building with the pointed top is a Sheraton hotel built

Ramapo Torne   **117**

on the site of the former Ford Mahwah Assembly Plant that closed in 1980.

Proceed ahead along the ridge of the Ramapo Torne, following the HTS Trail to another junction with the Seven Hills Trail, and continue straight ahead on a footpath marked with both blue-on-white and orange blazes. After a short climb onto an attractive rock outcrop, the two trails split. Bear left and follow the blue-on-white blazes of the Seven Hills Trail, which begins a steep but attractive descent. Be careful here, especially if it's wet or icy.

Before long you'll begin another climb to Torne View, another terrific spot. While the views here are slightly less expansive than at the previous overlook, there is little development to mar the vista. Just beyond, you may notice a junction with the black-on-white-blazed Raccoon Brook Hills Trail (the blazes are painted on the rocks). But continue ahead on the blue-on-white-blazed Seven Hills Trail, which descends to a valley and goes over a small hill to a second valley. Here, just before reaching the bottom, you'll reach a junction with the white-blazed Reeves Brook Trail.

Turn left here and follow the white blazes downhill, steeply in places, for the last 1.4 miles of the hike. The woods are mostly open but there are interesting rock outcrops and small streams. Toward the end, about 1 mile along (and depending on how wet it is), you may notice some attractive cascades in the stream. Finally, you'll reach a junction with the red-on-white-blazed Pine Meadow Trail. Turn left, and almost immediately you'll see the visitors center ahead and be back at your car.

Torne View

DANIEL CHAZIN

17

Breakneck Mountain Loop

Total distance: 6.9 miles

Walking time: 4 hours

Vertical rise: 900 feet

Maps: USGS 7.5' Thiells; NY–NJTC Harriman–Bear Mountain Trails #118

Trailhead GPS Coordinates: N 41° 11' 06" W 74° 04' 29"

This hike uses the Tuxedo–Mount Ivy, Breakneck Mountain, Suffern–Bear Mountain, and Red Arrow Trails to make a "lollipop-loop" hike (out and back on the same trail with a loop in the middle). The terrain is almost entirely through deep woods, with part of the route passing through dense stands of mountain laurel and traversing open rock slabs. Except at the start, the climbing is gentle, and the route makes for a leisurely saunter in a peaceful atmosphere embellished by birdsong. Rocky footing at the beginning and the end may pose a slight challenge to the inexperienced hiker.

HOW TO GET THERE

From the Palisades Interstate Parkway, take Exit 13 (US 202/Suffern/Haverstraw). Turn right at the bottom of the ramp onto US 202 West, and proceed for 1.7 miles to a junction with NY 306. Turn right onto NY 306, then right again at the stop sign just ahead. In 0.2 mile, turn left onto Mountain Road (at a sign for "Ramaquois"), then, in another 0.2 mile, turn left again onto Diltzes Lane. Continue on Diltzes Lane for 0.2 mile and, just before the overhead power lines cross the paved road, turn right into a gravel parking area with a sign indicating that parking for hikers is available.

THE TRAIL

Toward the rear of the parking area, at a green gate that blocks off the power line access road, you'll notice a triple-red-dash-on-white blaze that marks the start of the Tuxedo–Mount Ivy Trail. Follow this trail

Along the Breakneck Mountain Trail

DANIEL CHAZIN

uphill on a wide dirt road (used to access the nearby power lines). Bear right as you approach the power lines and continue along a dirt road, parallel to and below the power lines. After passing the next power line tower, bear left under the power lines to a Y-junction, and take the left fork uphill. A short distance beyond, the Tuxedo–Mount Ivy Trail leaves the service road and makes a right turn into the woods.

Continuing ahead, the Tuxedo–Mount Ivy Trail ascends gradually on an old woods road, bordered for part of the way with rough stone walls. After crossing a stream on stepping-stones, the road becomes rockier. Watch carefully for a left turn and follow the red-on-white blazes as the trail leaves the road it has been following and continues to climb rather steeply on another old

woods road. Near the top of the climb, the trail bears right and continues on a footpath.

Just below the summit of Eagle Rock, the trail reaches a viewpoint, with Limekiln Mountain visible across the valley to the north and the Hudson River to the east. The view is partially obscured by trees, but it is the only broad viewpoint on the entire hike. Beyond the viewpoint, the trail continues to climb, but much more gradually.

Soon, you'll reach a T-junction. The Red Arrow Trail, which will be your return route, begins on the right, but you should turn left to continue on the Tuxedo-Mount Ivy Trail, which now descends gently. After climbing a little, the Tuxedo–Mount Ivy Trail reaches a junction with the yellow-blazed Suffern–Bear Mountain Trail at the height of land. The junction is marked by an interesting rock outcrop

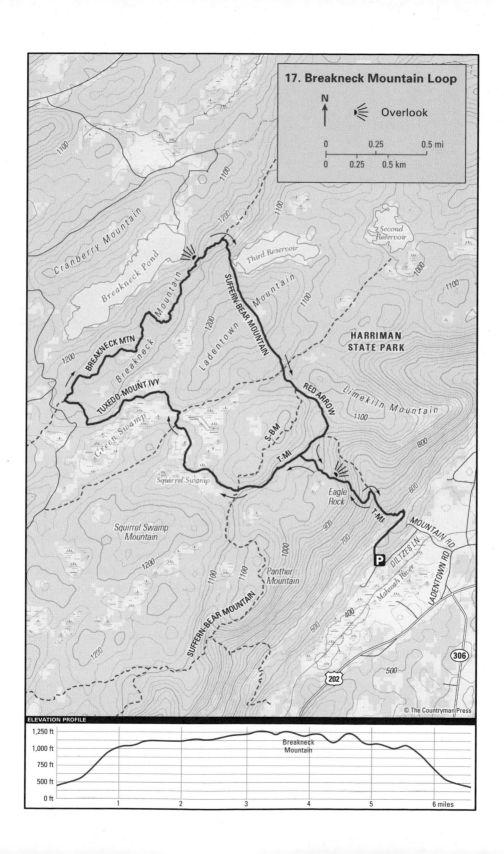

17. Breakneck Mountain Loop

N

Overlook

| 0 | 0.25 | | 0.5 mi |
| 0 | 0.25 | 0.5 km | |

Cranberry Mountain

Breakneck Pond

BREAKNECK MTN

Breakneck Mountain

TUXEDO-MOUNT IVY

Green Swamp

Squirrel Swamp

Squirrel Swamp Mountain

SUFFERN-BEAR MOUNTAIN

SUFFERN-BEAR MOUNTAIN

Ladentown Mountain

Third Reservoir

Second Reservoir

HARRIMAN STATE PARK

Limekiln Mountain

RED ARROW

S-BM

T-MI

Eagle Rock

T-MI

Panther Mountain

P

DILTZES LN

MOUNTAIN RD

LADENTOWN RD

Mahwah River

306

202

© The Countryman Press

ELEVATION PROFILE

1,250 ft	
1,000 ft	Breakneck Mountain
750 ft	
500 ft	
0 ft	

1   2   3   4   5   6 miles

West Pointing Rock

DANIEL CHAZIN

on the right (a good place to take a break) and an old stone fireplace on the left. The Suffern–Bear Mountain Trail, as its name implies, runs for just over 23 miles from Suffern to Bear Mountain. Proposed in 1924 by Major William A. Welch, then general manager of the Palisades Interstate Park Commission, the Suffern–Bear Mountain Trail is the longest trail in the park.

The Tuxedo–Mount Ivy Trail now levels off and passes through dense mountain laurel thickets. In places, the laurels arch over the trail. After going through these delightful laurels for about 0.5 mile, the trail reaches a T-junction with Woodtown Road, a woods road. It turns right and follows the road, crosses a stream on a wooden footbridge, and immediately leaves the road and turns sharply left into the woods. The trail now follows another old woods road which climbs gradually and soon levels off.

After crossing another stream on rocks, you'll notice the Green Swamp to the left of the trail. Toward the end of the swamp, after a short climb, follow the Tuxedo–Mount Ivy Trail as it turns right, leaving the woods road it has been following. A short distance beyond, you'll reach another junction, where a triple-white blaze on a tree and the letters BM painted on a rock mark the start of the Breakneck Mountain Trail. Turn right onto the Breakneck Mountain Trail.

Breakneck Mountain was once known locally as Knapp Mountain after the name of the original owner. This trail, too, was blazed at the suggestion of Major Welch in 1927. The trail proceeds northeast along the ridge of Breakneck Mountain, often emerging onto open rock slabs. Soon, it passes West Pointing Rock, a 10-by-14-foot boulder with a sharp projection on its west side. Further along the ridge, a particularly beautiful section traverses an open slab with large boulders left by the glacier that was once here. Notice the large cracks in the rock underfoot caused by winter's freeze-and-thaw cycles. As the trail approaches the northeastern end of Breakneck Pond, the pond can be glimpsed through the trees to the left.

In 1.5 miles, the Breakneck Mountain Trail ends at a junction with the yellow-blazed Suffern–Bear Mountain Trail. Do not turn left up the rocks, but continue straight ahead, following the yellow blazes downhill to the right toward Third Reservoir (which can be glimpsed ahead through the trees). The Suffern–Bear Mountain Trail passes the western end of the reservoir, which makes for an appealing spot to rest. The water is tranquil and inviting, but swimming is forbidden. The Third Reservoir, built in 1951, is the most recent of the three reservoirs built to serve Letchworth Village and the now-closed Letchworth Village State Developmental Center. Even with three reservoirs, Letchworth Village used to run out of water in dry years, and when this happened, a pipe was laid over Breakneck Mountain and water pumped out of Breakneck Pond.

The Suffern–Bear Mountain Trail now climbs over Ladentown Mountain and descends to Woodtown Road. It crosses the road and then a stream and soon reaches a junction with the Red Arrow Trail (the junction is marked by cairns). Turn left onto the Red Arrow Trail, which skirts the edge of a swamp and descends, passing old rock walls on the left and continuing through mountain laurel thickets. The trail bears right at a fork, then bears right again and continues uphill on a woods road.

Soon, you'll reach the end of the Red Arrow Trail, marked by a triple blaze. Turn left onto the Tuxedo–Mount Ivy Trail and follow it downhill to your car, now retracing the route you followed at the start of the hike.

18

Nurian/ Appalachian Trail Loop

Total distance: 7 miles

Walking time: 4.5 hours

Vertical rise: 900 feet

Maps: USGS 7.5' Sloatsburg; USGS 7.5' Monroe; NY–NJTC Harriman–Bear Mountain Trails #119

Trailhead GPS Coordinates: N 41° 15' 53" W 74° 09' 17.5"

This hike follows eight distinct trails— Arden-Surebridge, Stahahe Brook, Nurian, Dunning, White Bar, Ramapo-Dunderberg, Lichen, and Appalachian. You'll have the opportunity to clamber through the massive rocks in an area called the Valley of Boulders (on the Nurian Trail) as well as to explore the fascinating rock formation known as the Lemon Squeezer (on the Appalachian Trail [AT]). You'll walk by the beautiful, secluded Green Pond and the larger but also very scenic Island Pond. There are over 30 lakes and ponds in Harriman State Park, but nearly all of them were either created or have been greatly altered by the construction of dams. Green and Island Ponds are among the very few that remain in their natural state.

HOW TO GET THERE

From the Tuxedo railroad station, proceed north on NY 17 for 5.6 miles and turn right (east) onto Arden Valley Road at a sign for Harriman State Park. Cross over the New York State Thruway and make the next right into the Elk Pen parking area. If approaching from the north, take the New York State Thruway to Exit 16 (Harriman) and drive 4 miles south on NY 17 to reach the turn onto Arden Valley Road and the parking at the Elk Pen.

There once were approximately 60 elk penned here, hence the name for the parking area. The animals were brought from Yellowstone Park at the end of 1919, but they did not flourish; when their number gradually decreased, those remaining were sold in 1942.

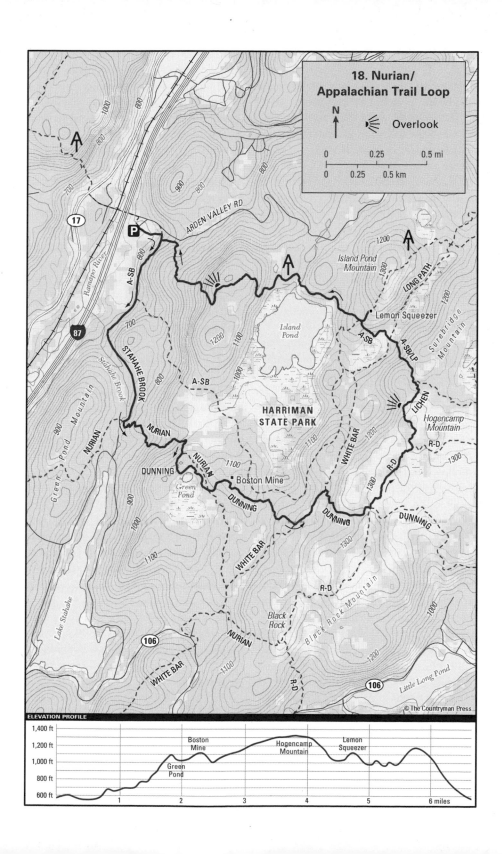

**18. Nurian/
Appalachian Trail Loop**

N

Overlook

| 0 | | 0.25 | | 0.5 mi |

| 0 | 0.25 | | 0.5 km | |

17

87

ARDEN VALLEY RD

P

A-SB

STAHAHE BROOK

Stahahe Brook

Ramapo River

700

600

800

700

1000

800

600

900

800

800

Island Pond
Mountain

1200

1300

LONG PATH

Lemon Squeezer

A-SB

A-SB/LP

1200

Surebridge
Mountain

Island
Pond

A-SB

1200

1100

1000

HARRIMAN
STATE PARK

LICHEN

Hogencamp
Mountain

R-D

1300

Green Pond Mountain

900

NURIAN

NURIAN

DUNNING

Green
Pond

NURIAN

DUNNING

Boston Mine

1100

1100

WHITE BAR

1200

R-D

1300

DUNNING

DUNNING

900

1000

1100

WHITE BAR

1300

R-D

Black
Rock

Black Rock Mountain

1300

1200

1000

Lake Stahahe

106

NURIAN

1100

R-D

106

Little Long Pond

WHITE BAR

© The Countryman Press

ELEVATION PROFILE

1,400 ft						
1,200 ft			Boston Mine	Hogencamp Mountain	Lemon Squeezer	
1,000 ft						
800 ft		Green Pond				
600 ft						
	1	2	3	4	5	6 miles

THE TRAIL

Begin the hike by heading east on the wide path through a grassy field toward the mountains, following the white blazes of the AT. At the end of the field, turn right onto a woods road known as the Arden Road (or the Old Arden Road). Just ahead, the AT turns left and begins to climb Green Pond Mountain, but you should continue ahead on the road, now following the Arden-Surebridge Trail, blazed with an inverted red triangle on a white background.

In 0.3 mile, the Arden-Surebridge Trail turns left, leaving Arden Road. Continue ahead on the road, now following the Stahahe Brook Trail, marked with red-stripe-on-white blazes. The route now is slightly uphill, and you begin to run closer to the New York State Thruway, so the noise of the traffic becomes increasingly intrusive.

Soon, you'll reach Stahahe Brook. The road formerly crossed the brook on a substantial wooden bridge, but this bridge was washed away by Hurricane Irene in August 2011, and the park does not plan to rebuild it. Follow the red-stripe-on-white blazes, which turn left just before the brook and proceed into the woods on a footpath parallel to the brook.

In about 0.5 mile, the Stahahe Brook Trail ends at a junction with the white-blazed Nurian Trail, named after Kerson Nurian, who first blazed this trail in the 1920s. Nurian, who was born in Bulgaria and was employed as an electrical engineer at the Brooklyn Navy Yard, was one of the first trail builders in Harriman State Park. In the 1930s, however, Nurian often found himself in conflict with others who also blazed hiking trails in the park. At that time, there was little regulation of the creation of trails or of their blazing, and hikers felt free to build and name their own section of trail. This practice led to the "Great Trail War," which eventually resulted in the dispute being settled by the New York–New Jersey Trail Conference.

Turn left and follow the Nurian Trail downhill. At the base of the descent, the trail crosses two branches of the outlet of Lake Stahahe and follows switchbacks uphill to the ravine of the Island Pond outlet brook—known as the Valley of Boulders—which features some impressively huge rocks.

Emerging from among these massive boulders, the trail descends slightly and then curves right, around the end of a long, sloping rock in a hemlock grove. Soon, you'll reach the start of the Dunning Trail, indicated by three yellow blazes on a tree to the right of the trail.

Turn right onto the Dunning Trail, which leads straight up a rocky pitch and over toward Green Pond. Pick your way down through the rocks in a fire-damaged area, taking your eyes from your feet long enough to appreciate the beauty of Green Pond. The Dunning Trail follows the northern shore of this pristine pond, while the Nurian Trail follows a parallel (but very different) route only a short distance away.

Beyond the pond, the Nurian Trail joins the Dunning Trail from the left for a very short stretch, but leaves to the right within 75 feet. Continue to follow the yellow blazes, and turn left when the Dunning Trail reaches Island Pond Road (a woods road). The trail now heads uphill. Watch carefully for a turn to the right that takes you to the Boston Mine—a large opening in the side of a hill that was last worked about 1880 and is now flooded. Ore from the mine was sent to the Clove Furnace at Arden, and many tailings remain in the area.

Turn right at the mine, and continue uphill. The trail undulates through hemlock and laurel and passes beneath a large rock outcrop. At 0.5 mile from the Boston Mine, the White Bar Trail joins from the right. You should turn left, now following both yellow and white blazes. When the trails diverge in 0.25 mile, turn right and continue uphill on the yellow-blazed Dunning Trail.

After climbing rather steeply over a rise, the Dunning Trail descends a little to reach a junction with the red-dot-on-white-blazed Ramapo-Dunderberg Trail. The Ramapo-Dunderberg Trail was the first trail to be built by the New York hiking clubs in Harriman State Park. Originally blazed in 1920, its route was suggested by Major William A. Welch, the general manager of the park at the time. Turn left onto the Ramapo-Dunderberg Trail, which passes through an area where the scars of a forest fire are quite noticeable, soon crossing a huge open rock surface known as the Whaleback. Just beyond, look for a plaque on a boulder to the right of the trail. It was placed in memory of George E. Goldthwaite, a member of the Fresh Air Club of New York, who was reputed to have hiked the entire 21-mile Ramapo-Dunderberg Trail in less than five hours—quite a feat for hiking this steep, rocky trail! The trail now steeply descends a rock face to cross a stream on a log bridge, and it climbs to a junction with the blue-L-on-white-blazed Lichen Trail.

Turn left and follow the Lichen Trail, which climbs to a west-facing viewpoint over Island Pond, then descends to end at a junction

Green Pond

DANIEL CHAZIN

Nurian/Appalachian Trail Loop

with the co-aligned Long Path (aqua) and Arden-Surebridge Trail (inverted red triangle on white). Turn left and follow the joint route of these trails, which descend rather steeply. In 0.3 mile, you'll reach a junction where the White Bar Trail begins on the left and then the Long Path leaves to the right. Continue ahead on the Arden-Surebridge Trail.

In another 0.25 mile, you'll reach a junction with the white-blazed AT. Just to the right on the AT is the Lemon Squeezer, where the trail is routed through a very narrow rock cleft. You should take a short detour to visit this fascinating feature, then return to the Arden-Surebridge Trail and turn right, briefly following both the Arden-Surebridge Trail and the AT.

When the trails diverge, leave the Arden-Surebridge Trail and continue ahead on the white-blazed AT, which descends rather steeply and briefly joins an old woods road, known as the "Crooked Road," near the shore of Island Pond. Soon, the AT turns left and climbs a knoll, with a limited view of Island Pond on the left. After descending, it passes the rusted remains of a rotary gravel classifier and crosses a wooden bridge over a stone spillway. Built by the Civilian Conservation Corps (CCC) in the 1930s as part of a project to increase the size of Island Pond, it was never completed, and Island Pond is one of the few lakes in the park that remain in its natural state.

In another 500 feet, you'll cross a gravel road that leads from Arden Valley Road to Island Pond. Soon, the AT turns left onto Island Pond Road, but in another 400 feet, it turns right and begins a steep climb of Green Pond Mountain. Near the summit, rock outcrops to the right of the trail offer limited west-facing views.

The AT now descends the mountain on switchbacks. At the base of the descent, turn right onto Arden Road, still following the white blazes, and in 100 feet turn left and cross the meadow where you began your hike. Continue to the Elk Pen parking area and your car.

19

Rockhouse Loop

Total distance: 7.3 miles (5.8-mile alternate)

Walking time: 4 hours (3-hour alternate)

Vertical rise: 1,000 feet (800-foot alternate)

Maps: USGS 7.5' Thiells; USGS 7.5' Peekskill; NY–NJTC Harriman–Bear Mountain Trails #119

Trailhead GPS Coordinates: N 41° 15' 11" W 74° 03' 58"

This relatively easy "lollipop-loop" hike goes through central Harriman State Park, an area once rich with farms and mines going back to colonial times. Circling but not climbing Rockhouse Mountain, the walking is easy, with just a few short climbs. However, at more than 7 miles, it can be a bit long for young children or beginning hikers. There are several interesting historic places to explore, so choose a nice day and start early. The hike is all on marked trails, except for a short section toward the end on an easy-to-follow woods road.

HOW TO GET THERE

The road to the parking area is closed to vehicles in winter (December 1st through April 1st). However, an alternative year-round access, which also shortens the hike by 1.5 miles, is available as an option (see Options).

Take the Palisades Interstate Parkway to Exit 16 (Lake Welch). Proceed for 0.5 mile to where the road splits. Bear right onto Tiorati Brook Road, and continue for 1.1 miles to a large parking area, just after a bridge, in a field on the right. You can also drive to the parking area from Tiorati Circle (see Options for directions to the circle). The parking area is 2.4 miles south on Tiorati Brook Road on your left.

THE TRAIL

Cross to the other side of Tiorati Brook Road, and begin hiking by following the blue-blazed Beech Trail, which heads southwest. This is one of the newer trails in the park,

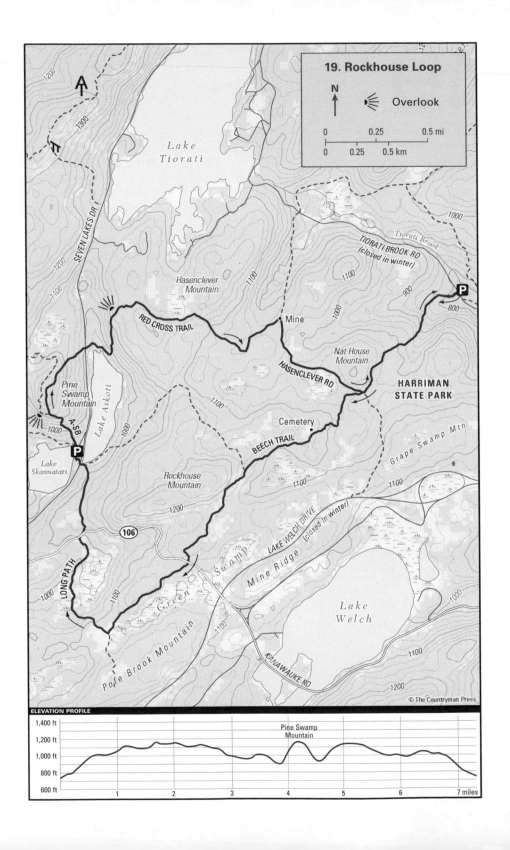

19. Rockhouse Loop

N

⚡ Overlook

| 0 | 0.25 | 0.5 mi |
| 0 | 0.25 | 0.5 km |

Lake Tiorati

Tiorati Brook

TIORATI BROOK RD
(closed in winter)

Hasenclever Mountain

Mine

RED CROSS TRAIL

SEVEN LAKES DR. 1

Pine Swamp Mountain

Lake Askoti

A-SB

P

Lake Skannatati

Nat House Mountain

HASENCLEVER RD

HARRIMAN STATE PARK

Cemetery

BEECH TRAIL

Grape Swamp Mtn

Rockhouse Mountain

LAKE WELCH DRIVE (closed in winter)

Mine Ridge (closed in winter)

Lake Welch

106

Green Swamp

LONG PATH

Pole Brook Mountain

KANAWAUKE RD

© The Countryman Press

ELEVATION PROFILE

Pine Swamp Mountain

| 1,400 ft |
| 1,200 ft |
| 1,000 ft |
| 800 ft |
| 600 ft |

1   2   3   4   5   6   7 miles

blazed in 1972 (most trails go back to the 1920s and 1930s). And though there are lots of beech trees along the route, it was really named after Art Beach, a tireless trail worker. The spelling was changed to circumvent a park policy against naming trails for living persons.

The trail follows a woods road, which soon reaches a fork. Bear right, and continue along the trail, which now runs alongside a gully. Soon you'll enter an area filled with blueberry bushes and mountain laurel; observe how the old road was built up from the surrounding ground. After crossing a small stream, the trail begins a steady climb. You may note a fine cascade just 0.3 mile from the start. Trail builders named it Arthur's Falls to honor a crew member.

After climbing just over 200 vertical feet, the trail reaches an intersection with the unmarked Hasenclever Road. Note this location because you will return here near the end of the hike. Continue ahead on the Beech Trail, which turns right, follows the road for only 15 feet, and then reenters the woods. The trail crosses another small stream and begins to climb again. You'll notice a change in vegetation as you near an old farmstead. Soon, you'll pass an old cemetery on your right. Cleaned and restored as an Eagle Scout project in 1990, the graves are from the Babcock, Youmans, and Jones families. Most of the readable inscriptions are from the mid- to late 1800s.

If you have the time and desire to explore the farm area, go back along the trail and look for a route through the barberry. In this area, you can find the remains of stone foundations and even an old root cellar. When you're ready to start hiking again, continue

Lake Skannatati from Pine Swamp Mountain

DANIEL CHAZIN

---

ahead on the blue-blazed Beech Trail, which levels off and passes a large glacial erratic to the left.

A little over 2 miles from the start of the hike, the trail crosses County Route 106. Just before reaching this crossing, be alert for the marked route to bear left, off the woods road and onto a narrower footpath. As you continue along, observe the attractive jumble of rocks to the right of the trail and the wonderful stand of mountain laurel, which in June will be ablaze with large white and pink blossoms.

About 0.5 mile after crossing County Route 106, the Beech Trail ends at a junction with the aqua-blazed Long Path. Turn right onto the Long Path, a major trunk trail, which currently extends over 300 miles from the George Washington Bridge north to John Boyd Thacher State Park just south of Albany. You, however, are not going that far—at least not today.

The Long Path traverses a wet area and emerges into a pine plantation, probably planted by the Civilian Conservation Corps (CCC) in the 1930s. Once again you reach County Route 106. The trail turns right and follows the road for about 250 feet, then turns left and renters the woods just before a bend in the road. Soon, the trail turns left onto a woods road which leads down to Seven Lakes Drive. On the way, you'll cross under a telephone line, where you'll notice an abundance of sweet fern. Pull off a leaf and crush it in your fingers for a pleasant smell.

At Seven Lakes Drive, the trail turns right and crosses a bridge over the outlet of Lake Askoti (Native American for "this side"), then turns left and climbs down an embankment to reach a large parking area at Lake Skannatati (Native American for "the other side"). This parking area is an alternative place to start the hike, especially when Tiorati Brook Road is closed for the winter (see Options).

Cemetery on the Beech Trail   DANIEL CHAZIN

Bear right and walk to the northern end of the parking area. Here, the Long Path enters the woods, but you should continue on the inverted-red-triangle-on-white-blazed Arden-Surebridge Trail, which begins here. The Arden-Surebridge Trail heads up Pine Swamp Mountain, a short but steep ascent of 200 vertical feet. After climbing over some rock outcrops, the trail levels off and reaches the trailhead of the Red Cross Trail (red cross on white background), which begins on the right. You need to turn right onto the Red Cross Trail, but about 100 feet ahead on the Arden-Surebridge Trail there is a fine viewpoint over Lake Skannatati that's worth the short detour.

The Red Cross Trail climbs briefly through open woods, then heads down to recross Seven Lakes Drive. It soon passes by a large rock slab jutting into Lake Askoti, which is a good place to take a short break. You've now hiked 4.7 miles—more than half of the total distance of the hike. The Red Cross Trail now makes a short, steep climb to another viewpoint. At 1,100 feet above sea level, you can look back across the road toward Pine Swamp and Surebridge Mountains.

After crossing under a telephone line, the trail climbs a little, descends, and traverses some wet areas. It soon reaches a woods road and turns left to follow it. A short distance beyond, you'll reach a junction with another woods road, known as the Hasenclever Road. You are now at the center of the Hasenclever Mine complex. You'll know that you're here when you spot the rusted debris on the side of the trail and the large mine pits—one of which is large enough to swallow a truck.

In 1765, Peter Hasenclever, while traveling through the area, discovered a large deposit of iron ore. He immediately bought 1,000 acres, including most of Cedar Ponds, now Lake Tiorati. His intention was to construct a furnace, but he was recalled to England before it could be built. However, mine operations under a succession of owners continued on and off for almost a hundred years. In the mid-1850s, one owner planned a railroad from the mine to the Hudson River at Stony Point. Though the railroad was never completed, the trench in which it was to run can still be seen—as can stone foundations and other remnants of the mining activity. At its peak, some 20 to 30 men worked in this area. The book *Iron Mine Trails* by Edward J.

Lenik (published by the Trail Conference in 1996 and now available online as an e-book) provides an extensive history and guide for exploring this area in depth.

Turn right, leaving the Red Cross Trail, and follow the unmarked Hasenclever Road. Although not blazed, this wide woods road is easy to follow. (If you'd rather not follow an unmarked route—especially if you're worried about darkness or weather—an alternative route is to stay on the marked Red Cross Trail, which reaches the paved Tiorati Brook Road in little more than 0.5 mile. Turn right and walk along the road for 1 mile back to your car.) Hasenclever Road soon crosses a bridge with concrete abutments and begins a gradual climb. In about 0.7 mile, you'll reach a junction with the blue-blazed Beech Trail. Turn left onto the Beech Trail, and head back to the parking area, which you'll reach in 0.9 mile.

OPTIONS
During the winter months, when Tiorati Brook Road is closed—or for those wanting a shorter hike (5.8 miles)—begin the hike at the Lake Skannatati access just off Seven Lakes Drive. To reach this parking area, take the Palisades Interstate Parkway to Exit 18 and the Long Mountain Circle. Go around the circle to Seven Lakes Drive (not US 6), and continue past Tiorati Circle (at 3.8 miles) for another 2.6 miles to a right turn down to the Lake Skannatati parking area. Begin the loop hike on the Arden-Surebridge Trail, as noted in the text above, and when you reach the intersection of Hasenclever Road with the Beech Trail, turn right (rather than left) to continue on the route of the hike that will lead you back to the parking area at Lake Skannatati.

20

Iron Mine Walk

Total distance: 8 miles
Walking time: 5 hours
Vertical rise: 1,050 feet
Maps: USGS 7.5' Monroe; USGS 7.5' Popolopen Lake; USGS 7.5' Thiells; USGS 7.5' Sloatsburg; NY–NJTC Harriman–Bear Mountain Trails #119
Trailhead GPS Coordinates: N 41° 14' 30" W 74° 06' 08"

Harriman State Park is full of historical walks, and this hike, which visits several of the region's 19th-century iron mines, blends good hiking with the annals of that time. Iron mining in the Ramapos actually dates back to 1742. At the onset of the Revolutionary War, the colonies were producing 14 percent of the world's iron, and they began exporting iron ore in 1817. Entrepreneurs were attracted not only by the iron ore of the Ramapo Hills, but by the nearby watercourses, needed to power the bellows for the furnaces, and by the heavily wooded slopes, whose timber yielded the necessary charcoal. Several nearby furnaces—including the Sterling Furnace near Sterling Lake, the Greenwood Furnace near the Ramapo River, the Queensboro Furnace, and the Forest of Dean Furnace—produced iron for guns during the American Revolution and the Civil War.

The mines varied in depth from 10 to 6,000 feet, the deepest being the Forest of Dean Mine (now located on the property of the United States Military Academy at West Point). Many of the mines are water filled and dangerous. This walk takes you past a few of the mines that can be inspected safely from the trail.

The mines you'll walk past are in the Greenwood group, so called because their ore was smelted at the Greenwood Furnace at Arden. This and other furnaces are described in *Vanishing Ironworks of the Ramapos* by James M. Ransom, a book to read if you wish to delve deeply into the history of the area. The Greenwood Furnace was established about 1810 and supplied

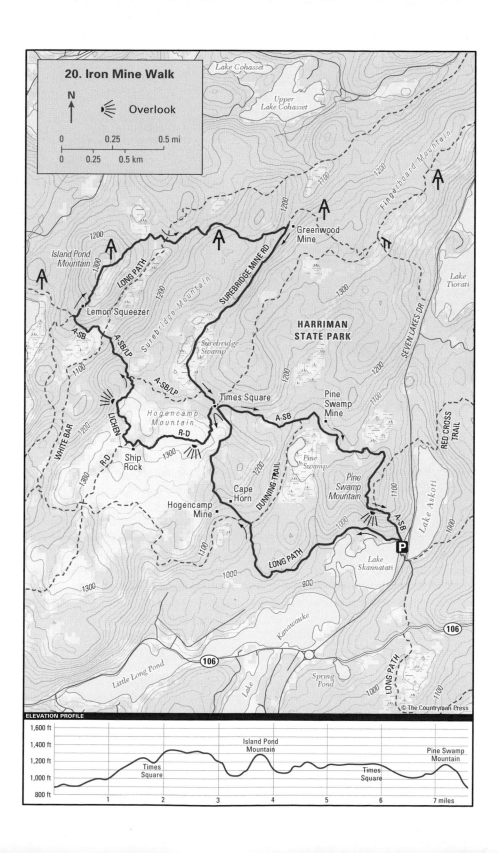

20. Iron Mine Walk

N

Overlook

0   0.25   0.5 mi
0   0.25   0.5 km

Lake Cohasset

Upper
Lake Cohasset

Fingerboard Mountain

Greenwood
Mine

Island Pond
Mountain

LONG PATH

SUREBRIDGE MINE RD

Lemon Squeezer

A-SB

A-SB/LP

Surebridge Mountain

Surebridge
Swamp

A-SB/LP

Times Square

HARRIMAN
STATE PARK

Lake
Tiorati

SEVEN LAKES DR

Pine
Swamp
Mine

WHITE BAR

LICHEN

R-D

Hogencamp
Mountain

R-D

Ship
Rock

A-SB

Pine
Swamp

RED CROSS
TRAIL

Cape
Horn

DUNNING TRAIL

Pine
Swamp
Mountain

Lake Askoti

Hogencamp
Mine

LONG PATH

A-SB

P

Lake
Skannatati

106

Kanawauke

Little Long Pond

106

LONG PATH

Spring
Pond

Lake

© The Countryman Press

ELEVATION PROFILE

1,600 ft
1,400 ft
1,200 ft
1,000 ft
800 ft

Island Pond
Mountain

Times
Square

Times
Square

Pine Swamp
Mountain

1   2   3   4   5   6   7 miles

Cape Horn

DANIEL CHAZIN

cannonballs to the American forces during the War of 1812. Robert Parrott acquired an interest in the furnace and surrounding lands in 1837, and he and his brother Peter managed the ironworks and became sole owners of it. With coal transported by the newly built railroad through the Ramapo Valley, the furnace's output increased until yearly production reached 5,000 tons of pig iron, destined for fine hardware and stoves. During the Civil War, the iron was used for the famous Parrott rifle, the most effective artillery weapon of the Union Army. This rifle was made at the West Point Foundry at Cold Spring under the direction of Robert Parrott. The ore supplied by the Greenwood, Surebridge, Pine Swamp, O'Neil, and Clove Mines was hauled to a kiln about 0.5 mile

above the Greenwood Furnace, where the ore was roasted to drive off sulfur, stamped to reduce the fragments to the size of a "pigeon's egg," and then smelted in the furnace, which was built in the charming glen beside the outlet of Echo Lake.

HOW TO GET THERE

The mine walk starts at the Lake Skannatati parking area off Seven Lakes Drive. To reach this parking area from the south, take the New York Thruway (I-87) to Exit 15A and proceed north on NY 17 for 2.7 miles, through and past the village of Sloatsburg, to a traffic light. Turn right onto Seven Lakes Drive and continue for about 7.8 miles to the parking area for Lake Skannatati, on the left side of the road. The turnoff to the parking area is 0.7 mile beyond the Kanawauke Circle.

You can also reach the start of the hike via the Palisades Interstate Parkway. Take the Parkway to Exit 18 and go around the Long Mountain Circle to the turnoff for the Seven Lakes Drive. Continue on Seven Lakes Drive for 2.6 miles beyond the Tiorati Circle to a signed right turn down to the Lake Skannatati parking area.

THE TRAIL

Two trails leave from the northwest corner of this parking area—the inverted-red-triangle-on-white-blazed Arden-Surebridge Trail, and the aqua-blazed Long Path. Follow the aqua blazes of the Long Path, which heads west and parallel to Lake Skannatati, and crosses an inlet stream near the northwest bay of the lake.

After climbing some more, the trail comes out on a woods road, the route of the yellow-blazed Dunning Trail. Turn left, briefly following both aqua and yellow blazes—but just ahead, when the two trails split, bear right and continue to follow the aqua blazes of the Long Path. Just before reaching a massive boulder (known as Cape Horn), you'll see remnants of 19th-century mining activity below to the left. Directly below the trail is a shaft of the Hogencamp Mine, which was active from 1870 to 1885.

The Long Path now begins to climb, passing a split boulder on a hill to the left. After a level section through a valley, the trail climbs slightly and passes stone foundations. A tramway from the Hogencamp Mine, used to transport the iron ore to a mine road, passed through this valley, and the stone foundations are probably remnants of structures built for the tramway.

The Long Path descends to a junction with the Arden-Surebridge Trail, marked with inverted-red-triangle-on-white blazes.

Turn left, now following both aqua and red-on-white blazes. In another 100 feet, you'll reach a large glacial erratic on the right known as "Times Square." Trails or woods roads extend in six directions from Times Square, thus providing its nickname.

Bear left just beyond Times Square onto the red-dot-on-white-blazed Ramapo-Dunderberg Trail, which heads southwest. It steeply climbs Hogencamp Mountain through hemlocks. Toward the top, you'll come out on a rock outcrop in an area that was ravaged by fire in 1988. You'll pass wonderful rock clefts and climb some more over bare rocks with glacial striations, with panoramic south-facing views over rolling terrain.

After reaching the summit of Hogencamp Mountain (1,353 feet), the trail continues across the broad summit ridge. It then zigzags down to Ship Rock, so named because it looks like a bottom-up prow of a boat. Just beyond, the trail makes a sharp right turn.

A short distance beyond, you'll notice a triple-blue-L-on-white blaze, which indicates the start of the Lichen Trail. Turn right and follow this picturesque trail, which proceeds through tall mountain laurel and hemlock, and over rock ledges. After passing a viewpoint to the northwest, the Lichen Trail drops sharply along an evergreen-covered hillside. At the base of the descent, it reaches an intersection with the co-aligned Arden-Surebridge Trail and Long Path, with inverted-red-triangle-on-white and aqua blazes. Turn left and follow the Arden-Surebridge Trail/Long Path, which passes a swamp on the right and heads down a pretty hemlock-covered hillside.

As the trail levels off at the bottom of the hill, it passes a wet area on the right and reaches another intersection. Here, the Long Path leaves to the right (northeast) and the White Bar Trail begins on the left.

Continue ahead on the red-on-white-blazed Arden-Surebridge Trail, the middle route, which crosses a small stream, follows it briefly, then begins to climb beside cliffs with massive rock formations. The hill to your right is recovering from the devastation of fires.

Soon, you'll notice a dramatic cleft at the edge of a cliff and reach a junction with the white-blazed Appalachian Trail (AT). Turn right, leaving the Arden-Surebridge Trail, and follow the white AT blazes, which lead under an overhanging rock and into a fascinating rock formation, aptly named the Lemon Squeezer. The trail climbs through a miniature chasm at the base of the cliff and then a steep rock face, where you will need to use both your hands and your feet. If the climb is too difficult, it is possible to bypass the steepest part by following a blue-blazed trail on the left.

After reaching the top of the Lemon Squeezer, the AT continues on a more moderate grade to the summit of Island Pond Mountain. Just north of the summit, you'll pass the ruins of a stone cabin built by Edward Harriman over a century ago.

The AT descends from the summit and enters an attractive hemlock grove. After winding through the hemlocks, you'll reach a junction with the aqua-blazed Long Path, marked by a wooden signpost. Continue ahead on the AT, which soon parallels a stream, crosses it, then turns right and climbs over the ridge of Surebridge Mountain.

At the base of the descent, the AT crosses Surebridge Brook and turns left onto Surebridge Mine Road. A few hundred feet beyond, you'll notice a 100-foot-long water-filled mine pit on the right, with an adjacent pile of tailings. This is the site of the Greenwood Mine, from which iron ore was extracted between 1838 and 1880. At the

Hiking through the Lemon Squeezer

DANIEL CHAZIN

north end of the mine pit, you can see a drill mark in the rock face, and several rusted pipes are visible nearby.

After examining these interesting features, turn around and head south on Surebridge Mine Road, continuing past the junction with the AT. Soon, you'll pass a large swamp, where signs of mining abound; tailing piles are everywhere, and a few pits of the Surebridge Mine lie to the east of the road. The road follows a causeway built up of tailings and heads south across Surebridge Swamp. An arch of rhododendron shades the causeway, from which there are glimpses of the twisted stumps and wildflowers in the sphagnum bog.

Near the south end of the swamp, the road climbs a little, and the co-aligned Arden-Surebridge Trail/Long Path joins from the left. Continue ahead, now following the inverted-red-triangle-on-white and aqua blazes along Surebridge Mine Road. Just ahead, you'll pass Times Square, where the red-dot-on-white-blazed Ramapo-Dunderberg Trail crosses and the Long Path leaves. Continue ahead on the Arden-Surebridge Trail, which begins a steady descent on an old mine road.

At the base of the descent, the yellow-blazed Dunning Trail begins on the right. Continue ahead on the Arden-Surebridge Trail, which crosses a stream. Just beyond, a large rectangular cut in the hillside to the left is a remnant of the Pine Swamp Mine, which operated from 1830 to 1880. You'll pass several other mine pits as you continue along the old mine road.

Just beyond these mine openings, the trail bears right and descends into the woods, passing a stone wall and stone foundations on the left. The Arden-Surebridge Trail now begins a steady ascent of Pine Swamp Mountain. Near the summit, a viewpoint to the south affords a panoramic view over Lakes Skannatati and Kanawauke. Continue along the Arden-Surebridge Trail as it descends steeply to the parking area at Lake Skannatati, where you left your car.

21

Black Mountain

Total distance: 4.5 miles

Walking time: 3 hours

Vertical rise: 900 feet

Maps: USGS 7.5' Popolopen Lake; NY–NJTC Harriman–Bear Mountain Trails #119

Trailhead GPS Coordinates: N 41° 17' 44" W 74° 03' 34.5"

In 1994, volunteers of the New York–New Jersey Trail Conference cleared and marked the Menomine Trail as a convenient connection between the Appalachian Trail (AT) and the Long Path. More importantly, it was the first marked trail to utilize the large Silvermine parking area that, unlike many others, is maintained (plowed) in winter.

This hike includes the 1,200-foot summit of Black Mountain. The route up the mountain features some lovely views, and the peak has an extensive view of the Hudson Valley down as far as the New York City skyline. The last part of the hike is not on a marked trail, but the route is pleasant and easy to follow (although it includes a short walk along Seven Lakes Drive).

HOW TO GET THERE

To reach the Silvermine parking area, take the Palisades Interstate Parkway to Exit 18. Proceed almost all the way around the traffic circle to Seven Lakes Drive (westbound). The parking area is on your left, 1.4 miles along the road. A fee is usually charged from Memorial Day to Labor Day.

THE TRAIL

Begin the hike on the yellow-blazed Memomine Trail by crossing the wide bridge at the bottom of the parking area and turning left on a dirt road, passing two small wooden outbuildings. After a short stretch through the woods, the trail begins to parallel the shore of Silvermine Lake.

Silvermine Lake has an interesting history. In the early 1900s, the area was called

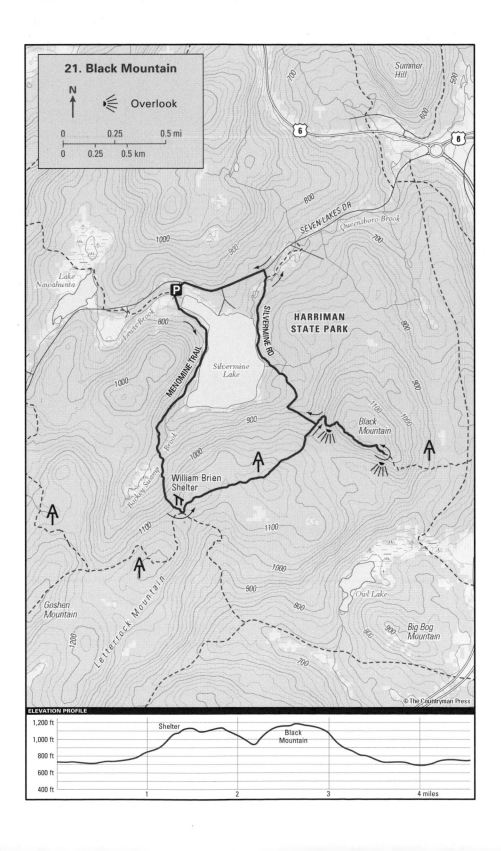

21. Black Mountain

N

☀ Overlook

0   0.25   0.5 mi
0   0.25   0.5 km

Summer Hill

700

500

600

6

6

800

SEVEN LAKES DR

Queensboro Brook

700

1000

900

Lake Nawahunta

Lewis Brook

800

P

SILVERMINE RD

HARRIMAN STATE PARK

800

1000

Silvermine Lake

900

Black Mountain

1100

1000

900

Brook

1000

Boskey Swamp

William Brien Shelter

1100

1100

1000

Owl Lake

900

800

Goshen Mountain

Letterrock Mountain

1200

900

Big Bog Mountain

700

© The Countryman Press

ELEVATION PROFILE

1,200 ft	Shelter		Black Mountain		
1,000 ft					
800 ft					
600 ft					
400 ft	1	2	3	4 miles	

Silvermine Lake from viewpoint on Black Mountain

DANIEL CHAZIN

Bockey Swamp, "bockey" being a local term for the woven baskets used by charcoal burners. During the 1920s, beavers—which had just been reintroduced—built a dam, killing many trees. The park cleared the dead trees and planted rice, which they hoped would attract birds to the area. Instead, deer ate the rice. In 1934, the Civilian Conservation Corps (CCC) built a 600-foot dam, and the new lake was named Menomine (wild rice) by Major William A. Welch, the first general manager of the park. In 1936, a ski slope and rope tow were installed, and the area was named Silvermine after a legendary Spanish silver mine on Black Mountain. In 1942 a second ski slope was added, and in 1951 the lake was renamed Silvermine. The parking lot was enlarged in 1968, but the ski area was closed in 1986. The name Menomine was brought back to the area when the trail was dedicated in 1994.

After about 20 minutes of walking, the trail heads away from Silvermine Lake and begins a modest 100-foot ascent on a woods road to a crest, where it makes a sharp left, crosses Bockey Swamp Brook (the inlet of the lake), and climbs rather steeply on a rocky woods road to the William Brien Memorial Shelter, 1.4 miles from the hike's start. Here, the Menomine Trail crosses the white-blazed AT, which is co-aligned with the red-dot-on-white-blazed Ramapo-Dunderberg Trail.

The William Brien Memorial Shelter, built in 1933, was later named for the first president of the New York Ramblers, a local hiking club. A short blue-blazed trail from the shelter leads to a well (all backcountry water should be treated before drinking). This area is popular with backpackers and long-distance AT hikers, as it is one of the few legal places to camp within the park.

From the shelter, look ahead about 100 feet to a boulder-covered hill. The AT and Ramapo-Dunderberg blazes will be clearly visible at the top of the hill. Continue ahead on the Menomine Trail for 50 feet, make a left onto the AT/ Ramapo-Dunderberg Trail, and climb up the hill. The trail meanders along the top of the ridge through open

hardwoods and, in about 1 mile, descends to a wide gravel road. Known as the Silvermine Road, it was built in 1934 as a fire road and will be the route you later use to complete this hike.

For now, cross the road and continue ahead on the AT/Ramapo-Dunderberg Trail as it climbs steeply up Black Mountain on a well-defined footpath. In about five minutes, you'll reach a good viewpoint from a rock outcrop over Silvermine Lake and the area you just traversed. Continue climbing more gently on the AT/Ramapo-Dunderberg Trail to the broad 1,200-foot summit of Black Mountain, which affords spectacular views over the Hudson River and the surrounding area. The small lake ahead of you is Owl Swamp. Farther afield, on the west bank of the river, are the dramatic shapes of the Tors (Hike 15) and Hook Mountain (Hike 14). On a clear day, the New York City skyline

William Brien Memorial Shelter

DANIEL CHAZIN

Black Mountain

is visible on the horizon. You'll want to linger here for a while and take in the panoramic view.

When you're ready to continue, retrace your steps down the mountain back to the gravel Silvermine Road. Turn right, downhill, toward the lake. The road is unmarked but very easy to follow. In 15 minutes, you'll pass by the dam (crossing is prohibited and unsafe), and five minutes later, you'll cross Queensboro Brook on a substantial bridge. Almost immediately after the bridge, two green-and-black-painted metal posts flank the road. Here, turn left and follow an unmarked trail about 100 feet to Seven Lakes Drive. Turn left and walk along the shoulder of the road for 0.4 mile back to the Silvermine parking area, where the hike began.

22

Anthony Wayne Loop

Total distance: 6 miles

Walking time: 4 hours

Vertical rise: 1,000 feet

Maps: USGS 7.5' Popolopen Lake; NY–NJTC Harriman–Bear Mountain Trails #119

Trailhead GPS Coordinates: N 41° 17' 54" W 74° 01' 40"

This hike uses portions of several trails in Harriman State Park, including the Suffern–Bear Mountain Trail, the longest trail in the park. It features a wonderful ridge walk with extensive views both to the east and west. The hike begins at the Anthony Wayne Recreation Area, opened in 1955, where the huge parking area once served visitors to two large swimming pools. The pools were closed in the 1980s and have since been demolished, leaving the parking area for use primarily by hikers.

HOW TO GET THERE

Take the Palisades Interstate Parkway to Exit 17, and drive past the tollbooth to park in the first lot on the right-hand side. Parking is normally free, except when special events take place during the summer. For information, call the Palisades Interstate Park Commission at 845-786-2701.

THE TRAIL

Walk back toward the tollbooth, turn left, and head toward two stone gateposts on the east side of the access road to the parking area. Signs on the metal barrier between the gateposts indicate that hiking trails start here. Our hike begins on the white-blazed Anthony Wayne Trail, which (like the recreation area) was named after the famous general "Mad Anthony" Wayne, who was believed to have marched with his men through the area in 1779 during the American Revolution. The Anthony Wayne Trail heads uphill on a gravel road (also marked with blue-on-white-diamond blazes as a bike

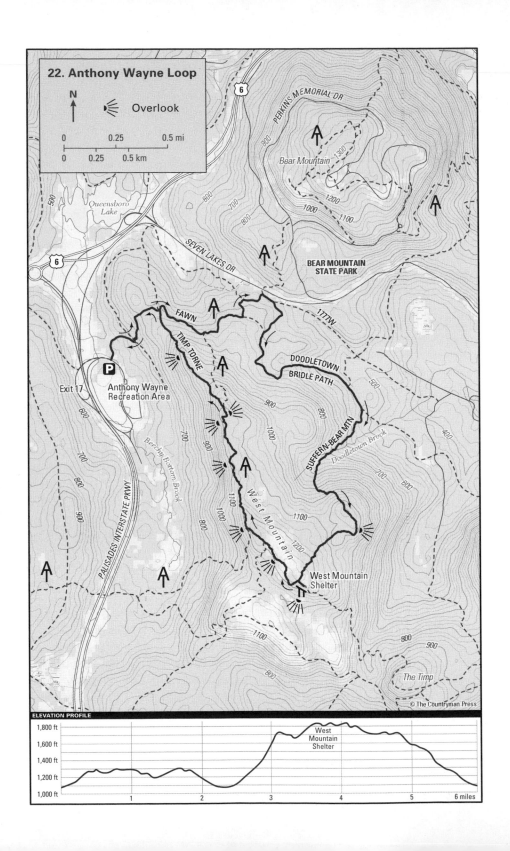

© The Countryman Press

trail), crosses a dirt road, and soon reaches a T-junction, where the Anthony Wayne Trail turns left. Look immediately to the left to find a triple-red-F-on-white blaze that marks the start of the Fawn Trail. This trail was shown on the first park map produced in 1920 and was badly damaged by bulldozers making a fire lane during the fire of 1988.

After climbing a switchback and then ascending more gradually, the Fawn Trail meets the blue-blazed Timp-Torne Trail at the height of land. Take note here because the hike will bring you back to this junction later on. Ahead (if there are no leaves on the trees) is a good view of Bear Mountain and the Perkins Memorial Tower. Continue on the Fawn Trail, which crosses the Timp-Torne Trail and bears left. It goes gently downhill at first and continues through a peaceful hardwood forest to its end at a junction with the Appalachian Trail (AT). Continue straight ahead, now following the white blazes of the AT through dense mountain laurel thickets. Soon, the AT turns left and descends, and it then turns right and joins the 1777W Trail. When the AT turns left before reaching Seven Lakes Drive, you should turn right and continue on the 1777W Trail. In 500 feet, you'll reach a junction, marked by a large number "5" on the left. Turn right here, leaving the 1777W Trail, and proceed uphill on an unmarked woods road, the route of the Doodletown Bridle Path.

The hamlet called Doodletown was first inhabited by the Junes (or Jouvins), descendants of the French Huguenots, probably from 1762 until 1965. Although records show that it had already been named

View of Bear Mountain from West Mountain

AUDRIUS JUSKELIS

West Mountain Shelter

DANIEL CHAZIN

"Doodletown" by the time of the British arrival, there are other suggestions for the derivation of the name. One of the most interesting is that the British derided the settlers by playing the tune "Yankee Doodle" as they marched through town. It is believed that over three hundred people once lived in Doodletown, and for many years after the hamlet's abandonment, the school remained standing. Today only foundations of the buildings can be discovered, sometimes covered by the nonnative barberry. The Doodletown Bridle Path, which circles the hamlet, was built in 1935 for use by horses and cross-country skiers, but its use by horses ended when the stables at Bear Mountain were demolished in 1961.

Follow the Doodletown Bridle Path for about 1 mile until the yellow-blazed Suffern–Bear Mountain Trail joins from the left. When the Suffern–Bear Mountain Trail turns right in 750 feet, leaving the Bridle Path, turn right and follow the yellow blazes uphill on a rocky woods road. After the Suffern–Bear Mountain Trail crosses the Doodlekill, the climb steepens. Soon after the trail bears left, leaving the woods road, it reaches a short, rocky climb over a talus slope, followed by a more gentle section. The Suffern–Bear Mountain Trail then passes through a small rock outcrop. Just off the trail to the left there is a limited view of the Timp and the Hudson River.

After descending into a hollow and continuing through a mountain laurel thicket, the trail climbs a talus slope and emerges in an open area, with a view of Bear Mountain on the right. A short distance beyond, you'll reach a junction with the blue-blazed Timp-Torne Trail, which takes its name from two prominent summits in the Harriman–Bear

Mountain State Parks: the Timp, which you have just seen (and will see again in a few minutes), and the Popolopen Torne, to the north. Turn left, following the blue blazes, and in about 500 feet you'll reach the West Mountain Shelter, built in 1928, with excellent views of the Timp and the Hudson River. This is a great place to take a break.

When you're ready to continue, retrace your steps back to the junction and turn left, now following both blue and yellow blazes. In 0.3 mile, the yellow-blazed Suffern–Bear Mountain Trail goes off to the left, and you continue ahead on the blue-blazed Timp-Torne Trail. Fire once consumed the area crossed by the trail, but now birch, cedar, and pines are thankfully making a comeback, and your route on the ridge is open to the sky.

In another 0.1 mile, the AT joins the Timp-Torne Trail at a junction marked with a wooden signpost. Your hike for the next 0.7 mile is along the spectacular west ridge of West Mountain, which offers many fine outlooks both to the west and to the east as the trails jog from one side of the ridge to the other, tempting you to linger.

The co-aligned blue-and-white blazes lead over open flat rocks and up a short climb before reaching a fork where the two trails split. Bear left and follow the Timp-Torne Trail, which heads downhill over rock slabs, passes through an interesting cleft in a rock, and finally reaches the junction with the Fawn Trail where you were previously. Turn left and retrace your steps back to your car.

23

Popolopen Torne

Total distance: 4.5 miles

Walking time: 3.5 hours

Vertical rise: 1,250 feet

Maps: USGS 7.5' Popolopen Lake;
USGS 7.5' Peekskill; NY–NJTC
Harriman–Bear Mountain Trails #119

Trailhead GPS Coordinates:
N 41° 19' 26" W 73° 59' 16"

This loop hike traverses both sides of a spectacular gorge and scrambles up an exquisite peak with a breathtaking 360-degree view of West Point, Bear Mountain, and the Hudson.

HOW TO GET THERE

From the traffic circle on the west side of the Bear Mountain Bridge, proceed north on US 9W for 0.2 mile to the Fort Montgomery State Historic Site on the east side of the road. Free parking is available, but there is a small admission charge to enter the visitors center (845-446-2134), which has displays and an interesting historic film. Self-guided tours of the area are available.

THE TRAIL

Begin the hike by walking back to US 9W, crossing the road, and heading south on a sidewalk over the Popolopen Viaduct (built in 1916 and widened in 1936). Just after the guardrail ends, you'll notice a triple-red-on-white blaze on a rock to the right, which marks the start of the Popolopen Gorge Trail. Turn right onto this trail, which soon begins to descend on a woods road, crossing under a power line on the way. At the base of the descent, it reaches the abutment of a former bridge over Popolopen Creek. Until the 140-foot-high Popolopen Viaduct was built in 1916, the iron bridge that was supported by this abutment—known as the Hell Hole Bridge—was the only way to cross the creek in this vicinity. To the left, you can see a spectacular waterfall which cascades over a stone dam built in 1901 to generate water power for a mill downstream.

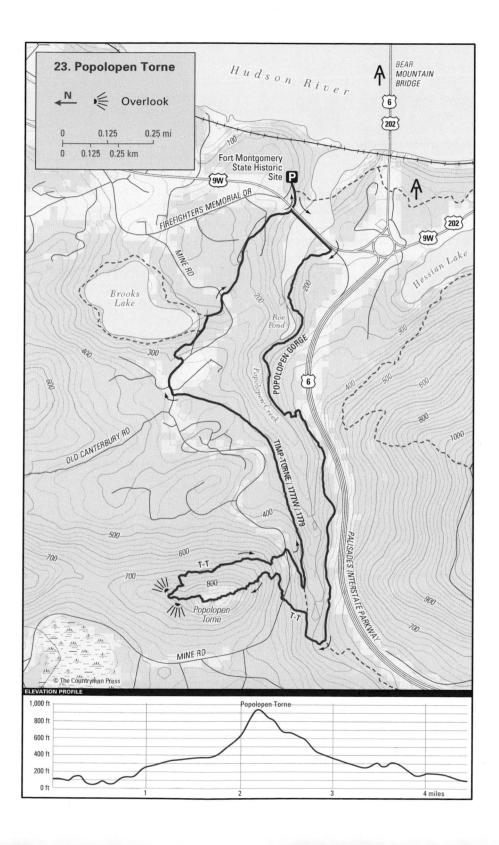

23. Popolopen Torne

N ◄—— ❇ Overlook

| 0 | 0.125 | 0.25 mi |
| 0 | 0.125 | 0.25 km |

Hudson River

BEAR
MOUNTAIN
BRIDGE

6
202

Fort Montgomery
State Historic
Site **P**

9W

FIREFIGHTERS MEMORIAL DR

202
9W

MINE RD

*Brooks
Lake*

*Roe
Pond*

Hessian Lake

100

200

200

300

400

600

300

POPOLOPEN GORGE

6

Popolopen Creek

OLD CANTERBURY RD

300

400

500

600

800

1000

TIMP-TORNE / 1777W / 1779

400

500

700

600

700

800

900

700

T-T

*Popolopen
Torne*

T-T

MINE RD

PALISADES INTERSTATE PARKWAY

© The Countryman Press

ELEVATION PROFILE

Popolopen Torne

1,000 ft
800 ft
600 ft
400 ft
200 ft
0 ft

1   2   3   4 miles

The Popolopen Gorge Trail now climbs on a footpath and begins to run parallel to Roe Pond, the body of calm water behind the dam. It continues on a woods road along the cascading Popolopen Creek.

About 0.5 mile from the site of the old bridge, watch carefully for a double blaze that marks a sharp left turn. The trail now climbs steeply on rock steps and switchbacks and reaches a wide woods road—the route of the Bear Mountain Aqueduct, built in 1930 to bring water from Queensboro Lake to the Bear Mountain Inn, and rebuilt in 2012. You are now high above the gorge; the water roars below. You may get glimpses through the trees of the Popolopen Torne, across the creek to the right, which is the high point of the hike. You'll also hear and see the traffic on the Palisades Interstate Parkway—just above you on the left—but for the most part, sounds of the traffic will probably be drowned out by the thundering sounds of the cascading stream below. You'll pass several large manhole covers, remnants of the original 1930 aqueduct.

After about 0.5 mile along the aqueduct, you'll come to a fork. The wide woods road—the route of the 2012 aqueduct—bears left here, but you should continue straight ahead onto a footpath, which follows the route of the 1930 aqueduct. You'll pass more manhole covers and exposed sections of pipe from the older aqueduct, which has now been abandoned. In another 0.25 mile, a woods road joins from the left, and the surrounding area flattens out.

Just beyond (about 1.5 miles into the hike), you'll come to a junction with the blue-on-white-blazed Timp-Torne Trail, as well as the 1777W and 1779 Trails. (The latter two

View of Bear Mountain Bridge and Hudson River from the Popolopen Torne   DANIEL CHAZIN

trails, which were marked by Boy Scouts in 1975 to commemorate the bicentennial of the American Revolution, roughly follow the routes taken by British and American troops during the Revolutionary War.) Turn right, leaving the Popolopen Gorge Trail, and follow the co-aligned Timp-Torne/1777W/1779 Trails down toward the stream.

At the base of the descent, the trails cross Popolopen Creek on a truss footbridge. The crossing of the creek here has been a challenge for many years. Until 1998, hikers crossed on a wooden bridge a short distance upstream, but that bridge was washed away by Hurricane Floyd. In 2004, funding was obtained for a new truss footbridge that was installed by volunteers of the New York–New Jersey Trail Conference. This bridge was built much higher than the previous one and was designed to withstand flooding. But the ferocious Hurricane Irene in August 2011 washed it away. In 2013, a new bridge of similar design was procured by the park and installed by Trail Conference volunteers.

After crossing the bridge, the trails head uphill on stone steps and soon reach a woods road—the route of the West Point Aqueduct, built in 1906 to carry water from Queensboro Lake to the United States Military Academy at West Point. The trails turn right and follow the aqueduct. In 300 feet, be alert for a double-blue blaze which marks a sharp left turn. Turn left and follow the blue-blazed Timp-Torne Trail, which leaves the aqueduct and begins its climb of the Popolopen Torne (the 1777W and 1779 Trails continue ahead along the aqueduct).

The Timp-Torne Trail crosses the unpaved Fort Montgomery Road and the paved Mine Road and climbs steadily through the woods. Soon, it comes out on open rocks. You'll need both your hands and your feet to negotiate some of the steep climbs. Pay careful attention to the blazes, which indicate the twists and turns of the best route.

As you get higher and climb through this fascinating terrain, views open up. At first, you can see Bear Mountain and the Hudson River to the east. A little higher, the view broadens to include the magnificent Bear Mountain Bridge across the Hudson, built privately in 1924. It was the first vehicular bridge built over the Hudson south of Albany and, when built, it had the longest main suspension span in the world. The bridge was not profitable, and it was sold to New York State in 1940. Behind the bridge is Anthony's Nose, the location of another hike (Hike 6) in this book. As you approach the summit, a west-facing view over the hills of the West Point Military Reservation opens up (the Harriman Park/West Point boundary is only yards away).

The summit of the Popolopen Torne is marked by a stone monument honoring members of the United States armed forces. The stones making up the monument were carried by volunteers from the base of the mountain. The summit offers a magnificent 360-degree view, and you'll want to take a break to rest from the climb and enjoy the panoramic view.

The Timp-Torne Trail continues beyond the monument and passes two more viewpoints—first to the west, then to the east—before reentering the woods. After a short descent over rocks, the route down the mountain follows a graded trail and is not as steep as the climb up the mountain. The trail passes one final east-facing viewpoint from a rock ledge and descends through the woods to Mine Road, reaching it about 500 feet east of where you crossed the road on the way up. Turn left and follow the road a short distance to a small parking area on the right. Turn right at the parking area onto a dirt road and, after passing a sign for the

West-facing view from Popolopen Torne DANIEL CHAZIN

United States Military Reservation, turn left onto a woods road that descends toward the Popolopen Gorge. When you reach the route of the aqueduct, turn left and rejoin the 1777W and 1779 Trails. For the rest of the hike, you'll be following three co-aligned trails: Timp-Torne, 1777W, and 1779.

The trails continue along the aqueduct for the next 0.7 mile. At first the route is level, supported by a stone retaining wall on the right, but you'll encounter a short, steep climb, followed by an equally steep descent. After crossing a stream, the trails climb to the paved Mine Road. Turn right onto Mine Road (passing Wildwood Ridge, a dead-end street) and continue for about 500 feet, then turn left at a double blaze and reenter the woods. The trails now descend, with Brooks Lake visible on the left through the trees.

At the base of the descent, the red-on-white-blazed Brooks Lake Trail joins briefly, and the trails cross a wet area on puncheons. At the next intersection, follow the Timp-Torne/1777W/1779 Trails as they turn right onto a grassy woods road, which leads in a short distance back to the paved Mine Road. Turn left, follow the road for only 150 feet, then turn right and reenter the woods on a footpath. Bear left at a fork in the trail, and you'll soon emerge onto a wide turn on a paved road. Take the right fork and head slightly downhill for a short distance until you see a double blaze, where the trails turn right and reenter the woods. Follow the coaligned Timp-Torne, 1777W, and 1779 Trails under the Popolopen Viaduct to their terminus at the Fort Montgomery Historic Site, where the hike began.

154   *Rockland County and Harriman Park*

24

Bear Mountain Loop

Total distance: 4.2 miles
Walking time: 3 hours
Vertical rise: 1,200 feet
Maps: USGS 7.5' Peekskill; USGS 7.5' Oscawana Lake; NY–NJTC Harriman–Bear Mountain Trails #119
Trailhead GPS Coordinates: N 41° 18' 44" W 73° 59' 20"

This loop hike climbs Bear Mountain on the steep Major Welch Trail and descends on a newly rebuilt section of the Appalachian Trail (AT). The original route of the AT on Bear Mountain was completed in 1923, but during the following years, the trail was relocated several times to avoid eroded sections.

By 2000, the AT route up the east face of Bear Mountain had become eroded and unattractive. Especially in view of the heavy use of this section of the AT by day visitors to the Bear Mountain Inn, the Trail Conference decided that it should be relocated to an entirely new route. The most attractive route required traversing an area of jumbled boulders to the northwest of the existing AT. To build a new trail through this area, the Trail Conference recruited professional trail builders to lead the construction effort and train hundreds of volunteers.

Construction of the new route up the east face of Bear Mountain began in 2006. By the time this relocation was completed and opened in 2010, more than 800 individuals had volunteered over 30,000 hours of their time to construct this section of the AT, which features stone steps and crib walls. Construction of this section required the same kind of masonry skills that were utilized by the Civilian Conservation Corps (CCC) in the 1930s to build roads, walls, and buildings in Harriman–Bear Mountain State Parks. Funding for the project was provided by the Trail Conference; the National Park Service; the Appalachian Trail Conservancy; the New York State Office of Parks, Recreation, and Historic Preservation; and the

Palisades Interstate Park Commission. As of this writing (September 2013), the new AT route on the east face of the mountain from the Scenic Drive to the summit was still under construction, with completion expected in 2015.

HOW TO GET THERE

From the traffic circle on the west side of the Bear Mountain Bridge (at the north end of the Palisades Interstate Parkway), proceed south on US 9W for 0.4 mile, then bear right at the traffic light and follow the ramp to the Bear Mountain Inn. Park in the large parking lot adjacent to the inn. An eight-dollar parking fee is charged on weekends year-round, and daily from Memorial Day to Labor Day.

THE TRAIL

From the parking area, proceed west (toward the mountain) on a paved path that runs along the south side of the Bear Mountain Inn. About 400 feet beyond the inn, you'll reach a junction of paved paths, marked by a trail sign. Turn right and follow the red-circle-on-white-blazed Major Welch Trail (named after the park's first general manager, who was instrumental in creating the extensive network of hiking trails in Harriman–Bear Mountain Parks). The Major Welch Trail proceeds north along a relatively level paved path, following the western shore of Hessian Lake and passing views of Anthony's Nose (across the river) and a tower of the Bear

View from the summit of Bear Mountain

DANIEL CHAZIN

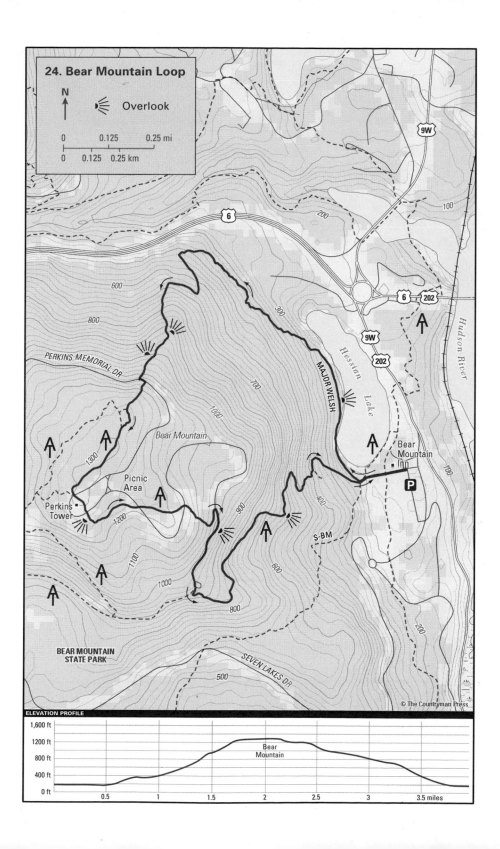

24. Bear Mountain Loop

N

☀ Overlook

0   0.125   0.25 mi
0   0.125   0.25 km

9W

6

200

100

6   202

9W

202

Hessian Lake

Hudson River

600

800

PERKINS MEMORIAL DR.

300

MAJOR WELSH

700

1000

Bear Mountain

1300

Picnic Area

Perkins Tower

1200

900

400

Bear Mountain Inn

P

S-BM

1100

600

1000

800

200

BEAR MOUNTAIN STATE PARK

500

SEVEN LAKES DR.

© The Countryman Press

ELEVATION PROFILE

1,600 ft	
1200 ft	Bear Mountain
800 ft	
400 ft	
0 ft	

0.5   1   1.5   2   2.5   3   3.5 miles

Stone steps along the Major Welch Trail

DANIEL CHAZIN

Mountain Bridge. In the 1700s, this lake was known as Lake Sinnipink, derived from the Native American name of the nearby Assinapink Creek. During the 19th century, blocks of ice were cut from the lake and shipped to New York City by the Knickerbocker Ice Company.

In about 0.5 mile, near the northern end of the lake, the trail bears left and climbs stone steps. Soon the trail levels off, then climbs more gradually on a rocky footpath. After passing a water tank, above on the left, the trail descends slightly on a dirt road, then bears left and continues on a relatively level (but very rocky) footpath through dense mountain laurel. If there are no leaves on the trees, below and to the right you may notice the flat-roofed Overlook Lodge, part of the Bear Mountain Inn complex.

In another 0.3 mile, the trail bears left and resumes its climb of Bear Mountain. The ascent soon steepens, with the trail following a rocky footpath through mountain laurel. Within a short distance, the trail turns left onto a well-graded footpath with stone steps, constructed in 2013 by a volunteer trail crew along with professional trail builders. In about 600 feet, the trail climbs a long flight of narrow stone steps wedged between large rocks and turns right at a large boulder, switching back toward the west.

At the end of the new trail section, the Major Welch Trail turns left and begins to climb several rock outcrops surrounded by mountain laurel. It then climbs a long rock outcrop studded with pitch pines, which affords a panoramic north-facing view. After climbing a little further, the trail emerges onto another rock outcrop with an even broader view, including the Hudson River. Brooks Lake is visible directly ahead, and the Bear Mountain Bridge is on the right, with Anthony's Nose behind it.

The trail continues ahead, briefly leveling off but soon resuming its ascent. Soon, you'll climb stone steps and reach the paved Perkins Drive—an auto route to the top of Bear Mountain. Follow the trail as it crosses the road diagonally to the left, climbs stone steps, and continues to climb over more rock outcrops through mountain laurel.

After climbing another 150 vertical feet, you'll reach a T-junction with a well-graded gravel path. A blue-blazed trail begins on the right, but you should turn left to continue on the Major Welch Trail. This handicapped-accessible trail section, opened in 2011, was skillfully constructed by a team of experienced professional trail builders to blend into the environment while making it possible for all users to enjoy a hiking experience.

At the next intersection, turn left again, now joining the white-blazed Appalachian Trail (AT), which runs concurrently with the Major Welch Trail, following a level path across the summit ridge of Bear Mountain. In 0.2 mile, you'll pass a massive boulder on the left. Atop the boulder are the concrete foundations of a former fire tower (replaced in 1934 by the Perkins Memorial Tower). This boulder marks the actual summit of the mountain (1,305 feet).

Just beyond, the trail crosses the paved loop road around the summit and reaches the Perkins Memorial Tower (the Major Welch Trail ends here). Built in 1934 to honor the memory of George W. Perkins, the first President of the Palisades Interstate Park Commission, the tower was originally used as a weather station, then as a fire lookout. In 1992, the tower was renovated, and new exhibits were installed. The staircases leading to the top of the tower feature tiles that detail historical events and include interesting snippets of information, such as the cost of a meal at the Bear Mountain Inn in 1920. The tower is usually open to the public without charge whenever the Perkins Memorial Drive is open to traffic (the road is closed during the winter and when the weather is inclement).

Continue past the tower, recrossing the paved loop road, and proceed ahead to a broad south-facing viewpoint, with Dunderberg Mountain jutting into the Hudson River to the left. Several rustic benches have been placed in this area for hikers to rest. After enjoying the view and taking a break, head back toward the tower, but bear right at a fork in the path. Directly ahead, on a rock, you'll notice a plaque placed to commemorate the service of Joseph Bartha as trails chairman of the New York–New Jersey Trail Conference from 1940 to 1955.

Bear right at the plaque and descend along the white-blazed AT, which soon levels off and begins to run along an old, rusted water pipeline atop a rock embankment. A short distance beyond, the trail crosses the paved Scenic Drive—a dead-end extension of Perkins Drive, which once continued down the mountain but was cut off by the construction of the Parkway in the 1950s. Soon, the trail recrosses the Scenic Drive and continues to descend, with views directly below over the Hudson River and Iona Island.

About 0.5 mile from the summit of Bear Mountain, the AT reaches the Scenic Drive for the third time. Here, it turns right and follows along the paved road, with excellent views of the Hudson River and Iona Island below. At the dead-end turnaround of the Scenic Drive, the trail continues ahead along the blocked-off paved road for 150 feet, then turns left into the woods and descends (the turn is marked by an arrow pointing to the "inn"). As you descend, you'll traverse over eight hundred hand-hewn stone steps, supported in places by stone crib walls.

In 0.75 mile, after passing a seasonal waterfall on the left, the trail curves to the left and reaches a panoramic viewpoint over Iona Island and the Hudson River. After descending a little further, it crosses a 28-foot-long wooden bridge and begins to descend more steeply on stone steps. Toward the base of the descent, you'll come to a junction where a blue-blazed side trail begins on the right. Bear left (following an arrow pointing to the "inn") and continue to follow the AT, which descends more gradually. After passing a stone building known as the Spider Hill House on the right, the AT reaches the trail junction behind the Bear Mountain Inn. Continue ahead past the inn and retrace your steps to the parking area where the hike began.

IV. The West Hudson Hills

Introduction to the West Hudson Area

New York's Orange County—known by hikers as the West Hudson area—has four distinct hiking areas: privately owned Black Rock Forest and Schunemunk Mountain, Storm King, and Sterling Forest State Parks.

BLACK ROCK FOREST

Black Rock Forest is a 3,800-acre preserve dedicated to scientific research, education, and conservation of the natural ecosystem that once covered this entire region. Only 50 miles north of New York City, the area is home to numerous ponds, wetlands, and great biological diversity.

The land remains relatively pristine, thanks to the foresight of Dr. Ernest Stillman, who in 1949 established and endowed it as a Harvard University research forest. In 1989, after Harvard decided the tract was no longer needed for its programs, the land was acquired by the late philanthropist William Golden, who established the not-for-profit Black Rock Forest Preserve.

Today, the forest is used as a field station by the Black Rock Forest Consortium, comprising 20+ private and public educational and research institutions, including the New York–New Jersey Trail Conference (NY–NJTC). The consortium provides a center for research and teaching at all levels and serves as an information network linking students, researchers, teachers, administrators, and institutions.

Public access continues. Hikers in the forest may notice distinctive plots of native trees, each with differing timber-management techniques. All but one of the half-dozen ponds are part of water systems for nearby towns, so laws prohibit use of them in any way. Dirt roads connect the various plots and are used by the forest's managers, but public vehicular traffic is not permitted. The Black Rock Fish & Game Club has sole permission to hunt the numerous deer that populate the forest. The property is closed to the public during deer season and may also be closed during times of high fire danger and for occasional special events. Call 845-534-4517 for information, or go to www.black rockforest.org. Organized groups such as hiking clubs must call to preregister.

SCHUNEMUNK MOUNTAIN STATE PARK

Schunemunk Mountain sits in solitary splendor, its long, gently rounded form isolated from the Hudson Highlands and the Shawangunks as completely as its rocks are separated by the ages from their surroundings. Light grayish and pinkish sandstones, shales, and conglomerates crown its summit ridge. Hikers marvel at the unique conglomerate bedrock, commonly called puddingstone, so apparent when walking along either of the two distinct ridges. In many places the bedrock has been ground down to a smooth surface by the movement of glaciers. The purplish hue of the main rock houses different sizes of pink- and lavender-colored rocks as well as attractive white quartz pebbles.

The name *Schunemunk* is believed to mean "excellent fireplace" and was given to the Leni-Lenape Native American village once located on the northern part of the mountain that is now a familiar sight to travelers on the adjacent New York State Thruway.

The northern half of the ridge was saved from development by Star Expansion Industries, the Ogden Family Foundation, and the Storm King Art Center, which, under the leadership of H. Peter Stern, formed the Mountainville Conservancy. In 1996, with the assistance of a grant from the Lila Acheson and DeWitt Wallace Foundation, the Open Space Institute acquired 2,100 acres that has become the core of the state park. The Nature Conservancy owns an additional 389 acres.

The hiking-only trails are open from dawn to dusk. Hunting is not permitted, but violations are not uncommon, so many hikers avoid the mountain during deer season, mid-November through mid-December.

STORM KING STATE PARK

To the east of Black Rock Forest stands mighty Storm King Mountain (Hike 30). In 1922 Dr. Ernest Stillman donated 800 acres to the Palisades Interstate Park Commission (PIPC) to ensure its preservation. Little did he know the controversy that would surround the mountain just four decades later when Consolidated Edison announced plans for a pumped storage power project that would have forever altered the area.

Prominent local citizens, the NY–NJTC, and The Nature Conservancy joined forces to fight the project. Along with others, they founded Scenic Hudson Inc., the organization that today is still working to preserve the Hudson Valley's natural heritage. The landmark legal battle that ensued—not finally settled until 1980—now forms the basis of the environmental law movement championed by organizations such as the Natural Resources Defense Council.

In the summer of 1999, the Storm King area was ravaged by a forest fire. It had been exceptionally dry, and the fire's heat went deep into the topsoil. To everyone's surprise, explosions followed. Long-forgotten unexploded shells detonated under the intense heat. Fortunately, no one was hurt. The park was closed, and a U.S. Army Corps of Engineers cleanup began in 2000. The park was reopened to the public in 2003.

Except for hiking trails, the park is undeveloped and managed from the administration building at Bear Mountain. Seasonal deer hunting is permitted only in the section of the park west of US 9W.

STERLING FOREST STATE PARK

Sterling Forest is known for its role in the early mining and smelting industry. Many woods roads crisscross the area. A score of historic mines and the remains of two 19th-century furnaces are found on the property, one visited on Hike 27. During the Revolutionary War, the ironmasters at Sterling forged a 500-yard-long chain that was stretched across the Hudson River at West Point to block British warships. The Sterling Ironworks also played a strategic role during the War of 1812 and the Civil War.

Once owned by the Harriman family, the land was offered to the state as parkland in the 1940s, but the offer was declined and the property sold to private interests. In the late 1980s, the corporate owners proposed a massive development: homes for 35,000 people, along with abundant office and commercial space. Hikers had a strong interest in preserving this rugged forest. Spearheaded by NY–NJTC Executive Director JoAnn Dolan and her husband, Paul, a public-private partnership to save Sterling Forest was formed. Thanks to generous appropriations by the states of New Jersey and New

York and the United States Congress, as well as substantial donations by the Open Space Institute, Scenic Hudson, the Doris Duke Charitable Foundation, and other groups and individuals, the PIPC acquired 14,500 acres of Sterling Forest in 1998. Subsequent acquisitions have increased the size of the park to nearly 22,000 acres.

A corridor of federal land surrounding the Appalachian Trail bisects the park at its northern end. Passaic County, New Jersey, owns a 2,000-acre tract in the south, acquired by eminent domain. Some hiking trails in Sterling Forest State Park follow footpaths (both Sterling Forest hikes in this book, Hike 25 and Hike 27, primarily use hiking trails routed along these footpaths), but many other trails follow woods roads, some of which are eroded. Some of the trails are multiuse. The park allows seasonal turkey and deer hunting (permit required).

A generous donation of $1.75 million from the family of the late U.S. Senator Frank Lautenberg (D-NJ) has endowed a visitors center at the south end of Sterling Lake, which also serves as the park's administrative headquarters. For more information, call 845-351-5907.

25

Sterling Ridge to the Fire Tower

Total distance: 7.4 miles, one-car hike
(5.5 miles, two-car hike)

Walking time: 4.5 hours, one-car hike
(3 hours, two-car hike)

Vertical rise: 700 feet, one-car hike
(400 feet, two-car hike)

Maps: USGS 7.5' Greenwood Lake;
NY−NJTC Sterling Forest Trails #100;
Sterling Forest State Park

Trailhead GPS Coordinates:
N 41° 11' 56" W 74° 15' 23.5"

This hike follows the Sterling Ridge Trail, with some moderate ups and downs, to an active fire tower with panoramic views. It then descends to Sterling Lake and passes historical remnants of the iron mining operations that took place in the area for over 150 years. It ends at the Sterling Forest State Park Visitors Center, which has a number of informative exhibits on the history of the area and its mining operations.

Today, Sterling Forest is a favorite destination for hikers. But it was not always that way. When the first edition of the *New York Walk Book* was published in 1923, most landowners did not object to hikers (then often referred to as "trampers") traversing their properties in rural areas; indeed, the 1923 *Walk Book* described many hiking routes that traversed private property. But it referred to the Sterling Forest area as "forbidden territory," stating that it "is posted against trespassers; and this prohibition is being enforced against trampers." The 1934 edition of the *Walk Book* reiterated that the area "is forbidden to trampers," who are "at the risk of arrest by the employes of the Sterling Iron and Railway Company," but added the hope "that some time it will come into public ownership, possibly by a western extension of the Palisades Interstate Park."

By the time the fourth edition of the *New York Walk Book* appeared in 1971, the Sterling Ridge Trail had already been established. Even then, "'no trespassing' signs were at both ends of the trail," although it was stated that the trail was "open to bona

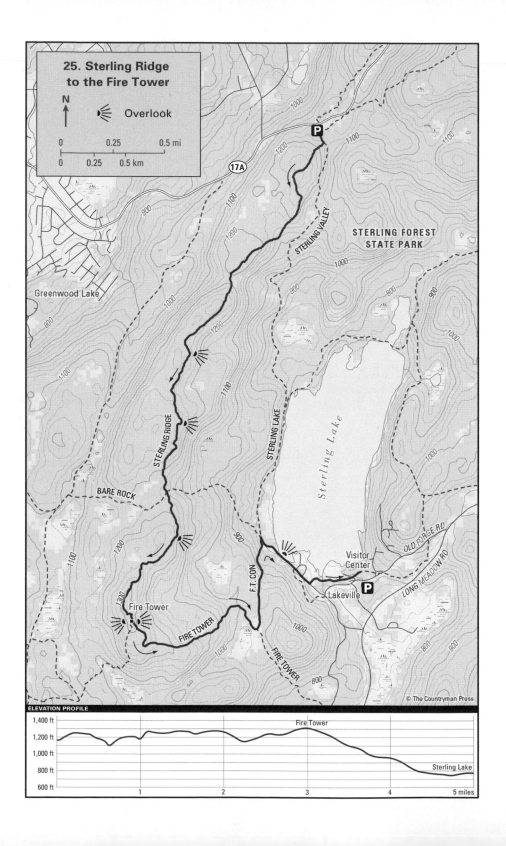

25. Sterling Ridge to the Fire Tower

N

Overlook

| 0 | 0.25 | 0.5 mi |
| 0 | 0.25 | 0.5 km |

17A

Sterling Valley

STERLING FOREST
STATE PARK

Greenwood Lake

STERLING RIDGE

STERLING LAKE

Sterling Lake

BARE ROCK

F.T. CON.

Fire Tower

FIRE TOWER

Visitor
Center

Lakeville

OLD FORGE RD

LONG MEADOW RD

FIRE TOWER

© The Countryman Press

ELEVATION PROFILE

1,400 ft
1,200 ft
1,000 ft
800 ft
600 ft

Fire Tower

Sterling Lake

1   2   3   4   5 miles

fide hikers, particularly those of the member clubs of the New York–New Jersey Trail Conference."

With the acquisition of Sterling Forest by New York State in 1998 and the creation of Sterling Forest State Park, the Sterling Ridge Trail was opened to all hikers, and additional trails were blazed in the area. But most of these newer trails follow woods roads, and the Sterling Ridge Trail remains one of the finest and most scenic trails in the park.

As described, this is a one-way hike, with two cars required. However, for those with only one car, it is possible to make a loop and return to the start via the Sterling Lake Loop and Sterling Valley Trail.

HOW TO GET THERE

If you have two cars available, take the New York Thruway to Exit 15A. Turn left at the bottom of the ramp onto NY 17 and head north for 1.4 miles to the exit for Sterling Forest. Follow Sterling Mine Road (County Route 72) west for 3 miles, then turn right onto Long Meadow Road (County Route 84). Proceed north on Long Meadow Road for 3.5 miles, then turn left onto Old Forge Road and continue for 0.5 mile until you reach the Sterling Forest State Park Visitors Center. Park in the parking lot on the right side of the road (you may wish to cross the road and stop at the visitor center, where

Sterling Lake

DANIEL CHAZIN

Sterling Forest Fire Tower

DANIEL CHAZIN

there are interesting exhibits and a free trail map is available). Leave one car here.

With the second car, continue ahead on Old Forge Road to its end at Long Meadow Road. Turn left onto Long Meadow Road and follow it for 3.6 miles to NY 17A. Turn left onto NY 17A (a divided highway at this point; make sure to cross the eastbound lanes before turning left onto the westbound lanes) and follow it for 4.1 miles to the trailhead of the Sterling Ridge Trail (marked by a small sign on the left side of the road). The trailhead is about 0.1 mile beyond a green-and-white sign indicating a hiker crossing. Turn left onto a dirt road and follow it past an open gate to a large parking area in a grassy field.

If you have only one car, proceed west on NY 17A from its intersection with NY 17 (2.5 miles north of Tuxedo) and continue for 5.5 miles to the trailhead of the Sterling Ridge Trail, on the left side of the road.

THE TRAIL

From the rear of the parking area, go around the gate and follow the woods road which leads south. This road is marked with the blue-on-white blazes of the Sterling Ridge Trail, the teal diamond blazes of the Highlands Trail, and the yellow blazes of the Sterling Valley Trail. In about 100 feet, turn right, leaving the road, and follow the blue-and-white and teal diamond blazes, which climb on a footpath (the yellow blazes continue ahead on the road). After reaching the top of a small rise, the trail levels off. Soon, the trail begins to run along the edge of a ravine, gradually descending, with limited views to the left through the trees. A short distance beyond, the trail crosses a seasonal stream and then begins to ascend. About 1 mile from the trailhead, it goes under a power line, with good views to the east and west.

After a short but steady ascent, the trail crosses a large rock outcrop. The trail continues along the ridge, now following a relatively level route. In about 0.5 mile, you'll come out on another large rock outcrop, with a limited east-facing view. After another level stretch, the trail continues on undulating terrain and then emerges onto a third rock outcrop, with a stunted red cedar tree growing out of a crack in the rock. There are only very limited views from the outcrop (which features a number of cairns), but after a brief descent, you'll reach a panoramic viewpoint over Sterling Lake to the east, with a log supported by stones serving as a bench.

The trail continues along the ridge. After descending a little, it crosses a woods road—the route of the orange-blazed Bare Rock Trail. The trail then climbs to another, more limited viewpoint over Sterling Lake from open rocks. It continues over undulating terrain, and after traversing an area dominated by hemlock and mountain laurel, reaches a ranger cabin and the Sterling Forest Fire Tower, about 3.5 miles from the start of the hike.

The view from the top of the fire tower, built in 1922, is well worth the climb. When open to the public, the tower provides an expansive view over the entire Sterling Forest. Sterling Lake is visible to the northeast, and a portion of the much larger Greenwood Lake can be seen to the west. On a clear day, North and South Beacon Mountains of the East Hudson Highlands may be seen in the distance to the northeast, and Schunemunk Mountain is visible to the north, with the Catskills on the horizon. A picnic table at the base of the tower makes it a good place to stop for lunch.

When you're ready to continue, find the white-stripe-on-red-blazed Fire Tower Trail and follow it as it descends from the ridge on a pleasant gravel road, with many grassy sections (do not follow the joint Fire Tower/Sterling Ridge Trail, which heads south on a footpath). After about 0.5 mile, as the road levels off, you'll come to a junction. The Fire Tower Trail turns off to the right on a branch road, but you should bear left and continue ahead on the main road, now marked with red-triangle-on-white blazes as the Fire Tower Connector Trail. The trail continues to descend, and after passing a private residence and going around a locked gate, it ends at a paved road near the shore of Sterling Lake.

If you have only one car and need to return to the trailhead on NY 17A, turn left onto the road, marked with the blue blazes of the Sterling Lake Loop. Just ahead, the paving ends and the road is blocked by a cable barrier. Soon, the road begins to follow the scenic shoreline of Sterling Lake. In about 0.75 mile, you'll come to a Y-junction. Bear left here and follow the yellow-blazed Sterling Valley Trail, another woods road that leads slightly uphill, away from the lake. After a level stretch, the road begins to climb. It passes under the same power line that you crossed earlier in the hike, and then continues to ascend steadily. In about 1.5 miles, it ends at the parking area where you began the hike.

If you have spotted a second car at the Sterling Forest State Park Visitor Center, turn right onto the paved road, following the blue blazes of the Sterling Loop Trail (the trail is very sparsely blazed along the road). Soon, the road begins to run along the shore of Sterling Lake, with panoramic views across the lake. A short distance beyond, you'll pass ruins of concrete and brick structures on the right. These are remnants of the former mining operations in the area. Sterling Forest was once a center of mining activity, with the first mines opened in the 1700s. The last active mine in the area closed down nearly one hundred years ago.

Just beyond (immediately past Building 28), follow the blue-blazed Sterling Lake Trail as it turns left, leaving the road, and enters the woods on a footpath. It soon crosses the outlet of Sterling Lake on a wooden bridge, with the ruins of the Sterling Furnace visible below on the right. After passing through an area with low, dense vegetation, the trail emerges onto a grassy field, passing the stone foundations of a former church. Continue to follow the blue blazes, which lead you to the Sterling Forest State Park Visitor Center, with its informative exhibits. From the visitor center, head uphill and cross the road to reach the parking area where you left your first car.

26

Mount Peter to Arden on the Appalachian Trail

Total distance: 12.3 miles (8.7-mile alternate)

Walking time: 9 hours (6.5-hour alternate)

Vertical rise: 2,050 feet (1,450-foot alternate)

Maps: USGS 7.5' Sloatsburg; Appalachian Trail Guide to New York–New Jersey, Map #2; NY–NJTC Sterling Forest Trails #100

Trailhead GPS Coordinates: N 41° 14' 38" W 74° 17' 15.5"

This arduous hike should not be attempted by anyone in poor physical condition or without motivation. It crosses several mountains with many false summits, includes some short sections of rock scrambling, and ends with a very steep descent down a precipitous hill—Agony Grind—that can be hard on tired knees. Fitzgerald Falls and Little Dam Lake are highlights of the trip, but some extremely beautiful sections, varied terrain, and vistas are also included. For its entire length, the hike follows the route of the Appalachian Trail (AT). Two cars are needed for a shuttle, and an option to shorten the hike is given.

HOW TO GET THERE

Drive two cars north on NY 17 through Sloatsburg and Tuxedo. Turn right onto Arden Valley Road 5.5 miles north of the Tuxedo railroad station, and continue for 0.3 mile to the ample parking at the Elk Pen on the right. Leave one car here. (During the early 1920s a herd of elk was indeed penned here. Transported from Yellowstone National Park in December 1919, the animals didn't flourish, and the survivors were sold in 1942.)

Now drive south on NY 17 for 2.8 miles to the junction of NY 17A. Bear right at the light and right again at the stop sign at the end of the commuter lot. Turn right, and continue west along NY 17A. The hiker sign you may notice about 5.5 miles down NY 17A indicates the trailhead of the Sterling Ridge Trail (Hike 25) and the Allis Trail. After 7.4 miles on NY 17A you'll reach a junction with

Fitzgerald Falls

DANIEL CHAZIN

NY 210. Bear right at the fork. Almost immediately at another fork you must decide whether to walk the 12.3-mile hike or the 8.7-miler. For the longer hike, bear left, staying on NY 17A toward Warwick. Continue for about 2 miles to the crest of Mount Peter, and park in the large dirt parking area for the AT on the left side of NY 17A.

For the shorter hike, take the right fork toward Monroe on Lakes Road. Continue straight ahead for 0.3 mile, paralleling Greenwood Lake on the right, to a stop sign. Drive straight ahead, now on County Route 5, and proceed 3.7 miles to a small parking area on the east side of the road close to a large power-line stanchion.

THE TRAIL

For the longer hike, proceed north on the AT from the parking area. Almost immediately, you'll notice a blue-blazed side trail on the left. Turn left and follow this trail, which leads in 0.2 mile to the Hawk Watch platform (used for monitoring spring and fall raptor migration), with views to the west and north. After taking in the views, retrace your steps to the AT and continue ahead. At first, the trail parallels the noisy NY 17A, but the road soon bends to the right, away from the trail.

The AT proceeds gently uphill, crosses a gas pipeline, and continues through an area with dense hemlock and mountain laurel. It

The West Hudson Hills

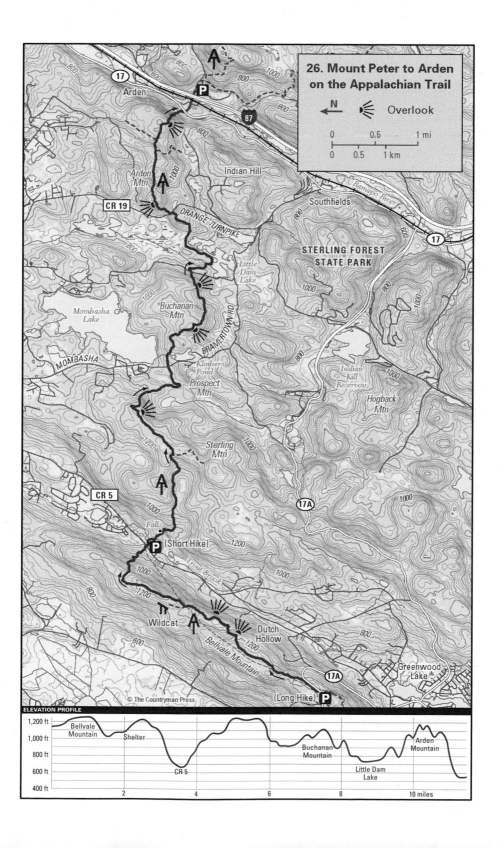

26. Mount Peter to Arden on the Appalachian Trail

N   Overlook

0   0.5   1 mi
0   0.5   1 km

Arden

Indian Hill

Southfields

Ranapo River

STERLING FOREST STATE PARK

Arden Mtn

CR 19

ORANGE TURNPIKE

Little Dam Lake

Mombasha Lake

Buchanan Mtn

BRAMERTOWN RD

MOMBASHA

Kloibers Pond

Prospect Mtn

Indian Kill Reservoir

Hogback Mtn

Sterling Mtn

CR 5

17A

Falls

(Short Hike)

Trout Brook

Wildcat

Dutch Hollow

Bellvale Mountain

17A

Greenwood Lake

(Long Hike)

© The Countryman Press

ELEVATION PROFILE

1,200 ft — Bellvale Mountain — Shelter — Buchanan Mountain — Arden Mountain
1,000 ft
800 ft
600 ft — CR 5 — Little Dam Lake
400 ft
         2   4   6   8   10 miles

Cat Rocks

DANIEL CHAZIN

then begins a gradual descent. About 1.3 miles from the start, you'll reach an outcrop of puddingstone rock known as the Eastern Pinnacles. You'll have to scramble up rocks to reach the top of this outcrop, which offers views to the north and east over the hills of Sterling Forest. Neither this scramble nor the next is particularly difficult, though both call for concentration and require the use of your hands as well as your feet.

There are alternatives to following the AT route up Eastern Pinnacles. A blue-blazed side trail avoids the climb by completely by-passing Eastern Pinnacles, and another blue-blazed trail, partway up the rocks, indicates an easier route. Unless the trail is wet or the weather is icy, by all means follow the white blazes, which offer the most scenic route.

The AT now heads gently downhill. It goes through dense mountain laurel thickets and traverses a wet area, then climbs to Cat Rocks—a dramatic rock outcrop with a steep drop. The east-facing view from Cat Rocks has largely grown in, but you'll want to take a break here to appreciate the fascinating puddingstone rock formations. Note particularly the deep crevice to the left of the trail. Again, an easier route that bypasses the steep climb is indicated by blue blazes. From Cat Rocks, the trail begins to descend.

Just over 2 miles from the start, a blue-blazed side trail on the left leads to the Wildcat Shelter. It is worthwhile to take the short side trip to the shelter—a favorite stop for many through-hikers on the AT. Return to the trail and turn left. The AT now climbs over a rise. After descending about 100 vertical feet, it turns sharply right and soon begins a steeper descent to Lakes Road, using rock steps for part of the way. When you reach Lakes Road, you've hiked for 3.6 miles. (The 8.7-mile hike begins here.) The teal-diamond-blazed Highlands Trail joins the AT here.

The AT crosses Lakes Road, descends through an area with dense vegetation, goes under a power line, and crosses a wooden bridge over Trout Brook. The trail proceeds across a flat expanse, climbs a rise, and continues through a hemlock grove. Soon, a blue-blazed high-water bypass trail, which avoids two crossings of the brook on rocks, begins on the left. A short distance beyond, the AT recrosses the brook on large boulders just below Fitzgerald Falls, a 25-foot waterfall in a rocky cleft. Water at the falls tumbles spectacularly through a split in the jagged rocks, and this is a good spot to take a break.

The AT now ascends steeply on rock steps to the right of the falls. The beautiful steps were constructed by volunteers of the New York–New Jersey Trail Conference in 2013. At the top, the trail briefly bears right, away from the stream, but soon bears left and crosses the stream on rocks (the blue-blazed bypass trail rejoins the AT just beyond). A short distance beyond, the trail crosses a gravel road, bears right, and begins a steady ascent, continuing to parallel the stream (below on the right). In another 0.25 mile, as the trail levels off, you'll notice several old stone walls on the left. These stone walls, and other walls encountered along the hike, are remnants of abandoned settlements in the area. After a level stretch, the trail continues to climb, crossing a boulder field along the way.

About 1.5 miles from Lakes Road, you'll reach a junction with the blue-blazed Allis Trail, which begins on the right. The Highlands Trail leaves the AT here and heads south on the Allis Trail. You'll notice a register box at the junction (please sign). The Allis Trail is named after a banker, J. Ashton Allis, who was an early treasurer of the Appalachian Trail Conference and a pioneer trail builder. There is an excellent west-facing viewpoint just 100 feet down the Allis Trail, and it's worth taking the short detour to this viewpoint, from which the High Point Monument in northwestern New Jersey can be seen on a clear day.

After another 0.8 mile of mostly level walking, you'll reach the summit of Mombasha High Point (elevation 1,280 feet), which offers limited south-facing views over the hills of Sterling Forest. On a clear day, you might be able to see the New York City skyline in the distance. You've now hiked 2.3 miles from Lakes Road and nearly 6 miles from NY 17A (if you've opted for the longer hike).

The AT now proceeds over rock slabs amid a forest of pitch pine—very different from the forest you've encountered so far on the hike. It curves sharply to the right and descends on a switchback, paralleling the escarpment that the trail followed above, then begins a steady descent. The trail passes through a gap in a stone wall, levels off, then continues to descend. At the base of the descent, it crosses several streams and wet areas on puncheons. After passing a small unnamed pond and crossing an overgrown field (a designated butterfly refuge), it reaches West Mombasha Road.

Walk across the road, cross a ditch on planks, and proceed ahead on what seems to be the top of an old rock wall. After crossing a dirt road, the trail follows another woods road. It soon bears right, leaving the road, crosses the outlet of Kloiber's Pond, and climbs over a rise. It descends to cross a stream in a valley lined with moss-covered rocks and hemlocks, then climbs steadily. After climbing steeply over jumbled rocks, the AT bears right and follows the edge of an escarpment which leads to the first summit of Buchanan Mountain (1,142 feet). The views from the summit are obstructed by trees, but a rock ledge a short distance beyond offers panoramic south-facing views. This is another good spot for a break. You've now hiked 4.4 miles from Lakes Road and 8 miles from NY 17A.

The AT descends into a valley, where it crosses four streams. Just beyond the fourth stream crossing, the trail climbs very steeply over large boulders to reach a limited viewpoint to the east from a secondary summit of Buchanan Mountain. The AT now descends steeply to East Mombasha Road. Cross the road and continue on a winding woods road to the inlet of Little Dam Lake, which is crossed on large boulders (the crossing may be impassable in times of high water). The AT follows the northern shore of the lake and proceeds over a ridge to emerge onto Orange Turnpike.

Turn left onto Orange Turnpike for 250 feet, and reenter the woods on the right-hand side of the road at the end of the guardrail. The AT now undulates over several shoulders of Arden Mountain, with the best views coming after the first rock climb. On the way, you'll pass a register box (please sign).

About 1 mile beyond Orange Turnpike, you'll see a triple blue blaze on the right, which marks the start of a connector to the Indian Hill Loop Trail (Hike 27). A short distance beyond, the blue-blazed Sapphire Trail begins on the left.

After climbing over a rise, you'll begin the steep downhill of Agony Grind. The trail is routed through two rock gullies but has no exposure because trees cover the area. The sounds of the busy traffic on NY 17 begin to intrude on the quiet of the wilderness. At the base of the descent, bear right, and parallel NY 17 before emerging from the woods and crossing the road to walk the 0.3 mile on Arden Valley Road back to your car at the Elk Pen.

27

Indian Hill Loop

Total distance: 4.3 miles

Walking time: 3 hours

Vertical rise: 900 feet

Maps: USGS 7.5' Monroe; NY–NJTC Sterling Forest Trails #100; Sterling Forest State Park (available online at http://newyork.sierraclub.org/nyc/ico/ Sterling_Trails.pdf)

Trailhead GPS Coordinates: N 41° 15' 11" W 74° 10' 59"

Although comprising part of Sterling Forest State Park, the Indian Hill tract traversed by this hike was not acquired by the State of New York directly from the Sterling Forest Corporation. Rather, the property was acquired by Scenic Hudson, which invited the New York–New Jersey Trail Conference to lay out and construct hiking trails on the land before it was transferred to the State of New York for inclusion in the park. The trails used by this hike, which, for the most part, follow footpaths, are among the most attractive in the park, as most other trails in Sterling Forest State Park are routed along woods roads, many of which are eroded.

The remains of the historic Southfields iron furnace, situated at the edge of the Indian Hill property, are along the trail near the start of the hike. The hike also passes by several viewpoints over other sections of the park, the Ramapo River Valley, and Harriman State Park.

Hunting is permitted in much of Sterling Forest State Park (845-351-5907), including Indian Hill. We suggest you hike elsewhere during deer season, usually mid-November to mid-December.

HOW TO GET THERE

From the south, take NY 17 north about 3.5 miles from Tuxedo. Just after passing the now-closed landmark Red Apple Rest, turn left onto Orange Turnpike (County Route 19). (If coming from the north, this junction is on the right, about 6 miles south of Exit 16 of the New York State Thruway, just past the

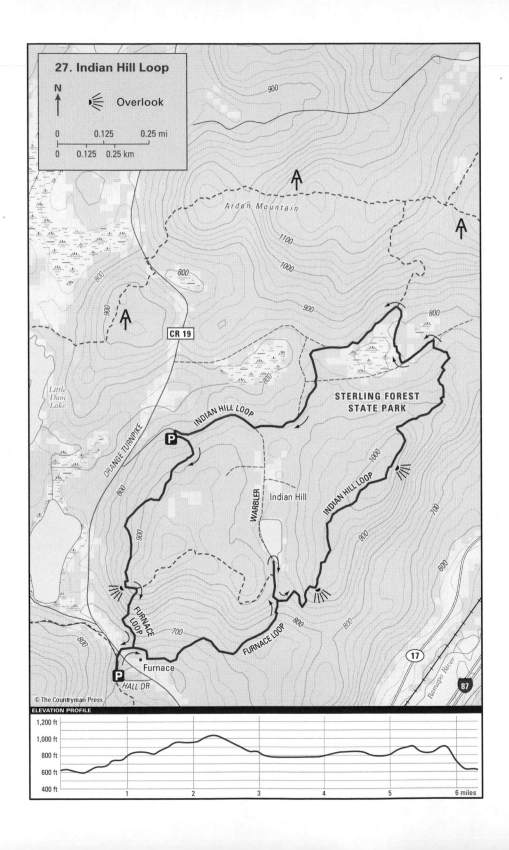

Tuxedo Heights Condominiums.) In 0.6 mile, turn left onto Hall Drive and park in a parking area on the left side of the road at a curve.

THE TRAIL

From the parking area, proceed ahead (north) on Hall Drive, following the white blazes of the Wildcat Mountain Trail. When you reach Orange Turnpike, turn right and cross the road, climb over the guardrail, and descend to cross a footbridge over Mombasha Creek. The trail now turns right and heads east, parallel to the stream.

Just beyond, the white-blazed trail ends, and you should continue ahead on the red-blazed Furnace Loop Trail. You now approach the historic Southfields Furnace, protected by a chain-link fence. Construction of the first furnace on this site began in 1804, and the furnace was "in blast" about a year later. By 1868, the Southfields Iron Works complex comprised not only a furnace but also a blacksmith shop, stamping mill, sawmill, gristmill, wheelwright, branch rail line, and manor house among other facilities. Although the charging bridge (supported by arches) and some of the walls of the casting room remain intact, the furnace has suffered decay from neglect and weathering. Its "last blast" was in the fall of 1887. The complex was acquired by the Scenic Hudson Land Trust in 1997 and was transferred in 2002 to the State of New York for inclusion in Sterling Forest State Park.

Footbridge over Mombasha Creek

DANIEL CHAZIN

Wide stone walls along the Indian Hill Loop Trail DANIEL CHAZIN

Some one to two hundred years ago, iron was produced in stone furnaces, like Southfields, by mixing iron ore, charcoal, and limestone. Once a furnace was lit, the blast would run continuously, producing as much as 25 tons of pig iron a week. In those days, a furnace might have required cutting 1 acre of hardwood forest a day to be used in making the charcoal. Today you would never know that almost the entire area of this hike had been clear-cut. Trees and other ground cover are again abundant. Nature has renewed and restored.

The Furnace Loop Trail continues along an old railroad bed, then turns left and begins to climb on a woods road. After descending a little, the trail climbs rock steps below rock outcrops on the left to reach a junction (marked by a cairn) with the white-stripe-on-yellow-blazed Indian Hill Loop Trail. You will be continuing north on this trail, but for now take a side trip by turning left and following both red and white-stripe-on-yellow blazes. The trail soon bends to the right and, in about three minutes, turns sharply left at a cairn. Continue ahead (do not turn left), now following the yellow-bird-on-green blazes of the Warbler Trail, and you'll soon reach the dam of a pond—a tranquil location worth a short visit.

When you're ready to continue, retrace your steps back to the junction of the red-blazed Furnace Loop and white-stripe-on-yellow-blazed Indian Hill Loop Trails and continue ahead, now following only the white-stripe-on-yellow blazes of the Indian

Hill Loop Trail. The trail crosses a stream on rocks and climbs to a panoramic south-facing viewpoint from a rock ledge. It then ascends to the ridgetop, which it follows north.

After a relatively level stretch, the trail climbs to the highest point on the ridge (1,047 feet). Turn right and walk a short distance to the edge of the ridge for a panoramic east-facing view over the Thruway and the Ramapo River Valley, with Harriman State Park beyond.

From the ridge, the trail descends gradually on switchbacks. Near the bottom, it briefly follows a stone wall, then turns right onto a woods road. At the base of the descent, it turns left onto a woods road between unusually wide stone walls. Now you've reached one of the area's mysteries.

The trail proceeds for some distance between two truly massive 8-foot-wide stone walls—much wider and larger than walls encountered elsewhere. Why were they built so wide? Did farmers just have lots and lots of rocks to clear? Did these walls have something to do with mining activity? So far, no one has been able to offer more than conjecture.

Soon the trail turns right, goes through a gap in a massive stone wall, and continues on a footpath. To the right, you'll notice a row of massive white oaks, over one hundred years old (one of the trees is adjacent to the trail). After crossing a stone wall, the Indian Hill Loop Trail reaches a junction with a blue-blazed trail that begins on the right and heads north to connect, in 0.4 mile, with the white-blazed Appalachian Trail (Hike 26). Here, the Indian Hill Loop Trail turns left

and begins to parallel the stone wall. It soon crosses two more stone walls, as well as a woods road lined on both sides with wide stone walls.

After passing through a wide gap in yet another stone wall, the trail turns left onto a grassy woods road. At a T-junction, it turns right onto another woods road, which it follows for about 0.25 mile to a barrier gate. Here, you'll see a triple blaze that marks the official end of the Indian Hill Loop Trail. Turn left and climb to the parking area, where you'll notice a kiosk on the left and a triple blaze that marks the start of the Indian Hill Loop Trail.

Turn left and reenter the woods on a footpath. The trail proceeds through a hemlock grove, bears right, and climbs to the crest of a rise. After descending a little, it climbs through mountain laurel to reach an open granite ledge, with west-facing views over the hills of Sterling Forest.

A short distance beyond, you'll reach a junction with the red-blazed Furnace Loop Trail (marked by a cairn). Turn right and descend steeply on this red-blazed trail, passing lichen-covered cliffs and interesting rock outcrops along the way. This is the steepest slope that you'll encounter along the hike, and you should use extreme care, especially if the trail is wet or covered with snow or ice. At the base of the descent, you'll reach a junction with the white-blazed Wildcat Mountain Trail. Turn right, now retracing your steps, and follow the white blazes across the stream and along Hall Drive back to the parking area where the hike began.

28

Schunemunk via High Knob

Total distance: 8 miles

Walking time: 6 hours

Vertical rise: 1,600 feet

Maps: USGS 7.5' Cornwall; NY–NJTC West Hudson Trails #114

Trailhead GPS Coordinates: N 41° 21' 41" W 74° 06' 29"

This hike traverses the spectacular ridge of Schunemunk Mountain for 3 miles, following slabs of the distinctive Shawangunk conglomerate which tops the mountain. It climbs to the summit on the Long Path via High Knob, follows the Jessup Trail along the ridge, and descends to Otterkill Road via the Trestle Trail. Because this is a one-way hike, it requires two cars for a shuttle.

The hike begins with a rather demanding climb of about 1,000 feet elevation gain up to the ridge. It continues with an undulating ridge walk, passing many panoramic viewpoints. After dropping into the valley between the two ridges of Schunemunk Mountain, it climbs rather steeply to the western ridge, then descends gradually to your second car. (If a second car is not available, it is still a splendid day's outing to walk to the summit and back—and perhaps hike to the summit from the other direction at another time.)

HOW TO GET THERE

Take the New York State Thruway (I-87) to Exit 16 (Harriman) and proceed north on NY 32 for 7.3 miles to the large black sign for the Black Rock Fish and Game Club. Turn left onto Pleasant Hill Road and left again onto Taylor Road. Taylor Road crosses Woodbury Creek and then I-87, and passes a hikers' parking area on the right. About 2 miles from NY 32, you'll reach a T-junction with Otterkill Road. Turn left and, in about 0.5 mile, you'll notice a massive railroad trestle ahead. There is space for a few cars immediately below the trestle, but the official parking area is another 0.2 mile farther down

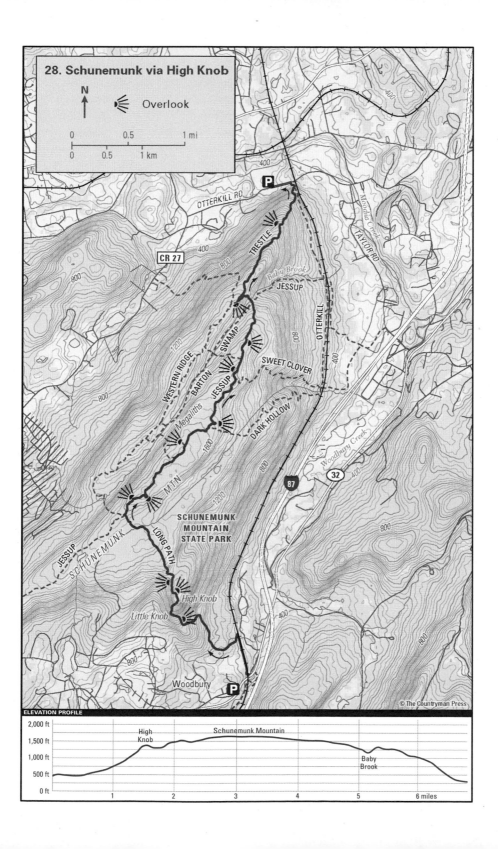

28. Schunemunk via High Knob

N

⟨⟨ Overlook

| 0 | 0.5 | 1 mi |
| 0 | 0.5 | 1 km |

OTTERKILL RD

CR 27

TRESTLE

JESSUP

Baby Brook

SWEET CLOVER

OTTERKILL

WESTERN RIDGE

BARTON

SWAMP

JESSUP

Megaliths

DARK HOLLOW

MTN

SCHUNEMUNK
MOUNTAIN
STATE PARK

JESSUP

SCHUNEMUNK

LONG PATH

High Knob

Little Knob

Woodbury

Woodna Creek

TAYLOR RD

Woodbury Creek

87

32

© The Countryman Press

ELEVATION PROFILE

2,000 ft						
1,500 ft	High Knob		Schunemunk Mountain			
1,000 ft					Baby Brook	
500 ft						
0 ft						
	1	2	3	4	5	6 miles

Otterkill Road, on the right-hand side of the road. Leave one car here.

Return in the second car to NY 32. Turn right and continue south on NY 32 for 3.3 miles, passing under another railroad trestle (known as the Woodbury Viaduct). Continue for another 0.2 mile beyond the trestle and park in the grassy area on the west side of NY 32, just before its intersection with Evans Road. (For those using one car and planning to walk to the summit and back, this parking area is 4 miles north of Exit 16 of I-87.)

THE TRAIL

Walk north on NY 32 for 0.2 mile and cross under the trestle. Just north of the trestle, at the end of the guardrail, a driveway goes off to the left. Turn left here and, almost immediately, you'll see a sign for the Long Path on the left. Turn left again and climb some rock steps, then turn left at the top of the first pitch and continue under the trestle. Immediately turn right, and again climb some rock steps until you reach the level of the tracks. Turn left and head north, following along the railroad tracks. Remember that this is an active railroad line, and a bend in the tracks behind you makes it impossible for the engineer of a northbound train to see you. You may find it easier to cross the tracks and head north with the tracks on your left. The Long Path is marked with aqua blazes, but there are relatively few Long Path blazes in the section along the tracks.

Just past a dirt road that leads down to an active quarry on the right, and as a chain-link fence begins on the right, watch carefully for a double aqua blaze on the west side of the

High Knob
DANIEL CHAZIN

tracks. Follow the Long Path as it leaves the railroad and turns sharply left onto a woods road. The road briefly parallels the tracks, but just before the road crosses a stream, the Long Path turns right, leaving the road. The trail crosses an old stone wall and soon bears right at a fork.

The Long Path now begins a steady climb, following a woods road for most of the way. After climbing about 500 vertical feet above the railroad, you'll notice a large rock outcrop on your right. This is Little Knob, which offers an east-facing view.

A little further up, the trail bends right and begins a very steep climb up a rock outcrop. At the top of the outcrop, amid pitch pines, you'll be afforded a panoramic south-facing view, with a relatively new housing development visible directly below. To the west, you can see the ridge of Schunemunk Mountain, where you'll soon be headed. You've now climbed nearly 1,000 feet from the trailhead, and you'll want to rest here and take in the view. Keep in mind, though, that this is only the first of four viewpoints that you'll encounter on High Knob.

The Long Path continues along the relatively flat summit ridge and soon arrives at the summit of the knob, which offers a spectacular view to the north and east. North and South Beacon Mountains and Breakneck Ridge are visible across the Hudson River, and you can see as far north as the Newburgh-Beacon Bridge. To the east, Storm King Mountain and the hills of Black Rock Forest can be seen on the other side of I-87. Just below you is the quarry that you passed as you walked along the railroad at the start of the hike.

When you're ready to continue, proceed ahead across the flat summit ridge. After descending just a little, the trail emerges on the edge of an escarpment, with views of the ridge of Schunemunk Mountain (note the communications tower). It follows rock slabs along the escarpment, studded with pitch pines, then turns left and descends into a valley. The trail now climbs a steep, rocky slope and turns right. It soon reaches yet another viewpoint—this one to the north. Beyond this viewpoint, the trail crosses several low ridges. A faded red paint blaze and a cairn mark an intersection with an unmarked trail that heads north, roughly paralleling Dark Hollow Brook, but you should continue ahead on the Long Path. After briefly paralleling the upper reaches of the brook and then crossing it, the Long Path climbs steadily to reach an intersection with the Jessup/Highlands Trail on the ridge of Schunemunk Mountain.

The Long Path turns left at this intersection, but you should turn right, now following the yellow blazes of the Jessup Trail and the teal diamond blazes of the Highlands Trail, and head north along the crest of the mountain. You'll immediately climb a large rock outcrop and emerge onto a large open area where the conglomerate bedrock has been smoothed by glacial action. The rock slabs here are so smooth that you can almost imagine that they were carefully evened out by heavy construction equipment! You'll also notice stunted pitch pines growing out of cracks in the bedrock.

The trail now reenters the woods. Soon, you'll emerge onto another open area of smooth conglomerate bedrock with a panoramic west-facing view. A short distance beyond, you'll reach the base of a steep rock outcrop. You'll need both your hands and your feet to climb this one! When you reach the top, you'll be rewarded with a broad east-facing view.

You'll be following the Jessup Trail along the eastern ridge of Schunemunk Mountain for the next 3 miles. Open slabs of smooth conglomerate rock studded with pitch pines alternate with wooded areas. Along the ridge, the trail is marked not only with paint blazes and metal markers, but also with cairns. In addition, in some places along the ridge, lines of small rocks have been placed to indicate the trail route. You'll encounter a number of viewpoints on both sides of the ridge, making this stretch of trail one of the most spectacular in the entire region.

About 1 mile from the Long Path/Jessup Trail junction, you'll reach a junction with the blue-dot-on-white-blazed Ridge-to-Ridge Trail, which begins on the left and heads over to the western ridge of the mountain. Continue ahead on the Jessup/Highlands Trail, which soon reaches the summit of the mountain (1,664 feet), marked with white paint on the bedrock. Although there once was a 360-degree view from the summit, the view has largely grown in.

The Jessup/Highlands Trail now bears left and descends, almost immediately reaching a junction with a white-blazed side trail (also marked by cairns) that leads to the Megaliths—a group of huge blocks of conglomerate rock that have split off from the bedrock. The Megaliths also offer a fine west-facing view. This is a good place for a lunch break. If you have not spotted a second car, this should be your turnaround point.

If you have left a car at Otterkill Road, return to the Jessup/Highlands Trail and turn left. Almost immediately, the trail drops down into an attractive laurel grove that arches overhead. Soon, you'll reach a junction with the black-dot-on-white-blazed Dark Hollow Trail, which begins on the right and descends the east face of the mountain, but you should continue ahead on the Jessup/Highlands Trail. In a short distance, you'll come out onto another spectacular viewpoint over the Hudson River and the East Hudson Highlands.

About 0.5 mile beyond, after passing yet another viewpoint, the white-blazed Sweet Clover Trail joins from the right.

Continue ahead along the ridge, now following the white blazes of the Sweet Clover Trail, the yellow blazes of the Jessup Trail, and the teal diamond blazes of the Highlands Trail. The trail drops down to cross an intermittent stream and soon emerges onto a panoramic viewpoint. To the west, you can see the western ridge of Schunemunk Mountain in the foreground, with the Shawangunks and Catskills visible beyond on a clear day. You can also see the Hudson River to the northeast, with North and South Beacon Mountains and Breakneck Ridge across the river.

A short distance beyond, the Sweet Clover Trail departs to the left at a viewpoint over the western ridge. If you carefully scan the ridge to the left, you may be able to see the High Point Monument at the northwestern tip of New Jersey. Continue ahead on the Jessup/Highlands Trail, which soon begins a gradual descent, with more views along the way. After reaching another panoramic viewpoint to the west and north, the trail bears left and descends more steeply.

At the base of the descent, the Jessup/Highlands Trail reaches a woods road in the valley. Here, the Jessup/Highlands Trail turns right, but you should cross the road and continue ahead, now following the red-dot-on-white-blazed Barton Swamp Trail, which comes in from the left. Almost immediately, you'll cross Baby Brook on rocks and begin a rather steep climb. Soon, the trail turns left and follows along a rock ledge, with a sharp drop-off to the left. It then turns right, climbs through a cleft in the rock, and emerges onto a large expanse of conglomerate rock, with views to the northeast over the Hudson River. Continue ahead a short distance to a junction with the white-blazed Trestle Trail.

Turn sharply right and follow the Trestle Trail downhill on a relatively smooth footpath. After about five minutes, you'll notice a side trail on the right that leads to a viewpoint.

Along the Jessup Trail on Schunemunk Mountain

DANIEL CHAZIN

This is the first northeast-facing view you get when you climb the mountain on the Trestle Trail, but you've already seen a number of broader views, so you might want to skip this viewpoint. Continue downhill on the Trestle Trail, and in another 0.7 mile you'll come to a viewpoint on the left with a bench. From here, you can see the trestle that gives the trail its name.

The official name for the trestle is the Moodna Viaduct. It was built between 1904 and 1908 as part of a new freight bypass constructed by the Erie Railroad. Until the 1980s, the trestle was used only for freight service. Regularly scheduled passenger trains used this spectacularly scenic trestle for the first time in 1983, when the original Erie Railroad main line through Goshen and Middletown was abandoned. Today, Metro-North operates 13 passenger trains in each direction over the trestle every weekday (service is also provided on weekends). Most of these trains run between Port Jervis, New York, and Hoboken, New Jersey.

Continue heading downhill on the Trestle Trail, and in another 0.5 mile, you'll reach a junction where a triple-red blaze marks the start of the Otterkill Trail. Turn left to continue on the Trestle Trail, which soon approaches the trestle on the right. The trail bears left, away from the trestle, and descends to Otterkill Road. Turn left and follow the white-blazed trail along the road until you reach the parking area on the right where you left your car.

29

Schunemunk Loop

Total distance: 7.8 miles

Walking time: 5.5 hours

Vertical rise: 1,700 feet

Maps: USGS 7.5' Cornwall; NY–NJTC West Hudson Trails #114

Trailhead GPS Coordinates: N 41° 24' 28" W 74° 04' 53"

Schunemunk, a mountain that sits in solitary splendor, is a hikers' favorite. The light sandstones, shales, and conglomerates that crown its summit provide a solid surface for a ridge walk replete with distinctive scenery, long views, gnarled trees, and uncommon rock formations.

This loop walk from the north will highlight the deep cleft that creases Schunemunk Mountain as well as take you to vantage points on both the long eastern and western faces.

HOW TO GET THERE

To reach the trailhead, take the New York State Thruway (I-87) to Exit 16 (Harriman), and drive north on NY 32 for 7.3 miles to a sign for the Black Rock Fish and Game Club. Turn left here onto Pleasant Hill Road (County Route 79). At the bottom of the hill, turn left again onto Taylor Road, then bear right and cross the bridge over I-87. The trailhead parking area is on the right side of the road, just beyond the junction with Creekside Lane.

THE TRAIL

From the western end of the parking area, cross the road and proceed south on the joint Jessup (yellow blaze), Sweet Clover (white blaze) and Highlands (teal diamond blaze) Trails, which climb gently to the crest of a field and then descend to a woods road. To the right, you can see Schunemunk Mountain, which you'll soon climb.

Turn right on the woods road, going past a chain that blocks off the road. When the white-blazed Sweet Clover Trail leaves to

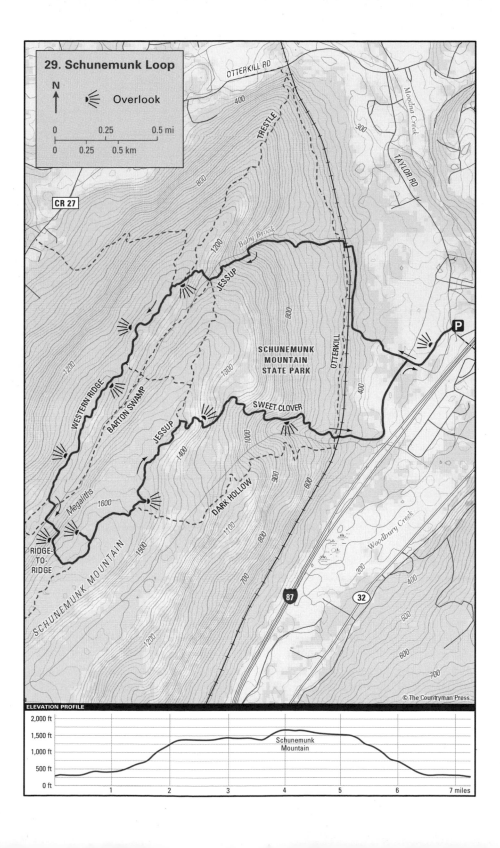

29. Schunemunk Loop

N

☀ Overlook

| 0 | 0.25 | 0.5 mi |
| 0 | 0.25 | 0.5 km |

CR 27

OTTERKILL RD

400

300

Moodna Creek

TRESTLE

TAYLOR RD

800

Baby Brook

1200

JESSUP

800

SCHUNEMUNK
MOUNTAIN
STATE PARK

OTTERKILL

P

1200

WESTERN RIDGE

BARTON SWAMP

1300

JESSUP

SWEET CLOVER

400

1000

1400

Megaliths

900

1600

DARK HOLLOW

600

1500

1100

800

RIDGE-
TO-
RIDGE

SCHUNEMUNK MOUNTAIN

1500

700

Woodbury Creek

300

87

32

400

1200

500

600

700

© The Countryman Press

ELEVATION PROFILE

2,000 ft							
1,500 ft				Schunemunk			
1,000 ft				Mountain			
500 ft							
0 ft							
	1	2	3	4	5	6	7 miles

East-facing view from Schunemunk Mountain

DANIEL CHAZIN

the left, continue ahead, now following the yellow blazes of the Jessup Trail. (You're also following the Highlands Trail, but the teal-diamond Highlands Trail blazes appear mainly at intersections.) The Jessup Trail crosses a field diagonally to the right, crosses a footbridge over a stream, reenters the woods, and soon climbs to a woods road, where it turns right.

Follow the yellow blazes along the woods road for about 0.5 mile. Watch for a sharp left turn, where the trail leaves the road and climbs to cross the railroad tracks. This is an active rail line, so be sure to stop, look, and listen for approaching trains before crossing.

On the other side of the tracks, the Jessup Trail turns right, briefly joining the red-blazed Otterkill Trail. It soon reaches the cascading Baby Brook and turns left to parallel the brook. The Otterkill Trail turns right and crosses the brook on a wooden footbridge, but you should continue ahead along the yellow-blazed Jessup Trail, which climbs steadily along the brook. In the next 0.75 mile, you'll climb about 700 feet. If you're taking this hike in the spring, wild oats, spring beauty, and trailing arbutus line the way.

After joining a woods road, the trail detours to the right to pass by a beautiful cascade. Continue ahead along the Jessup Trail, which soon reaches a junction with the red-on-white-blazed Barton Swamp Trail. Turn right and follow the Barton Swamp Trail, which crosses Baby Brook on rocks and begins a steep climb up the western ridge of the mountain. At the top, the trail turns left and follows a rock ledge, with east-facing views over Storm King Mountain and Black Rock Forest. The trail continues to climb through a cleft in the rock and emerges onto a large expanse of conglomerate rock studded with pitch pines, with even broader views to the northeast over the Hudson River. The Newburgh-Beacon Bridge is visible in the distance. Near the top of the western ridge of Schunemunk Mountain, northwest-facing views to the Shawangunks and Catskills begin.

Continue to follow the red-dot-on-white blazes, passing a junction where the white-blazed Trestle Trail leaves to the right, until the Barton Swamp Trail ends at a junction with the orange-blazed Western Ridge Trail. Bear left here and proceed south along the Western Ridge Trail, which follows the western ridge of Schunemunk Mountain over conglomerate rock outcrops studded with pebbles of white quartz and pink sandstone. This unusual rock has been smoothed by glacial action, sometimes resembling a level sidewalk. Pitch pines grow out of cracks in the rock. Soon, views appear to the left over the eastern ridge of the mountain, separated from the western ridge by the valley of Baby Brook. In about ten minutes, the Western Ridge Trail reaches a panoramic west-facing viewpoint. A short distance beyond, you'll come to a junction with the white-blazed Sweet Clover Trail, which leaves to the left.

Continue ahead on the orange-blazed Western Ridge Trail for about 1 mile, passing more viewpoints as well as a fascinating

The Megaliths

DANIEL CHAZIN

deep fissure in the rock to the right of the trail. After a brief descent, you'll reach a junction with the blue-dot-on-white-blazed Ridge-to-Ridge Trail. Turn left, leaving the Western Ridge Trail, and follow the Ridge-to-Ridge Trail, which descends to the valley between the two ridges. Here, it turns right onto a woods road, briefly joining the red-dot-on-white-blazed Barton Swamp Trail.

In about 500 feet, turn left and continue to follow the blue-dot-on-white-blazed Ridge-to-Ridge Trail as it crosses a wet area and then steeply ascends the eastern ridge of the mountain. After a very steep pitch, the trail turns right along a ledge and reaches a panoramic west-facing viewpoint. The trail continues to climb more gradually. After traversing an open area of exposed conglomerate bedrock, the Ridge-to-Ridge Trail ends, on the crest of the eastern ridge, at a junction with the yellow-blazed Jessup Trail and the teal-diamond-blazed Highlands Trail.

Turn left and follow the joint Jessup/Highlands Trail, which reaches the 1,664-foot-high summit of Schunemunk Mountain—marked on the rock with white paint—in another 0.1 mile. The Jessup/Highlands Trail bears left and descends, almost immediately reaching a junction with a white-blazed side trail (also marked by cairns) that leads to the Megaliths—a group of huge blocks of conglomerate rock that have split off from the bedrock. This is a good place for a break, as the interesting geologic features are complemented by a fine viewpoint to the west.

When you're ready to continue, return to the Jessup/Highlands Trail and turn left. In another 0.3 mile, the black-on-white-blazed Dark Hollow Trail leaves to the right. This trail descends the mountain and could be used as an alternate return route. But for now, continue ahead on the Jessup/Highlands Trail, soon coming out onto another spectacular viewpoint over the Hudson River and the East Hudson Highlands.

About 0.75 mile beyond, after going by yet another viewpoint, you'll reach a junction with the white-blazed Sweet Clover Trail. Turn right, leaving the Jessup/Highlands Trail, and follow the Sweet Clover Trail downhill. After passing an east-facing viewpoint, the trail descends on rock steps, crosses the northern branch of Dark Hollow Brook, then again approaches the brook just above a series of cascades. The trail descends some more, follows along the side of a hill, then resumes its descent, with portions of the trail having been relocated to avoid eroded sections.

Having descended over 1,200 feet from the summit, the Sweet Clover Trail arrives at a junction with the red-blazed Otterkill Trail just before reaching the Metro-North railroad tracks. Turn left onto the Otterkill Trail, then almost immediately turn right and cross the railroad tracks (use extreme caution, as the crossing is on a curve in the tracks, and it is difficult to see or hear approaching trains). Continue to follow the Sweet Clover Trail as it descends through the woods, turns right onto a woods road, then bears left and follows a grassy road through fields. When you reach the junction with the yellow-blazed Jessup Trail (also the route of the teal-diamond-blazed Highlands Trail), turn right, then left, following the joint Sweet Clover/Jessup/Highlands Trails back to the parking area where the hike began.

30

Mighty Storm King

Total distance: 2.5 miles
Walking time: 2.5 hours
Vertical rise: 700 feet
Maps: USGS 7.5' Cornwall; USGS 7.5' West Point; NY–NJTC West Hudson Trails #113
Trailhead GPS Coordinates: N 41° 25' 23" W 74° 00' 03"

"The Montaynes look as if some Metall or Minerall were in them. For the trees that grow on them were all blasted, and some of them barren with few or no trees on them." Thus did Robert Juet describe his view of the Hudson Highlands in September 1609 after his first trip up the Hudson in Henry Hudson's vessel the *Half Moon,* anchored in what is now Newburgh Bay. The centuries have done little to alter the view.

The noble ring of hills through which the Hudson flows south of Newburgh is as impressive as any range in the state. Storm King guards the west bank, and Beacon Mountain—giving way to Breakneck Ridge and Bull Hill on the south—guards the eastern shores. They are all mountains you will want to climb again and again.

Storm King and Butter Hill form a semicircular crest, which noted American historian Benson Lossing believed the Dutch skippers thought of as a huge lump of butter, hence the original name "Boterberg." Nathaniel Parker Willis, who settled at Idlewild at the foot of Storm King in present-day Cornwall, wrote weekly letters to the *Home Journal* in the 1850s, describing his bucolic surroundings. It was he who was able to change the name of part of the mountain to the more romantic Storm King.

Storm King Mountain is also linked to a major environmental court case. In the early 1960s, the Consolidated Edison Company (Con Ed) announced plans to build a hydroelectric plant at the base of the mountain, with a pumped storage reservoir in the adjacent Black Rock Forest. What is now known

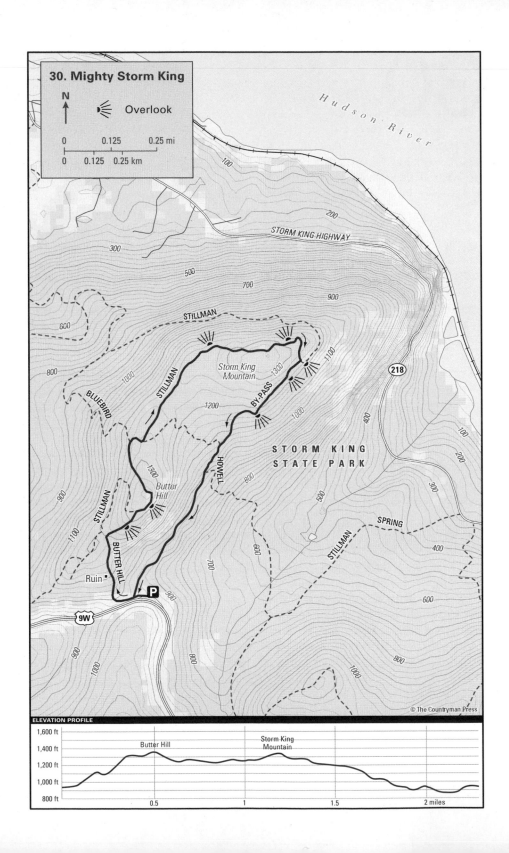

30. Mighty Storm King

N

☀ Overlook

0 — 0.125 — 0.25 mi
0 — 0.125 — 0.25 km

Hudson River

STORM KING HIGHWAY

100

200

300

500

700

900

600

STILLMAN

800

1000

STILLMAN

Storm King
Mountain

1300

1100

BY-PASS

1200

1000

218

400

BLUEBIRD

HOWELL

STORM KING
STATE PARK

100

200

300

900

1300

Butter
Hill

800

500

SPRING

400

STILLMAN

1100

BUTTER HILL

600

700

600

STILLMAN

Ruin

P

9W

900

800

1000

800

1000

600

© The Countryman Press

ELEVATION PROFILE

1,600 ft				
1,400 ft	Butter Hill		Storm King Mountain	
1,200 ft				
1,000 ft				
800 ft	0.5	1	1.5	2 miles

as Scenic Hudson was formed by the New York–New Jersey Trail Conference and others to fight this project. A 17-year legal fight ended with a settlement in which Con Ed basically gave up. This court case established the right of citizens' groups to take government agencies to court to protect scenic beauty and recreational interests. For more on this historic case, see http://library.marist.edu/archives/mehp/scenicdecision.html.

HOW TO GET THERE

From the circle at the west end of the Bear Mountain Bridge, proceed north on US 9W for 8.5 miles to a parking area on the right, at a sharp bend in the road. (This is the second parking area along US 9W in Storm King State Park, but the only one which is designated by a blue parking area sign; it has a yellow-on-blue historical marker entitled FREEDOM ROAD and an adjacent marker commemorating the completion of the Storm King Bypass Highway.) This parking area cannot be accessed from the southbound lanes of US 9W. If you are coming from the north, go to the junction of US 9W and NY 293/NY 218, and use the underpass to turn around and head back north 3.1 miles to the parking area.

THE TRAIL

From the parking area, walk north along the grassy shoulder of the road. Soon, you will see a triple-orange blaze, which marks the start of the Butter Hill Trail. Follow the orange blazes as they bear right, away from the road, and begin to ascend steeply. Soon, views over the Hudson River begin to appear to the right. The mountain across the river is Bull Hill (Mount Taurus), and the point of land jutting into the river is Little Stony Point.

In 0.2 mile, you'll reach three stone pillars, with a stone foundation behind the pillars. These are the remains of Spy Rock

House, the summer cottage of Dr. Edward L. Partridge, who served on the Palisades Interstate Park Commission from 1913 to 1930.

The trail now descends slightly into a rugged, stone-filled valley, then continues to climb Butter Hill, first gradually, then more steeply. At the top of the steep climb, you'll reach open rock ledges that afford a wide panorama to the east, south, and west. US 9W is visible straight ahead to the south, with the fire-scarred North Ridge of Crows Nest Mountain to its left. The Hudson River is to the east.

After a short level stretch, the Butter Hill Trail ends at a junction with the yellow-blazed Stillman Trail and the teal-diamond-blazed Highlands Trail. Turn right and follow the Stillman Trail up to the summit of Butter Hill. A rock outcrop to the left of the trail offers a 360-degree view. The East Hudson Highlands are visible across the river, with towers marking the summits of North and South Beacon Mountains to the north. Bull Hill is directly to the east. On the west side of the river, the north ridge of Crows Nest Mountain is directly to the south, with Black Rock Forest visible to the southeast. Schunemunk Mountain may be seen to the west, with the Moodna Viaduct (on the Metro-North rail line to Port Jervis) towering over the valley just north of the mountain. Some 3,200 feet long and 193 feet high, the viaduct was constructed from 1904 to 1908 by the Erie Railroad and is the highest and longest railroad trestle east of the Mississippi River. In the distance to the northwest are the Shawangunks and, behind them, the Catskills. To the north, the Newburgh-Beacon Bridge spans the Hudson River.

After enjoying this spectacular view, continue ahead on the yellow-blazed Stillman Trail, which descends slightly. Soon, you'll reach a junction with the blue-and-red-blazed

Bluebird Trail, marked by a large cairn. Turn right, uphill, and continue on the Stillman Trail. A short distance ahead, after passing through a burned-out area, you'll reach the northern end of the blue-blazed Howell Trail, which leaves to the right. Bear left here, continuing along the yellow-blazed trail, which follows a relatively level route for the next 0.7 mile. After a short, steep climb, you'll reach a limited view to the north. About five minutes ahead, though, you'll come to a much better viewpoint looking north over the Hudson River. Pollopel Island is directly below, with the ruins of Bannerman's Castle on its high point.

This mysterious island, now a state park, has been named Pollepel (or some variant thereof) as far back as the 1600s, when the Dutch governed the area. The name appears on a Dutch map of the Hudson River valley that dates back to the mid-1600s. Jasper Dankers, a minister, recorded in 1680 that it was called *Potlepels Eylant,* Dutch for Potladle Island. Another version of the origin of the name is that a young girl named Polly Pell was rescued from the breaking river ice near the island by her sweetheart, to whom she was promptly married. In 1777, General Henry Clinton fortified Pollepel Island, along with Constitution Island to the south. In the 1850s, Benson Lossing reported that it contained a solitary house that looked like a wren's nest, inhabited by a fisherman with an insane wife who thought herself to be

North-facing view from Storm King Mountain

DANIEL CHAZIN

The West Hudson Hills

the queen of England. Francis Bannerman bought the island in 1900 to house his arsenal of secondhand military supplies—arms captured in the Spanish-American War. To store his surplus military supplies, he constructed a Scottish-style "castle," which became a landmark along the river. The castle was damaged by an explosion in 1920, and it was essentially abandoned after 1950. It was acquired by New York State in 1967, but two years later a fire destroyed much of its interior. The shell remained largely intact until December 2009, when a large portion of the castle collapsed during a storm. For more history and a tour schedule, go to www.bannermancastle.org.

Continue ahead, past the summit of Storm King Mountain, with some more views from rock ledges to the left. After a short descent, you'll reach a panoramic north-facing viewpoint with superb views. To the east, Breakneck Ridge (marked by the rail tunnel) is visible across the river. The stone building at the foot of Breakneck Ridge (partially obscured by the vegetation) caps a shaft of the Catskill Aqueduct, which tunnels 1,100 feet below the river. North Beacon Mountain (with communications towers) and South Beacon Mountain (with a fire tower) are to the northeast. To the northwest, the village

of Cornwall can be seen along the west bank of the river.

The Stillman Trail now continues to descend, soon reaching a junction with the white-blazed Bypass Trail. Turn left at this junction and walk about 25 feet to a rock ledge that affords a broad south-facing view down the Hudson River. The village of Cold Spring is visible across the river to the southeast, and Constitution Island juts into the river just beyond.

Now return to the junction and continue along the white-blazed Bypass Trail, which descends along the side of the mountain—first gradually and then more steeply, with several limited views of the river from rock ledges on the left. After crossing a seasonal stream, the Bypass Trail climbs briefly to end at a junction with the blue-blazed Howell Trail, which comes in from the right.

Bear left and continue ahead on the Howell Trail, which soon begins to follow an old road. In about 500 feet, the blue-blazed trail turns sharply left, leaving the old road, but you should continue ahead on the road. Although it is now unmarked, the road is distinct and easy to follow. It climbs briefly, then descends steadily. As it approaches US 9W, the old road climbs rather steeply to end just beyond the parking area where the hike began.

31

Black Rock Forest– Northern Loop

Total distance: 5.5 miles

Walking time: 3.5 hours

Vertical rise: 1,000 feet

Maps: USGS 7.5' Cornwall; NY–NJTC West Hudson Trails #113; Black Rock Forest

Trailhead GPS Coordinates: N 41° 24' 7.5" W 74° 02' 51.5"

While not a primary access point, there is a small trailhead for Black Rock Forest on its northwestern side that is ideal for this loop hike. For an online sketch map, go to www .blackrockforest.org/html-files/imagemap .html (a much better copy is available from the forest office and at kiosks at the main trailheads). Please note that the forest is closed to public use during deer hunting season. If unsure, call the Black Rock Forest office at 845-534-4517 (emergencies only: 914-755-2348).

HOW TO GET THERE

To reach the trailhead, drive north on US 9W to Angola Road near Cornwall. Head southwest onto Angola Road for 1.6 miles, turn left onto Mine Hill Road, and continue for 0.9 mile to the parking turnout on the right side of the road, just beyond a very sharp, steep hairpin turn.

From the New York State Thruway (I-87), take Exit 16 and follow NY 32 north for 7 miles to Mountainville, where you turn right onto Angola Road. After 0.8 mile, you will come to a stop sign. Turn left to continue on Angola Road. In another 0.8 mile, turn right onto Mine Hill Road. Follow Mine Hill Road uphill for 0.9 mile to the parking turnout described above. Note: Trailhead parking is very limited (maximum five vehicles), and roadside parking is not permitted. Please make sure that you do not block the road or hamper access by emergency vehicles. The parking area often fills up early on weekends, so you might want to plan this hike for a weekday.

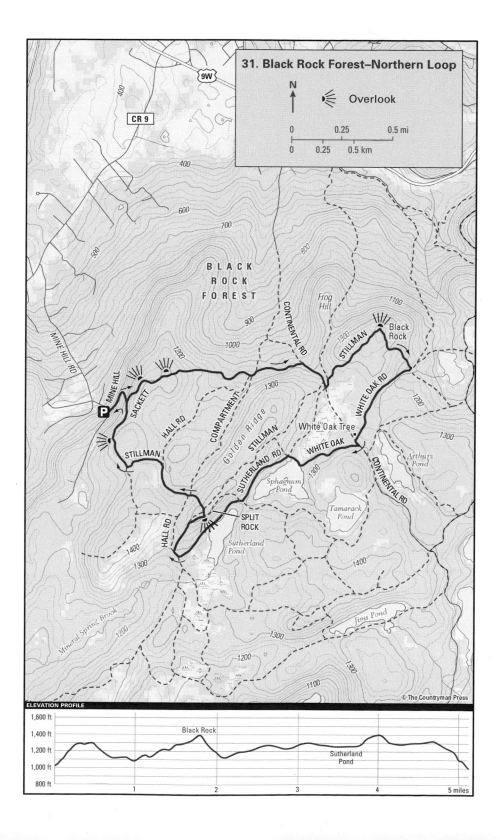

31. Black Rock Forest–Northern Loop

N

Overlook

| 0 | 0.25 | 0.5 mi |
| 0 | 0.25 | 0.5 km |

9W

CR 9

400

400

600

700

500

800

B L A C K
R O C K
F O R E S T

Frog
Hill

900

1000

1100

1200

MINE HILL RD

MINE HILL

SACKETT

Black
Rock

STILLMAN

1300

P

HALL RD

COMPARTMENT

Golden Ridge

STILLMAN

STILLMAN

WHITE OAK RD

1200

1300

White Oak Tree

WHITE OAK

Arthurs
Pond

SUTHERLAND RD

Sphagnum
Pond

1300

CONTINENTAL RD

CONTINENTAL RD

SPLIT
ROCK

Tamarack
Pond

HALL RD

1400

1300

Sutherland
Pond

1400

Mineral Spring Brook

1200

Jims Pond

1300

1200

1100

© The Countryman Press

ELEVATION PROFILE

1,600 ft
1,400 ft
1,200 ft
1,000 ft
800 ft

Black Rock

Sutherland
Pond

1   2   3   4   5 miles

THE TRAIL

The hike begins by following the yellow-diamond-blazed Mine Hill Trail, which starts on the opposite side of the road, just beyond the parking turnout. The trailhead is marked by a triple blaze. Follow the trail uphill, steeply in places. At a switchback turn, there are views over Schunemunk Mountain, the Moodna Viaduct, the Shawangunks, and the Catskills from open rocks to the left of the trail. The Mine Hill Trail now heads south and soon ends at a junction with the yellow-circle-blazed Sackett Trail. (You'll encounter four different yellow-blazed trails on this hike, so it's important to note the shape of the blazes, in addition to their color.)

Turn left and follow the Sackett Trail, which soon reaches a viewpoint from an open rock ledge, then climbs to another viewpoint. The trail now levels off and begins a steady descent. After crossing two streams in a wet area, you'll notice a stone chimney to the left of the trail—the remnant of an old cabin, built many years ago as a family camping retreat.

A short distance beyond, the yellow blazes turn left and follow the grassy Hall Road for about 300 feet. Where the road bears left, continue along the yellow-blazed trail as it bears right, leaving the road. It descends to a low point, with many fallen trees, then ascends gradually, traversing several rocky areas along the way. About 1.5 miles from the start of the hike, the Sackett Trail turns right onto Continental Road, another woods road, which it follows for a short distance to its junction with Hulse Road (Continental Road is blocked off with a cable immediately before this junction).

Here, the Sackett Trail ends. You should turn left onto Hulse Road, now following the route of the Stillman Trail, blazed with yellow rectangles, which is co-aligned with the Highlands Trail (teal-diamond blazes). The trail follows the road for only 150 feet. Just past a stream crossing, watch carefully as the yellow and teal blazes bear right, leaving the road, and continue ahead on a footpath. Follow the Stillman and Highlands Trails through a thick stand of mountain laurel and then steadily but gradually uphill. About 0.4 mile from the last intersection, the trail climbs steeply over a rock outcrop and reaches the 1,410-foot summit of Black Rock Mountain, after which the forest is named. The summit affords expansive views to the north and east over the Hudson River.

After you've rested for a while, turn right and follow the teal and yellow blazes as they descend rather steeply on a wide footpath. At the base of the descent, the trail makes a sharp left turn. Here, you should turn right, leaving the yellow-and-teal-blazed trail, onto a grassy path that leads 50 feet down to White Oak Road, a wide gravel road. Turn right on White Oak Road and follow it as it climbs gently, paralleling the outlet stream from Arthurs Pond to the left. In 0.5 mile, you'll reach a T-junction, with a giant white oak tree (after which the road is named) in the middle of the intersection.

Turn left at the road intersection onto Continental Road, passing a pine plantation on the left. In 200 feet, you'll reach a junction with the white-blazed White Oak Trail. Turn right and follow the white blazes, which run along a grassy woods road for a short distance, then continue ahead where the main woods road turns left. The White Oak Trail soon narrows to a footpath and goes through dense mountain laurel thickets, with an understory of blueberry bushes. In about 0.3 mile, it crosses a stream and reaches the stone impoundment of Sphagnum Pond. The trail skirts the dam; crosses a wet, grassy area on puncheons; and climbs to Sutherland Road.

Sutherland Pond from the Split Rock Trail

DANIEL CHAZIN

Turn left onto the road, which parallels Sphagnum Pond, visible below on the left. At the next intersection, Chatfield Road begins on the left, but you should bear right to continue on Sutherland Road. Just beyond, you'll pass on the right the trailhead of the white-blazed Split Rock Trail and a large cut into the hillside—the site of an abandoned mine.

The road now begins to parallel the shore of Sutherland Pond, the only natural pond in Black Rock Forest (the other ponds were created by the construction of dams). As the road moves away from the pond, keep your eyes open for an unmarked trail on the left that leads to a rock ledge overlooking the pond. Swimming (at your own risk) is permitted in Sutherland Pond, but not in the other ponds in Black Rock Forest, which are reservoirs for nearby towns.

When you're ready to resume the hike, return to Sutherland Road and turn left. In about 0.25 mile, you'll reach an intersection with Hall Road—the route of the blue-blazed Compartment Trail and the teal-diamond-blazed Highlands Trail. Turn right onto Hall Road and, almost immediately, you'll go around a gate. Just beyond, the Compartment/Highlands Trail turns right, leaving the road. Follow the blue and teal-diamond blazes, which climb steadily on a footpath through mountain laurel thickets.

Near the crest of the rise, you'll reach an intersection where the white-blazed Split Rock Trail begins on the right. Turn right and follow the Split Rock Trail, which soon climbs to the top of a huge boulder with a panoramic view to the southeast. Sutherland Pond is directly below, and the New York

View from the summit of Black Rock Mountain   DANIEL CHAZIN

City skyline is visible in the distance. This is a good spot to take a break.

When you're ready to continue, look for a yellow diamond blaze on a tree. Here, you should turn left and proceed for 100 feet to again intersect the blue-blazed Compartment Trail, near its intersection with the yellow-rectangle-blazed Stillman Trail, which comes in from the right.

From this intersection, head downhill (northwest), following both blue and yellow blazes. Just before reaching an intersection with the grassy Hall Road, the Compartment Trail leaves to the right. Bear left and follow the yellow rectangle blazes, which in 100 feet turn right and continue along Hall Road.

(Note that the yellow-triangle-blazed Short Cut Trail begins at this intersection; make sure that you follow the yellow rectangles, not the yellow triangles.)

Near the crest of a slight rise, follow the yellow-rectangle-blazed Stillman Trail as it turns left, leaving the road, and proceeds through dense mountain laurel thickets. The Stillman Trail soon reaches a T-junction, where the yellow-circle-blazed Sackett Trail begins. Turn right and follow the Sackett Trail past another west-facing viewpoint. When you reach the next intersection, turn left and follow the yellow-diamond-blazed Mine Hill Trail down to Mine Hill Road, where you began the hike.

32

Black Rock Forest– Southern Ledges

Total distance: 9 miles

Walking time: 6.5 hours

Vertical rise: 1,300 feet

Maps: USGS 7.5' Cornwall; NY–NJTC West Hudson Trails #113; Black Rock Forest

Trailhead GPS Coordinates: N 41° 25' 07" W 74° 00' 39"

The hiking trails in Black Rock Forest are among the region's least used. They wind around and over a dozen peaks with elevations of more than 1,400 feet. But generally these peaks rise less than 400 feet from the high plateau that is a westward continuation of the Storm King intrusion of the Hudson Highlands. That plateau drops precipitously to the west and north, with the summit of Black Rock Mountain, namesake of the forest, standing out above the valley near Cornwall.

This hike starts at the forest's main parking area and winds along the southern ledges that border on the lands of the United States Military Academy at West Point. For an online sketch map, go to www.blackrock forest.org/html-files/imagemap.html (a much better copy is available from the forest office and at kiosks at the main trailheads). Please note that the forest is closed to public use during deer hunting season, usually mid-November to mid-December. If unsure, call the Black Rock Forest office at 845-534-4517 (emergencies only: 914-755-2348).

HOW TO GET THERE

From the traffic circle at the western side of the Bear Mountain Bridge, proceed north on US 9W for 8.8 miles. About 0.5 mile beyond a parking area marked with a blue sign, turn right onto Mountain Road. Immediately turn right again and proceed through a very narrow underpass beneath US 9W (large vehicles may not fit in this underpass). Continue ahead for 0.2 mile to a parking area on the

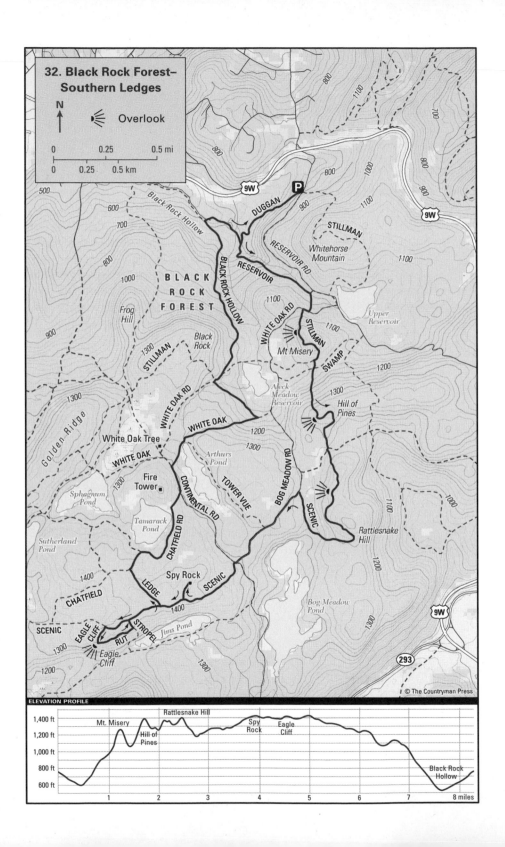

32. Black Rock Forest–Southern Ledges

N

≋ Overlook

0   0.25   0.5 mi
0   0.25   0.5 km

800
1100
700
900
9W
800
DUGGAN
P
900
1100
9W
500
600
Black Rock Hollow
700
RESERVOIR RD
STILLMAN
Whitehorse Mountain
1100
800
RESERVOIR
BLACK ROCK FOREST
1000
BLACK ROCK HOLLOW
1100
Upper Reservoir
Frog Hill
900
1300
STILLMAN
Black Rock
WHITE OAK RD
Mt Misery
STILLMAN
SWAMP
1100
1300
1300
Aleck Meadow Reservoir
Hill of Pines
1200
1300
Golden Ridge
WHITE OAK RD
WHITE OAK
1200
1300
Arthurs Pond
BOG MEADOW RD
White Oak Tree
WHITE OAK
Fire Tower
TOWER VUE
1300
Sphagnum Pond
CONTINENTAL RD
SCENIC
Rattlesnake Hill
1100
1000
Tamarack Pond
Sutherland Pond
CHATFIELD RD
1200
1400
Spy Rock
SCENIC
Bog Meadow Pond
1300
LEDGE
1400
CHATFIELD
SCENIC
EAGLE CLIFF
STROPEL
RUT
Jims Pond
9W
1300
Eagle Cliff
293
1200
1300
© The Countryman Press

ELEVATION PROFILE

Rattlesnake Hill
1,400 ft
Mt. Misery
Spy Rock
Eagle Cliff
1,200 ft
Hill of Pines
1,000 ft
800 ft
Black Rock Hollow
600 ft
1   2   3   4   5   6   7   8 miles

right side of the road, just before a locked gate.

THE TRAIL

From the kiosk at the end of the parking area, proceed ahead on the red-blazed Duggan Trail. In about 0.5 mile, the red trail ends at a junction with the blue-blazed Reservoir Trail. Continue ahead on the blue trail, which immediately crosses Ben's Bridge (a wooden footbridge) and climbs along a picturesque stream, with cascades and waterfalls, following an old woods road. When the blue trail ends, bear right and continue ahead on the yellow-blazed Stillman Trail.

Soon the Stillman Trail reaches the dirt White Oak Road. Here it is joined by the teal-diamond-blazed Highlands Trail, which comes in from the left. The joint Highlands/Stillman Trail now turns right and follows the road for 100 feet, then turns left and begins a steep climb of Mount Misery on a footpath. At the top (elevation 1,268 feet), you'll reach a limited viewpoint to the west and northwest. Continue ahead for a short distance, and you'll come to a much better viewpoint, with Black Rock Mountain visible directly ahead and Aleck Meadow Reservoir below to the left. This is a good place to take a break (you've climbed nearly 700 vertical feet from Ben's Bridge).

Continue ahead on the yellow/teal-diamond trail, which begins its descent of Mount Misery, first gradually and then more

Bog Meadow Pond from Rattlesnake Hill

DANIEL CHAZIN

steeply. In a rugged, boulder-strewn area at the base of the descent, you'll notice a triple-white blaze, which marks the start of the Scenic Trail. Turn left and follow the white-blazed Scenic Trail, which crosses the blue-blazed Swamp Trail at the end of the rocky area and begins a steady climb of the Hill of Pines, passing through attractive mountain laurel and hemlock.

At the top of the climb, the trail comes out on open rocks, with a spectacular west-facing view. Black Rock Mountain may be seen on the right, and the Black Rock Forest fire tower is to its left. (Despite the name "Hill of Pines," there are only two pine trees near the summit, which is mostly covered with oaks.)

The trail climbs a little to the true summit (elevation 1,400 feet), descends the hill, and soon crosses the dirt Carpenter Road diagonally to the right. It now begins a gradual climb of Rattlesnake Hill. After about 10 minutes, you'll reach a viewpoint to the right of the trail (the best view is from a rock ledge adjacent to a large pine tree). The fire tower may be seen straight ahead, and Bog Meadow Pond is to the left. After a short but steep descent and a relatively level stretch, you'll reach a second viewpoint—this one marked by a cairn and a gnarled, nearly horizontal pine tree.

Continue ahead through a dense mountain laurel thicket to the third viewpoint on Rattlesnake Hill, which offers a panoramic view from open rocks. Bog Meadow Pond is below on the left, with the rolling hills of Orange County beyond. Continue ahead on the white trail, which begins to descend—first steeply, then more gradually. The trail briefly runs along the southern boundary of Black Rock Forest, with Bog Meadow Pond visible through the trees to the left. After crossing the inlet stream of the pond, the

trail reaches the dirt Bog Meadow Road. Turn left onto the road, continuing to follow the white-blazed Scenic Trail. In 0.25 mile, the yellow-blazed Tower Vue Trail begins on the right, but continue ahead on the road, following the white blazes. Soon you'll reach a T-junction with Continental Road. Continue to follow the white-blazed Scenic Trail, which reenters the woods and begins to climb gradually.

When the trail levels off, watch carefully for a cairn. Here, the blue-blazed Spy Rock Trail leaves to the right. Turn right and follow this short trail, which leads in about 1,000 feet to Spy Rock, marked by a single pitch pine. This is the highest point in Black Rock Forest (1,461 feet), but there are only limited views of the Shawangunk Mountains to the north and the Hudson River to the northeast.

Retrace your steps to the white-blazed Scenic Trail and turn right. Soon you'll pass the yellow-blazed Ledge Trail, which begins on the right, and then the Stropel Trail (also yellow blazed), which goes off to the left. Proceed ahead on the white-blazed Scenic Trail, but a short distance beyond, turn left onto the blue-blazed Eagle Cliff Trail, which leads in a short distance to Eagle Cliff—a huge rock outcrop with glacial striations—that offers a panoramic south-facing view. On a clear day, you may be able to see the New York City skyline in the distance. Wilkins Pond is straight ahead, and Jim's Pond is to the left. This is a good place to take a break.

When you're ready to continue, bear right onto the orange-blazed Rut Trail, which runs near the edge of the escarpment, with views through the trees on the right. Be alert for a sharp left turn, where the trail turns slightly away from the cliff edge and goes down through a narrow passage between boulders. Soon you'll reach a trail junction, where the Rut Trail ends. Turn left onto the

View from Hill of Pines

DANIEL CHAZIN

yellow-blazed Stropel Trail, which leads in a very short distance to the white-blazed Scenic Trail. Turn right and rejoin the Scenic Trail.

In another 0.2 mile, the yellow-blazed Ledge Trail begins on the left. Turn left onto this trail, which climbs over a rise and descends gently to end at a T-junction with the blue-blazed Chatfield Trail. Turn right onto the Chatfield Trail and descend to Chatfield Road. Turn right onto the road and follow it past Tamarack Pond to the intersection of Chatfield and Continental Roads.

At this intersection, you'll see an old stone building with a distinctive bulging chimney, indicative of a beehive oven inside. This is the Chatfield House, built in 1834. The house was gutted by fire in 1908 and restored in 1932 by Dr. Stillman. The lands nearby were once pastures and orchards,

and Tamarack Pond, originally called Orchard Pond, was used as a cranberry bog.

Turn left onto Continental Road, but follow it for only 0.2 mile and turn right onto the white-blazed White Oak Trail, which passes the northern end of Arthurs Pond. Here, the yellow-blazed Tower Vue Trail begins on the right, but you should continue ahead on the white-blazed White Oak Trail, which descends to White Oak Road near the Aleck Meadow Reservoir. Turn left onto the road and head toward Black Rock Mountain (visible in the distance). Just beyond a stream crossing (the stream is the outlet of Arthurs Pond), the road curves to the left. Here, to the right, you'll notice a short unmarked trail which leads up to the yellow-blazed Stillman Trail (also the route of the teal-diamond-blazed Highlands Trail). Turn right onto this short connector trail, then turn right onto the Stillman/Highlands Trail, which follows a woods road. A short distance beyond, the yellow and teal-diamond blazes turn right, but you should continue ahead on the road, now following the white-blazed Black Rock Hollow Trail. The trail descends along the road, with portions rerouted to bypass very eroded sections of the road.

At the base of the descent, the white-blazed trail ends at a filtration plant. Turn right onto the blue-blazed Reservoir Trail and follow it around the plant and along the brook to a junction with the red-blazed Duggan Trail just before Ben's Bridge. Turn sharply left onto the red-blazed trail and follow it uphill to the parking area where the hike began.

V. The Shawangunks

Introducing the Shawangunks

The Shawangunks (pronounced "shon-gum" and commonly called "The Gunks" by local folks and visiting climbers) is a continuation of the northern end of the ridge that is called the Kittatinnies in New Jersey and the Blue Mountains in Pennsylvania. The long ridge of the Northern Shawangunks, edged with sparkling white cliffs, is visible to the west of I-87 and has been designated a "Last Great Place" by The Nature Conservancy. Mohonk Mountain House's Sky Top Tower atop the ridge can be seen from many miles away.

The Shawangunks—which has been translated as "white rock"—are world famous for rock climbing. Oft-told legend has it that Fritz Wiessner—a celebrated and accomplished climber who had emigrated from Germany—became aware of these dazzling cliffs one afternoon in 1935 from across the Hudson while on Breakneck Ridge after a thunderstorm. Climbing first at Sky Top, he and his friend Hans Kraus were responsible for many of the first climbs of the Shawangunk cliffs.

Recreation opportunities abound. Cross-country skiing and snowshoeing are popular in winter, when the high elevation of the ridge attracts snow that remains longer than in lower-lying areas. Mountain bikes are allowed on many of the carriage roads.

This picturesque 30,000-acre preserved area can be divided into four jurisdictions: Mohonk Preserve, Mohonk Mountain House, Minnewaska State Park Preserve, and the Sam's Point Preserve—each with its own trails, access points, and fee structures. The area is a delight throughout the year, with its combination of white rock slabs and cliffs, green pitch pines, blueberry bushes that turn bright red in the fall, sheep laurel, mountain laurel, and rhododendron blooming in June—and, with luck, a clear, blue sky as a backdrop. The ridge contains five "sky lakes" and several waterfalls.

There has long been a human presence on the Shawangunk Ridge. Arrowheads have been found, indicating use of caves and rock shelters by Native Americans. Trees on the ridge were consumed for the production of charcoal and barrel hoops, hemlock trees were cut for their bark and used to tan hides, and millstones were hammered out of the bedrock. Among the best-known residents are the berry pickers, whose shacks can still be seen along the Smiley Road, which runs 7 miles from Ellenville to Lake Awosting. Berry pickers invaded the area each summer as early as 1862. Their practice of setting fires to handicap the growth of competing vegetation resulted in improved berry crops for them and the development of a pygmy pine forest probably unique in the world.

The Shawangunks owe their development to the vision of Alfred Smiley, who first saw the Shawangunk escarpment in 1869. Alfred was so impressed by the spectacular beauty of the area that he persuaded his twin brother Albert, the principal of a Quaker boarding school, to purchase the 300-acre property at Mohonk Lake for $28,000. To finance the cost of running the property, they opened a hotel the following year. In 1876, Alfred purchased 2,500 acres at Lake Minnewaska, and he opened a hotel there three years later. By Albert's death in 1912, the property had grown through more than one hundred purchases to encompass 5,000 acres. The brothers transformed a boulder-strewn land into a premier resort by the systematic construction of carriage roads and walking paths.

MOHONK PRESERVE

Organized in 1963 as the Mohonk Trust, the Mohonk Preserve is New York State's largest privately owned nonprofit nature sanctuary. Its lands are open to the public for recreational activities compatible with preservation. Hikers on Mohonk Preserve lands need to be either Mohonk Preserve members or to have purchased a day pass, which they may be required to show to a ranger. The per-person day fee is currently $12. Day passes, memberships, and trail maps are available for purchase at the visitors center. To reach the visitors center, drive west about 6 miles on NY 299 from the village of New Paltz to its end at a T-junction with US 44/NY 55. Turn right, continue for 0.5 mile, and turn right onto the entrance road to the Mohonk Preserve Visitors Center. Inside the center is a small gift shop and much information on the natural history of the area. Outside there are nature trails to be walked.

MOHONK MOUNTAIN HOUSE

This elegant building is a private hotel that reflects the leisure and elegance of Victorian vacations. The trails that surround the hotel were laid out with the same 19th-century attitude that fostered the resort. Today, these paths are a marvel of rock climbs, lovers' lanes, deep-woods walks, and vantage points that reflect their builders' humor. Every spot is named—but the fun and sense of discovery are still there. A Mohonk Preserve annual or day pass is honored on Mountain House lands, but day visitors are requested not to enter the hotel.

You may easily become infatuated with the area and wish to return to the Mountain House. Delicious meals are provided for overnight guests as well as for those reserving in advance by purchasing "A Day at Mohonk." This allows you to drive to the hotel, hike their lands, and enjoy a meal and entry to the hotel. A day pass is also available that allows you to take a shuttle bus (seasonally) directly from the main parking lot to the area of the hotel.

MINNEWASKA STATE PARK PRESERVE

This spectacular state park preserve owes its existence to a chain of events beginning in 1879, when Alfred Smiley opened the first of two hotels overlooking Lake Minnewaska. The Smileys constructed many carriage roads and walking trails for the guests at their hotels. In the 1950s, Kevin Phillips, the general manager of the hotels at Lake Minnewaska, bought the property and endeavored to update the facilities by adding a golf course and a downhill-ski slope. However, financial difficulties forced the sale of part of the acreage, including Lake Awosting, to New York State in 1971, creating Minnewaska State Park Preserve. Continuing financial problems and a proposal by the Marriott Corporation to build condominiums, a 450-room hotel, an 18-hole golf course, and other amenities resulted in a long legal battle. In 1987, a 1,200-acre parcel that includes Lake Minnewaska was added to the Minnewaska State Park Preserve. Today Minnewaska, administered by the Palisades Interstate Park Commission, is one of New York State's most beautiful parks. Thanks to the work of the Open Space Institute, additional lands have been added to the park, which now includes 22,123 acres.

Lakes Awosting and Minnewaska are renowned for their aquamarine color and exceptionally clear water. Swimming is allowed in designated areas in both lakes, and bicycles are allowed on many of the carriage roads. In winter, when snow conditions permit, the carriage roads are groomed for cross-country skiing. There is an $8 parking fee, with a $6 per-person entrance fee charged when cross-country skiing is available.

SAM'S POINT PRESERVE

The Sam's Point area was formerly owned by the village of Ellenville, with Lake Maratanza—the highest of the "sky lakes"—serving as the village's water supply. For three decades, some 4,800 mountaintop acres were leased to Ice Caves Mountain, Inc., a private corporation, and public access was limited to the ice caves on the escarpment, southeast of the Sam's Point promontory. In 1997, with the assistance of the New York-New Jersey Trail Conference, the land was acquired by the Open Space Conservancy. It has subsequently been transferred to the State of New York and added to Minnewaska State Park Preserve. Known as the Sam's Point Preserve, the property is managed by The Nature Conservancy, which has built a conservation center at the entrance. A $10 parking fee is charged. Lake Maratanza, near Sam's Point, is still part of the water supply system of the village of Ellenville, and no recreational use of the lake is permitted.

33

Shawangunk Ridge

Total distance: 6.2 miles

Walking time: 4.5 hours

Vertical rise: 1,350 feet

Maps: USGS 7.5' Wurtsboro

Trailhead GPS Coordinates:
N 41° 40' 09" W 74° 24' 20"

The Shawangunk Ridge is part of the same ridge that in New Jersey is called the Kittatinny Ridge. This route for the Long Path was created as a more natural alternative to the suburban lowland route through Orange County. During the trip from NY 52 to Ferguson Road (formerly Roosa Gap–Summitville Road), the hiker often walks on Shawangunk slabs above the scrub oak, blueberry, and pitch pine so prevalent on the ridge and is thus afforded many good views. In addition, the trail passes an attractive cascade and some fascinating free-standing rocks.

HOW TO GET THERE

A car shuttle is needed. Leave the New York State Thruway (I-87) at Exit 16 (Harriman), and drive two cars west on NY 17 (I-86) for 29 miles to Exit 114 (Wurtsboro, Highview). Exit 114 is only available going westbound. Turn right at the end of the exit ramp onto Old NY 17 (County Route 171), and proceed for 0.5 mile. Turn left onto Shawanga Lodge Road, and follow it for about 3 miles to a stop sign at Pickles Road. Continue ahead, but almost immediately turn left onto Ferguson Road. Continue for 0.1 mile and turn left into a parking area at a sign for the Wurtsboro Ridge State Forest. Leave one car here.

Drive the second car back to the stop sign at the end of Ferguson Road and turn right, then immediately turn left onto Pickles Road. In 0.7 mile, turn left at a stop sign onto the unsigned Roosa Gap Road. (Pickles Road changes its name to Ski Run Road on the other side of Roosa Gap Road.) Continue

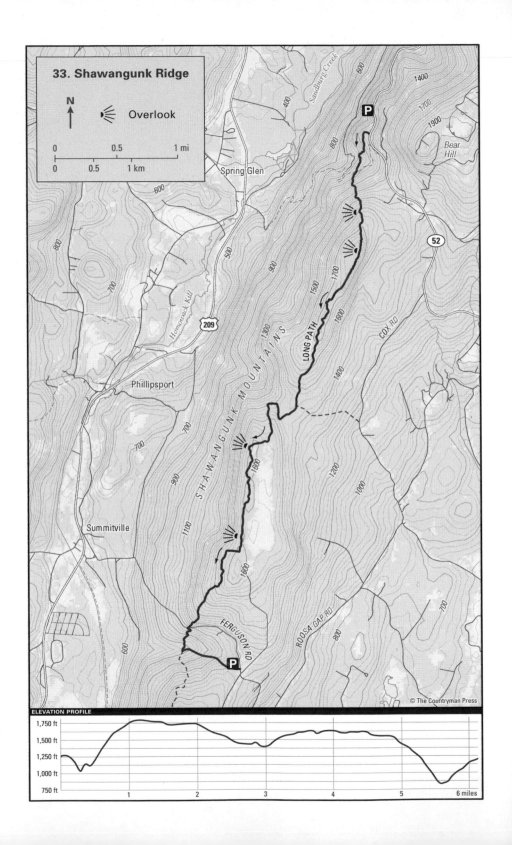

33. Shawangunk Ridge

N

☀ Overlook

0 — 0.5 — 1 mi
0 — 0.5 — 1 km

Spring Glen

Sandburg Creek

Bear Hill

52

LONG PATH

SHAWANGUNK MOUNTAINS

COX RD.

209

Phillipsport

Summitville

FERGUSON RD.

ROOSA GAP RD.

© The Countryman Press

ELEVATION PROFILE

1,750 ft
1,500 ft
1,250 ft
1,000 ft
750 ft

1   2   3   4   5   6 miles

on Roosa Gap Road for 2 miles. When you reach an intersection where Frey Road begins to the right, bear left to continue on Pleasant Valley Road, and cross a bridge. In 0.2 mile, bear left at another stop sign onto Cox Road. Follow Cox Road for about 2 miles to NY 52. Turn left onto NY 52, and continue for 1.7 miles to a scenic overlook on the left side of the road. Park the second car here.

THE TRAIL

After enjoying the panoramic view from the overlook, walk back along NY 52 (proceeding southeast) for about 750 feet. When you reach the end of the guardrail, you'll see the start of a yellow-blazed trail on the right. Turn right and follow the yellow trail. The trail climbs a little, with views of the valley on the right when there are no leaves on the trees, then descends steadily through a deciduous forest with a dense understory of blueberry and mountain laurel. It crosses an intermittent stream and continues to descend to a woods road. The trail turns right onto the road, then immediately turns left and continues downhill to a magnificent cascading stream. Use care when crossing the rock slabs, as they are often slippery. Once on the other side, turn sharply left, paralleling the stream uphill. (If the water is high, the crossing may be impassable. If so, continue uphill along the stream; you should be able to cross it on rocks just above the top of the steep climb.)

The yellow trail now climbs steeply, then bears right, away from the stream. After a

Along the Shawangunk Ridge Trail

KEITH SHANE

West-facing view from the Shawangunk Ridge Trail   KEITH SHANE

short level section, the yellow trail ends at a woods road. Turn right and follow the road for only 20 feet, then turn sharply left and reenter the woods on a footpath—the route of the aqua-blazed Long Path (do not follow the Long Path straight ahead on the woods road). You will follow the Long Path for the next 5 miles. In addition to aqua paint blazes, this section of the Long Path is marked with blue circular plastic discs of the New York State Department of Environmental Conservation (DEC), as you are now on state land.

For the next 0.5 mile or so, you'll be climbing, steeply in places, toward the crest of the Shawangunk Ridge. The trail proceeds through a dense understory of blueberry and mountain laurel—particularly beautiful in June, when the mountain laurel is in bloom. Soon you'll reach an open area with pitch pines, which offers a broad west-facing view. After taking in the view, continue climbing to the crest of the ridge. You'll be climbing about 500 vertical feet in only 0.6 mile.

About 1 mile from the start the trail levels off, and you'll soon reach a panoramic viewpoint from the west side of the ridge. This is a good place to take a break—a welcome respite from the steep climb up the ridge.

After taking in the view, continue ahead on the Long Path, which follows exposed slabs of Shawangunk Conglomerate along the west side of the ridge. You'll notice pitch pines growing from cracks in the bedrock. After a while, the trail moves over to the east side of the ridge, where it runs along the edge of a 30-foot-high escarpment. Many interesting rock pinnacles are visible just to the left of the trail, and at one point there is a panoramic northeast-facing view. The rock formation to the north is Bear Hill, and the microwave towers at Lake Maratanza are visible beyond. Beyond this viewpoint, the trail switches back to the west side of the ridge, with more views. It goes back and forth, crossing from one side of the ridge to the other several times.

The trail follows the ridge for about 1 mile, then bears left and descends gradually through a deciduous forest. Soon you'll come to a stone wall—evidence of the former agricultural use of the area. The next section of the trail is relatively level and often wet. You'll cross a number of stone walls and pass a stand of barberry, an invasive species. This entire route of the Long Path from NY 52 to Ferguson Road is remarkably free of invasives, and this one large patch of barberry is the only instance you'll encounter of invasive species along this entire segment of the Long Path.

After descending a little more and then climbing briefly, the Long Path bears right and follows the base of a rock escarpment on the left, descending gradually. It crosses an intermittent stream and soon bears left, climbing through a crack in the escarpment. The trail now continues to climb toward the crest of the ridge.

As the trail approaches the ridge, scrub oak becomes the predominant vegetation. Because the scrub oak tends to grow relatively high, the views are limited in this section. Soon the trail descends to a col, then climbs to a rise (with limited views) marked by two glacial erratics. A short

distance beyond, you'll reach another large erratic, known as Jack's Rock, which offers a broader west-facing view.

For another 0.5 mile, you'll walk high along the western escarpment, with occasional views through the dense scrub oak. The end of this section is marked by a plaque in memory of Jack Hennessey, a dedicated volunteer trail maintainer of this trail section. The trail now descends slightly from the ridge, then levels off.

In another 0.5 mile, you'll reach a panoramic viewpoint to the southwest—the most spectacular viewpoint you've encountered so far on the hike. The Wurtsboro Airport is visible in the valley below; the huge building just beyond is a Kohl's distribution center. The large wetland in the distance is the Basha Kill, and on a clear day the High Point Monument can be seen in the distance.

The Long Path now begins a steady descent. The first part of the descent is on a graded footpath, but as you approach Ferguson Road, the trail descends more steeply along rock slabs, which can be slippery when wet. The trail crosses Ferguson Road and continues to descend on switchbacks.

At the base of the descent—just before the Long Path crosses a stream—a yellow-blazed trail begins on the left. Turn left and follow the yellow trail, which ascends steadily—first paralleling the stream, then crossing several tributaries. Near the top of the climb, just beyond a stream crossing, the trail approaches a spectacular waterfall that cascades down into the valley below. The yellow trail ends at the parking area where you left the first car.

34

Verkeerder Kill Falls Loop

Total distance: 9.6 miles

Walking time: 6.5 hours

Vertical rise: 1,200 feet

Maps: USGS 7.5' Ellenville; USGS 7.5' Napanoch; NY–NJTC Shawangunk Trails #104

Trailhead GPS Coordinates:
N 41° 40' 13.5" W 74° 21' 40"

This hike loops around the Sam's Point Preserve, home to the world's largest area of ridgetop dwarf pitch pines. It has been designated by The Nature Conservancy as one of the "Last Great Places" in the world. The first part of the hike follows a gravel road still used by service vehicles to access radio towers, but for most of the way, you'll be following narrow footpaths that traverse dense pitch pine forests.

The Sam's Point area was first publicized as a tourist attraction by Thomas Bosford, who acquired land in the area in 1858. In 1871, he built an observatory at the top of the promontory, as well as a hotel that used the cliff as one of its walls. The hotel burned down after its first season. Then, in 1922, the tract was acquired by the village of Ellenville for watershed protection. Subsequently, the village leased a portion of the property to an entrepreneur who permitted visitors (for a fee) to enter the lighted ice caves. Several groups worked together for the protection of this site, and after many years of negotiations, it was acquired by the Open Space Conservancy in 1997, with management provided by The Nature Conservancy. In 2007, the Open Space Conservancy conveyed 3,800 acres of the Sam's Point Preserve to the State of New York, and the remaining 1,000 acres were transferred to the state in 2013.

The Sam's Point Conservation Center, which opened in 2005, is a dramatic "green" building which contains exhibits that highlight the unique landscape and spectacular

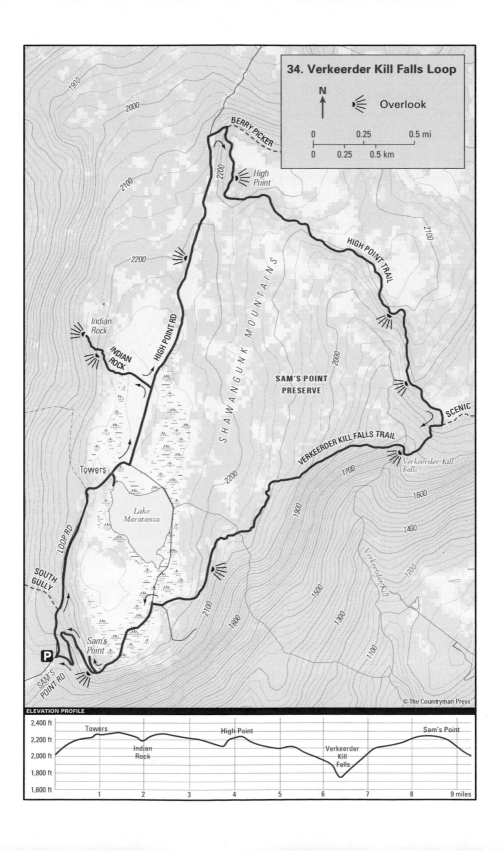

34. Verkeerder Kill Falls Loop

N

≋ Overlook

0   0.25   0.5 mi
0   0.25   0.5 km

BERRY PICKER

High Point

HIGH POINT TRAIL

2100

2000

Indian Rock

INDIAN ROCK

HIGH POINT RD

S H A W A N G U N K   M O U N T A I N S

SAM'S POINT PRESERVE

SCENIC

VERKEERDER KILL FALLS TRAIL

Verkeerder Kill Falls

1700

1600

1400

Towers

Lake Maratanza

2200

1900

1500

1300

1200

1100

Verkeerder Kill

LOOP RD

SOUTH GULLY

Sam's Point

P

SAM'S POINT RD

2100

1800

© The Countryman Press

ELEVATION PROFILE

2,400 ft									
2,200 ft	Towers			High Point				Sam's Point	
2,000 ft		Indian Rock					Verkeerder Kill Falls		
1,800 ft									
1,600 ft									
	1	2	3	4	5	6	7	8	9 miles

scenery. For more information, go to www
.nature.org.

HOW TO GET THERE

Take NY 17 (I-86) to Exit 119 and continue
north on NY 302 for 9.6 miles to Pine Bush,
where NY 302 ends. Turn left onto NY 52
and continue for 7.3 miles. Just before the
crest of the hill, turn right onto Cragsmoor
Road. In 1.3 miles, turn right in front of the
Cragsmoor post office, then take the next
right onto Sam's Point Road and follow it for
about 1.2 miles to its end at the parking area
for the preserve. A parking fee of $10 per
car is charged.

THE TRAIL

From the parking area, walk around the gate
and take the left fork of the Loop Road (a
gravel road, closed to private vehicles but
open to service vehicles). Follow the road
uphill, passing several dilapidated shacks on
the left built to house the "berry pickers" who
lived there seasonally while harvesting the
blueberries and huckleberries that are found
in abundance in the area. The berry picking
industry in the area started in the 1860s and
continued for over one hundred years.

In 0.3 mile, a wooden sign on the left
marks the start of the South Gully Trail, the
route of the aqua-blazed Long Path. Continue ahead on the gravel Loop Road, which
passes the site of a former quarry on the
right and levels off.

About 1 mile from the start, you'll notice several radio towers on the left. These
towers—an unwelcome intrusion on the pristine beauty of the area—predate The Nature
Conservancy's stewardship of the property.
Service vehicles are allowed to use the
Loop Road to access the towers, and you
may be passed by one of these vehicles
along the way. Soon an unmarked side trail
begins on the right (opposite a road on the

left that leads to one of the towers). Follow
this side trail a short distance down to the
scenic Lake Maratanza, which still serves as
the water supply for the village of Ellenville
(swimming is not permitted). The lake served
as a tourist attraction around 1900, and a
hotel was built along its shore.

Return to the Loop Road and turn right.
When you reach a junction marked by a
wooden sign, turn left onto the High Point
Road, a wide gravel road constructed by the
Civilian Conservation Corps (CCC) in the
1930s. In 0.4 mile, you'll notice a wooden
sign on the left. Turn left and follow the yellow-
blazed Indian Rock Trail, which crosses a wet
area on a long set of puncheons and continues on a level, narrow footpath through pitch
pines with a dense understory of blueberries.
This footpath is a welcome change of pace
from the wide gravel road that you have been
following up to now.

In about 0.3 mile, as the trail curves to
the right, an open rock ledge straight ahead
offers panoramic views to the west and
north, with the Catskill Mountains visible to
the right. The Indian Rock Trail now begins
to descend—emerging, in another 0.25 mile,
onto an exposed rock ledge. The blazes lead
down through a narrow crevice and out to
Indian Rock—a large, fractured boulder balanced on a smaller boulder, which offers
views to the west and north.

After taking a break, retrace your steps
back to the High Point Road and turn left.
In about 0.7 mile, the improved gravel road
ends and the road becomes grassier and
somewhat narrower. Just beyond, you'll
pass a west-facing viewpoint with a bench.
A short distance ahead, you'll notice in the
distance on the right a rock outcrop that
marks High Point, which you'll soon climb.

In another 0.5 mile, you'll come to a junction marked by a wooden sign. Ahead, High
Point Road is somewhat overgrown, and

Indian Rock

DANIEL CHAZIN

you should turn right—now following the red-blazed High Point Trail, which will be your route for the next 2.5 miles. Most of the blazes are painted on the rocks on the footpath, but you will also notice some blazes on trees along the way. At times, the trail maintainer has placed rows of smaller rocks to keep the walker on track.

The trail begins by climbing rather steeply to a T-junction, where the blue-blazed Berry Picker Trail begins on the left. Turn right, continuing to follow the red-blazed High Point Trail, which is now joined by the Long Path (along the route of the High Point Trail, the Long Path is marked only by occasional logo blazes). In a short distance, you'll emerge onto a panoramic viewpoint from an open rock ledge, with views to the west

and north. This was once the location of the High Point fire tower. Continue along the High Point Trail, which ascends very gently through dense stands of pitch pine. Some of these pitch pines are hundreds of years old. Their growth is stunted by the wind and the thin and unfertile soil.

In about 0.25 mile, you'll reach High Point, the highest point in the area (2,240 feet), marked by a USGS benchmark. High Point offers a panoramic 360-degree view. To the north, you can see the Catskills, with Slide Mountain (the highest peak in the Catskills) and the Burroughs Range in the foreground, and the peaks of the Devil's Path (Plateau, Sugarloaf, Twin, and Indian Head Mountains) to the right in the distance. The radio towers you passed previously are

Verkeerder Kill Falls

DANIEL CHAZIN

visible to the southwest, and to the northeast you can see Gertrude's Nose in Minnewaska State Park Preserve. The Hudson Highlands can be seen to the east, and on a clear day, you might even get a glimpse of the Hudson River.

After taking a break to admire the spectacular view, continue along the High Point Trail, which steeply descends from the rock ledge and continues through a dense stand of pitch pines, with an understory of blueberries. There are several short but steep descents in the next section of the trail, and you'll need to use both your hands and your feet to negotiate these steep pitches. After about 1 mile, you'll come out onto a rock outcrop, with panoramic views to the west and south. To the southwest, across the valley, you can see the radio towers that you passed earlier in the hike, and the Wallkill Valley is visible to the south. For the next 0.5 mile, you'll be following a dramatic escarpment, with many views along the way. Finally, the High Point Trail goes back into the woods and descends to reach a T-junction, marked by a sign.

The light-blue-blazed Scenic Trail begins on the left, but you should turn right onto the Verkeerder Kill Falls Trail (also the route of the Long Path), marked with aqua blazes. You will note that the pitch pines that you've seen for most of the hike have been replaced by deciduous trees in this area. A short distance ahead, you'll come to a fork. The main trail bears left here, but you should take the right fork, which leads to an exposed rock ledge, with two glacial erratics, that offers views to the west and south.

Return to the main trail and follow it as it descends, steeply in places, toward the falls. As you approach the falls, the trail turns right, but you should continue ahead to a rock ledge overlooking the 180-foot-high Verkeerder Kill Falls—the highest waterfall

in the Shawangunks. Use extreme care, as there is a sheer drop from here to the bottom of the falls! The falls are most dramatic after heavy rains, and might be reduced to a trickle in times of drought. They're particularly fascinating in winter when ice forms on the cliff.

When you're ready to continue, turn left on the Verkeerder Kill Falls Trail/Long Path, which almost immediately crosses the braided Verkeerder Kill above the falls (the crossing can be difficult if the water is high) and soon begins a gradual climb. At first, you'll pass through an area dominated by tall oak, birch, and maple trees, but after gaining some elevation, the pitch pine/blueberry forest returns.

Just beyond, the trail makes a sharp left turn (the overgrown path to the right, now abandoned, once led to the Loop Road near Lake Maratanza). The trail now levels off, and the vegetation soon changes to a birch forest with an understory of ferns. After the trail crosses an intermittent stream (the outlet of Lake Maratanza), the pitch pine/blueberry forest returns, and the trail resumes its ascent.

Soon views appear to the northeast over Minnewaska State Park Preserve. The three rock formations that you see are (left to right) Castle Point, Hamilton Point, and Gertrude's Nose. A short distance beyond, the Verkeerder Kill Falls Trail ends at a junction with the road that leads to the Ice Caves. Turn right, head uphill to the Loop Road, and turn left, following the sign that points to the Conservation Center.

Follow this deteriorated paved road for about 0.5 mile until a wide road leaves on the right. Turn right and follow this road a short distance to Sam's Point, a large open rock slab with protective rock walls, which offers panoramic views to the southwest. Sam's Point was once called the Big Nose of Aioskawasting. The legend surrounding the current name of this magnificent promontory is that Samuel Gonsalus, a famous local hunter and scout constantly at odds with his Native American neighbors, was once alone at this promontory when he was surprised by a group who started in pursuit, as Sam ran away. Sam—a big man and always a good runner—outpaced his enemies and flung himself from the brink to land in a clump of bushes that broke his fall. His enemies retreated, mistakenly assuming that Sam had been killed by the fall.

Return to the Loop Road, turn right, and follow the road as it descends on switchbacks below the cliffs of Sam's Point and returns to the Conservation Center and the parking area where the hike began.

35

Minnewaska Loop

Total distance: 9.2 miles

Walking time: 6 hours

Vertical rise: 1,000 feet

Maps: USGS 7.5' Gardiner; USGS 7.5' Napanoch; NY–NJTC Shawangunk Trails #104

Trailhead GPS Coordinates: N 41° 44' 04" W 74° 14' 39"

Although it does not pass by either Lake Minnewaska or Lake Awosting, this hike traverses some of the most spectacular scenery in Minnewaska State Park Preserve. It begins by following the cascading Peters Kill, continues to climb over conglomerate rock slabs with pitch pines, and reaches Castle Point, with panoramic views. It follows along magnificent rock ledges, passes the fascinating Rainbow Falls, and climbs to a broad viewpoint over the Catskill Mountains. Although the hike can easily be completed by the average hiker in six hours, the amazing sights you'll see along the way will tempt you to linger, and you might want to allow even more time to savor all the special features of this hike into the backcountry of Minnewaska State Park Preserve.

HOW TO GET THERE

Take the New York State Thruway (I-87) to Exit 18 (New Paltz). After paying the toll, turn left onto NY 299 and continue west through the village of New Paltz. When you cross the bridge over the Wallkill River at the west end of the village, continue ahead on NY 299 (do not turn right toward the Mohonk Mountain House). In another 5.6 miles (from the Wallkill River bridge), NY 299 ends at a T-junction with US 44/NY 55. Turn right and follow US 44/NY 55 as it negotiates a very sharp hairpin turn and climbs to pass under the Trapps Bridge (a steel overpass). Continue for 3 miles past the Trapps Bridge to the entrance to Minnewaska State Park Preserve, on the left side of the road (an eight-dollar parking fee is charged at the

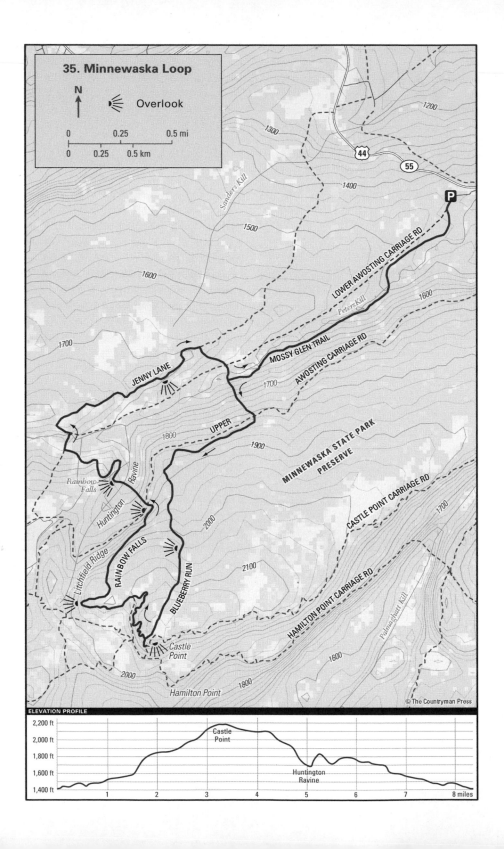

35. Minnewaska Loop

N

Overlook

0   0.25   0.5 mi
0   0.25   0.5 km

Sanders Kill

1200

1300

44

55

1400

P

1500

LOWER AWOSTING CARRIAGE RD

Peters Kill

1600

1600

1700

MOSSY GLEN TRAIL

AWOSTING CARRIAGE RD

JENNY LANE

1700

UPPER

1800

1900

MINNEWASKA STATE PARK PRESERVE

Rainbow Falls

Ravine

Huntington

2000

CASTLE POINT CARRIAGE RD

1700

Litchfield Ridge

RAINBOW FALLS

BLUEBERRY RUN

2100

HAMILTON POINT CARRIAGE RD

Palmaghatt Kill

Castle Point

2000

1600

Hamilton Point

1800

© The Countryman Press

ELEVATION PROFILE

2,200 ft
2,000 ft
1,800 ft
1,600 ft
1,400 ft

Castle Point

Huntington Ravine

1   2   3   4   5   6   7   8 miles

gatehouse). Immediately turn right and proceed for 0.2 mile to the Awosting parking area. Make a note of the park closing time, which is closely observed. On a fine weekend, it's advisable to arrive early because the lot has been known to fill up and close by 10 am.

THE TRAIL

From the kiosk at the rear of the parking area, continue past the gate onto the Lower Awosting Carriage Road. Almost immediately, turn left onto the yellow-blazed Mossy Glen Trail, built by volunteers of the NY–NJTC in 1999 as a scenic alternative to the carriage road. In 0.5 mile, after passing through an attractive forest of hemlock and mountain laurel, the trail approaches the carriage road, then turns sharply left and descends to the Peters Kill, which it crosses on a wooden footbridge. The bridge built in 1999 was washed away by Hurricane Irene in August 2011, but it was replaced by the park in 2013.

The Mossy Glen Trail now turns right and parallels the stream, which is tinged with brown from tannic acid in the trees. The Peters Kill rushes along through chutes, cascades, and falls, often slowing into deep pools. For part of the way, the trail follows polished rock slabs, smoothed by the glaciers, that slope toward the stream. These slabs can be very slippery, so care should be exercised, especially if they are wet or

View of Hamilton Point and the Wallkill Valley from Castle Point DANIEL CHAZIN

covered with pine needles. Rhododendron and white pine may be found along the trail, together with hemlock and mountain laurel. At one point, the trail tunnels under dense rhododendron.

In another 1 mile, the Mossy Glen Trail ends in an open area, with stunted pitch pines and an understory of blueberries. Turn left here onto the blue-blazed Blueberry Run Trail, which climbs steadily through mountain laurel and blueberries. After a while, the grade moderates, and the trail crosses the Upper Awosting Carriage Road.

A short distance after heading back into the woods, the Blueberry Run Trail turns right and begins to parallel the carriage road on a level footpath, passing through dense mountain laurel thickets (in full bloom in late June). Puncheons have been placed across several wet areas. In 0.5 mile, the trail crosses under a power line, with the foothills of the Catskills and the Rondout Reservoir—one of the links in New York City's water supply chain—visible to the right.

After descending a little, the trail bears left and begins a gradual climb through mountain laurel, hemlock, blueberries, and pitch pines. During the next mile, the trail gains about 300 feet in elevation. Along the way, the trail traverses a number of rock slabs, with cairns indicating the route. After passing an interesting cliff on the right, the Blueberry Run Trail climbs more steeply and emerges onto an expansive conglomerate rock slab covered with stunted pitch pines and blueberries. To the north, you can see the Catskill Mountains in the distance. From the right, the peaks you see are Overlook Mountain and Indian Head, Twin, Sugarloaf, and Plateau Mountains of the Devil's Path. The trail continues to climb, soon emerging on another large conglomerate slab, with several large cairns.

After reaching an open rock ledge at the highest point on the trail, the Blueberry Run Trail descends slightly to end at the Castle Point Carriage Road. Turn left onto the carriage road, and almost immediately you'll reach Castle Point, a steep promontory with panoramic views. Lake Awosting is below to the west, and Sam's Point may be seen to the southwest (to the left of the communications towers visible in the distance). Directly ahead (south) you can see Hamilton Point, another rock promontory, with the Wallkill Valley beyond, and the cliffs of Gertrude's Nose may be seen across Palmaghatt Ravine to the east. Over to the left is the gorge of the Hudson River between Breakneck Ridge and Storm King. The hills of Harriman–Bear Mountain and Sterling Forest State Parks may also be visible on a clear day. You'll want to take a break here to savor the views from this spectacular point—the highest viewpoint in the park.

When you're ready to continue, turn left onto the carriage road, marked with blue Shawangunk Ridge Trail logo blazes and blue diamonds. This carriage road is open to bicyclists, as well as hikers, and you should be alert for approaching bicycles. You'll immediately pass the trailhead of the Blueberry Run Trail on your right and soon begin to head downhill, passing more magnificent viewpoints over Sam's Point, Lake Awosting, and the Catskills. A short distance beyond the second hairpin turn on the Castle Point Carriage Road, watch carefully on the right for two rock steps that climb up into the woods just before another bend in the road. Turn right here onto the orange-blazed Rainbow Falls Trail (also the route of the Shawangunk Ridge Trail), which immediately bears left and follows along rock ledges, with the cliffs of Battlement Terrace visible on the other side of the Castle Point Carriage Road.

View of the Catskills from the Rainbow Falls Trail

DANIEL CHAZIN

After steeply descending a rock ledge, the trail follows along low cliffs. Soon you'll come out on wide, open rock ledges that afford a panoramic view of Lake Awosting, with Sam's Point on the left and the Catskills on the right. This is another special place where you'll want to spend some time exploring the area and savoring the views.

When you're ready to continue, follow the orange-blazed Rainbow Falls Trail as it reenters the woods and makes several short but steep climbs over rock ledges. Soon the trail begins to descend over slabs of conglomerate rock studded with pitch pines. It continues downhill through mountain laurel thickets and dense hemlock groves. On the way down, you'll pass a rock ledge on the left that offers a panoramic north-facing view, with Huntington Ravine below and the Catskills in the distance.

The Rainbow Falls Trail continues to descend. As it approaches the Upper Awosting Carriage Road, it bends sharply to the left and descends along a cliff of fractured conglomerate blocks. The trail crosses the road, descends rock steps, and continues downhill through a stand of hardwoods and large hemlocks, crossing a stream on the way. Soon the sounds of the falling water at Rainbow Falls can be heard.

At the base of the descent, the trail crosses another stream and climbs over rocks to reach the base of the falls, where the water drops from overhanging rock ledges, forming a cool mist. Use caution as you approach the falls, as the wet rocks may be slippery.

Leaving the falls, the trail descends to the stream and parallels it for a few minutes, with cliffs above on the left. Pay careful attention to the trail blazes, as in a short distance the trail bears left, away from the stream, and steeply climbs through a gap in the cliffs. At the top, the trail turns left and comes out on open rocks, with south-facing views across Huntington Ravine. After climbing a little more, the trail emerges at the top of a sloping face of conglomerate rock dotted with pitch pines, with panoramic north-facing views of the Catskill Mountains. The Rainbow Falls Trail descends along the rock slabs, then bears left and crosses a stream just below a cascade (the stream crossing can be tricky if the water is high). It briefly bears left and climbs a little, then continues to descend. With Fly Brook in view to the right, the Rainbow Falls Trail bears left and climbs to its terminus at the Lower Awosting Carriage Road.

Turn right onto the carriage road and cross over Fly Brook on a concrete bridge. The road formerly crossed an earthen causeway over the stream, but the causeway was destroyed during Hurricane Irene and has been replaced by the bridge. Just beyond, turn left onto the blue-blazed Jenny Lane Trail (also the route of the Shawangunk Ridge Trail), which follows an old woods road. The road soon bears right and climbs rather steeply, then levels off. For part of the way, the road follows slabs of conglomerate rock.

In 0.5 mile, the trail turns right under power lines. For a short distance, it runs parallel to the power lines, but just beyond the next power line tower, the trail turns left and reenters the woods. Soon the trail begins to run close to the edge of the ridge, coming out occasionally on open rocks, with views to the southeast across the valley of the Peters Kill.

After bearing left, away from the edge of the ridge, you'll reach a junction with the Blueberry Run Trail (also blazed blue), marked by a sign on the right. Turn right onto the Blueberry Run Trail, which soon begins a rather steep descent. At the base of the descent, it turns left and passes through a hemlock grove, crossing a stream on rocks. A short distance beyond, the trail reaches the Lower Awosting Carriage Road.

Here you have two options. If you want to head directly back to your car, turn left and follow the carriage road for 1.5 miles to the parking area. The road is relatively uninteresting (although you will get a few glimpses of the Peters Kill, below on the right), but it is the shortest and fastest route back to your car.

If you have enough time and want to return by a more interesting route, you can continue along the Blueberry Run Trail, which descends to cross the Peters Kill on a log bridge and climbs to a junction with the Mossy Glen Trail. Turn left at the junction and retrace your steps back to the parking area on the Mossy Glen Trail. You've already hiked this trail on your way in, but it is certainly a nicer way to conclude your hike than walking on the rather boring carriage road.

36

The Trapps to Gertrude's Nose

Total distance: 10.1 miles

Walking time: 6 hours

Vertical rise: 1,100 feet

Maps: USGS 7.5' Gardiner; USGS 7.5' Napanoch; NY–NJTC Shawangunk Trails #104; Mohonk Preserve–Northern Section

Trailhead GPS Coordinates: N 41° 44' 15" W 74° 11' 51"

For a special look at this geologically intriguing area known as the Gunks, try the hike along the Trapps to Gertrude's Nose. The hike uses trails on the escarpment edge as well as some easy walking on carriage roads, ending with a stroll through deeply forested areas. The route includes a visit to spectacular Millbrook Mountain and Gertrude's Nose. The beauty of the Shawangunks lies in the way the views continuously unfold, enlivening every few feet of each walk.

It is the rock—and its history—that is so impressive about this hike. The Shawangunks were formed about 450 million years ago. The sediments that form the shining white conglomerates were once deposited along the shores of an inland sea, whose waters tumbled and smoothed the quartz pebbles that were later embedded in these gleaming white rocks. These sediments were shaped by heat and pressure, faulted and bent, and uplifted about 280 million years ago to form the magnificent cliffs of the Shawangunks' southwestern face, where the horizontal layers of deposits are worn away. The dip to the northwest produces the long slopes so characteristic of the area. The age of the uplift makes the Shawangunks one of the youngest formations in the East.

HOW TO GET THERE

Take the New York State Thruway (I-87) to Exit 18 (New Paltz). After paying the toll, turn left onto NY 299 and continue west through the village of New Paltz. When you cross the bridge over the Wallkill River at the west

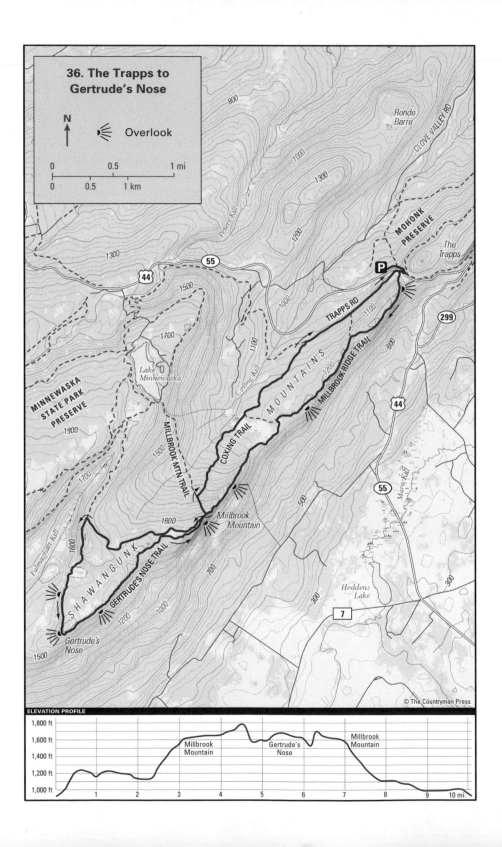

36. The Trapps to Gertrude's Nose

N

↑

🜋 Overlook

| 0 | 0.5 | 1 mi |
| 0 | 0.5 | 1 km |

Ronde Barre

CLOVE VALLEY RD

MOHONK PRESERVE

The Trapps

P

299

TRAPPS RD

MILLBROOK RIDGE TRAIL

MOUNTAINS

44

55

COXING TRAIL

Mud Kill

MILLBROOK MTN TRAIL

Lake Minnewaska

MINNEWASKA STATE PARK PRESERVE

Peters Kill

Coxing Kill

Millbrook Mountain

S H A W A N G U N K

GERTRUDE'S NOSE TRAIL

Palmaghatt Kill

Gertrude's Nose

Heddens Lake

7

© The Countryman Press

ELEVATION PROFILE

1,800 ft									
1,600 ft			Millbrook Mountain			Gertrude's Nose		Millbrook Mountain	
1,400 ft									
1,200 ft									
1,000 ft									
	1	2	3	4	5	6	7	8	9	10 mi.

end of the village, continue ahead on NY 299 (do not turn right toward the Mohonk Mountain House). In another 5.6 miles (from the Wallkill River bridge), NY 299 ends at a T-junction with US 44/NY 55. Turn right and follow US 44/NY 55 as it makes a very sharp hairpin turn and climbs to pass under the Trapps Bridge (a steel overpass). Continue for 0.3 mile past the Trapps Bridge and turn right into the West Trapps Trailhead parking area. A $12 per person daily use fee will be collected by the attendant (a $55 annual membership is also available).

THE TRAIL

The hike begins on lands of the Mohonk Preserve. It heads southwesterly, following the Millbrook Ridge Trail, which runs close to the edge of dramatic cliffs. The thrill that a nonclimber gets following this route can be compared to that which a climber gets from climbing the famous Shawangunk cliffs.

From the eastern end of the parking area, follow the yellow-blazed West Trapps Connector Trail, a gravel road which leads east parallel to US 44/NY 55. In about 0.25 mile, you'll reach the Trapps Bridge. Ascend the rock stairway that leads up to the bridge, turn right, and cross the bridge, continuing ahead on the Trapps Road.

About 150 feet down Trapps Road from the steel bridge, watch for three light-blue blazes on the left that mark the start of the Millbrook Ridge Trail. Turn left and follow this trail—marked with paint blazes on the rocks—which steeply climbs over rock slabs dotted with pitch pines. Soon you'll reach a north-facing viewpoint (the first of many along the ridge).

A short distance beyond, after some more climbing, you'll reach the crest of the ridge (known as the Near Trapps). Here there is an even-broader view from a point called the Hawk Watch. To the left, you can see Dickie Barre, with the Catskill Mountains in the distance beyond. To the right, there is a sweeping view over the Wallkill Valley, with New Paltz visible in the distance. This is a good spot to rest and take a break from the climb.

Almost immediately the cleft in the Shawangunk ridge becomes apparent. The eastern ridge meets the western one near Minnewaska, a resort whose lands once encompassed most of the central Shawangunks. The cliffs and tower of the Mohonk Mountain House—a hotel whose grounds, together with Mohonk Preserve lands, make up the northern Shawangunks—are visible as you climb the trail. These cliffs and the Sky Top tower frame the high peaks of the central Catskill range—a view that reappears many times during this walk.

Follow the light-blue blazes of the Millbrook Ridge Trail as it undulates along the top of the ridge, alternating between rock slabs and soft pine-needle-covered paths. The trail now levels off and continues through a wooded area along the ridge, with scrub oak and pitch pine and an understory of blueberry bushes. Soon you'll reach another viewpoint on the left, with the Sky Top tower of the Mohonk Mountain House visible to the north, and the intersection of NY 299 and US 44/NY 55 directly below.

About 1 mile from the start, you'll descend slightly and reach a junction with the red-blazed Bayards Trail, which begins on the right. Continue ahead on the light-blue-blazed Millbrook Ridge Trail, which bears left and climbs to the top of the next ridge, known as the Bayards. After passing several viewpoints over the Wallkill Valley, you'll traverse a long, relatively level section. Suddenly, the trail emerges onto a rounded outcrop with a view ahead (through the trees) of the dramatic cliff of Millbrook Mountain—the next destination of the hike.

The Trapps to Gertrude's Nose

After bearing right and descending through mountain laurel and hemlock, the Millbrook Ridge Trail arrives at a junction with the red-blazed Millbrook Cross Trail, about 2 miles from the start. Continue ahead on the light-blue-blazed trail, which bends left and climbs to regain the crest of the ridge. Soon it crosses a rock outcrop with several small glacial erratics. It continues on a relatively level footpath through laurel and hemlocks and emerges onto an open area.

The trail now follows a rocky path through hemlocks, soon arriving at the base of a cliff. It climbs over rocks to the right of the cliff and continues on a footpath below the crest of the ridge. Soon the trail bears left, climbs through a boulder field, and proceeds through an open area, with blueberries and pitch pines, to reach the crest of the ridge.

The trail turns right and continues to climb along exposed rock outcrops, with views to the south and east over the Wallkill Valley as far as the Hudson Highlands. Sky Top may be seen to the northeast, and the Catskills in the distance to the north. Just beyond, the trail follows a narrow path to the right of a sloping rock slab. Next the trail climbs to the very edge of the cliff, with a sheer 300-foot drop. Using extreme caution, you can peer over the sharp cliff edge and see the vast boulder field below—probably the moraine of a small glacier that remained after the main ice sheet had melted away.

Continue to follow the Millbrook Ridge Trail along the cliff edge. Soon the trail heads slightly inland. Finally—a little over 3 miles from the start—you'll arrive at a junction with the red-blazed Millbrook Mountain Trail

Along the Gertrude's Nose Trail

DANIEL CHAZIN

(marked by a sign for "Lake Minnewaska"). Continue ahead on the trail (now blazed red) for a few hundred feet to a sign reading ENTERING MINNEWASKA STATE PARK PRESERVE, turn left, and climb the rock slab to the edge of the cliff—the summit of Millbrook Mountain, which offers an even broader view than those you've seen until now.

After taking in the view, walk down the slabs to the Millbrook Mountain Carriage Road and turn left. It's easy walking, even a bit dull, but the quickest way to make a loop walk around Gertrude's Nose. The carriage roads are the marvel of Mohonk and Minnewaska—miles and miles of graded pathways that today make for superb walking. They all are paved with Martinsburg shale, a 2,000-foot layer of which underlies the Shawangunks. The shale weathers to a dense but surprisingly soft and smooth walking surface. Except on the trails, the shale is unnoticeable, for almost everywhere it is topped with the white conglomerate. You may encounter mountain bikers along this road.

After a gentle downhill, the carriage road bends to the right before ascending slightly and then resuming its downhill trend. In about 1 mile, you'll reach a junction with the red-blazed Gertrude's Nose Trail, which begins on the left. The junction is marked by a sign.

Follow the Gertrude's Nose Trail as it descends toward Palmaghatt Ravine, the deep cleft between the trail you are following and the Hamilton Point Road. For part of the way the trail follows the edge of hemlock-covered ledges, sometimes on the white sloping slabs of the cliff tops, yielding views ahead to Gertrude's Nose. In places the trail is routed into the woods away from the cliff edge to protect the islands of fragile plants growing on the rock slabs. After a 20-minute walk, the trail descends steeply through deep and shady hemlock woods to cross under a power line at a small stream.

Head out to the white slabs, and stop to admire some of the glacial erratic boulders that dot the cliff tops. Observe also the deep clefts that fissure the cliffs, created as the soft shale foundations weathered and became displaced. Admire the wind-sculpted rock wonders as you walk the 40 minutes it may take to cover the 1 mile from the carriage road to the Nose. Here the evidence of another geological force is clear: the glaciers that once covered the Shawangunks to a depth of 4,000 to 5,000 feet. As the ice mass moved along the northwestern slopes, the rocks it pushed along scraped the conglomerate, leaving striations—long, thin scratch marks—that can be seen occasionally. The smooth polish of many surfaces is also the work of the glaciers, achieved as the ice mass moved over a layer of mud.

Pause at the promontory of Gertrude's Nose for another break, and enjoy the panoramic views to the east and south. Take note of signs along the way emphasizing that the area is ecologically sensitive and requesting that walkers remain on the marked trail and tread only on bare rock surfaces. Look around and wonder at the large tumbled rocks, the many cracks and crevices, freestanding boulders, and smooth slabs that make Gertrude's Nose such a special place.

After taking in the spectacular views, begin the return trip by continuing around the point and heading northeast, following the red blazes along the ridge. This part of the ridge is not as dramatic as the western section that you just traversed, as it lacks the many open rock slabs. However, there are a number of good viewpoints over the Wallkill Valley to the east from rock ledges to the right of the trail. In little more than 30 minutes, the trail again crosses on rocks underneath the power line. Just as the trail begins to climb after the power line, look for

Wallkill Valley from the Millbrook Ridge Trail DANIEL CHAZIN

a herd path to the right that will take you to a deep hole in the rocks. Stand here for a few moments to feel the cold air escaping upward, then return to the trail, which now climbs along ledges amid stunted trees and rocks.

About 0.5 mile from the power line crossing, you'll notice that the Millbrook Mountain Carriage Road begins to parallel the trail just to the left. Soon you'll reach the end of the road, just below the summit of Millbrook Mountain. Continue ahead, following the red blazes, until you reach a sign pointing to Lake Minnewaska. This sign marks the start of the red-blazed Millbrook Mountain Trail, which begins on the left. Turn left here and follow this red-blazed trail as it descends steadily

into the valley of the Coxing Kill. In about 0.25 mile, the blue-blazed Coxing Kill Trail begins on the right. Leave the red-blazed Millbrook Mountain Trail, and turn right onto the Coxing Trail, following it downhill at first on slabs and then through hemlocks and laurel. Walking here is very different from the preceding ridge traverse and is a peaceful end to an exhilarating outing. After strolling through a wet area, watch for an attractive spring to the west (left) of the trail.

The spring, bordered and protected by a rock wall, is called the James Van Leuven Spring, after one of the early settlers of the land. Old maps dated 1865 indicate that part of the Coxing Trail was once a public road and that the James Van Leuven cabin was probably located on the hump above the spring.

Cross the outlet of the spring on stepping-stones and the subsequent swampy area on planks. The Coxing Trail becomes wider, and the rock walls that can be seen show where the land was once cleared and farmed. There are muddy sections. Blazes are few, but the area is quiet and serene and the footpath easily followed. This old road you are following runs parallel to the Millbrook Ridge Trail and passes by the two red-blazed connectors seen earlier: the Millbrook Cross Trail and the Bayards Trail.

After following the Coxing Trail for about an hour, you'll come to a junction with the Trapps Road. Turn right, and be aware that mountain bikers use the Trapps Road. After a while you may notice traffic on US 44/NY 55 down to the left. Just past the trailhead of the Millbrook Ridge Trail, you'll reach the steel Trapps Bridge. Cross the bridge, turn left, descend the stairway, and follow the connector trail back to the parking area where you began the hike.

37

Undercliff/Overcliff Carriage Roads

Total distance: 5.7 miles

Walking time: 2.5 hours

Vertical rise: 350 feet

Maps: USGS 7.5' Gardiner; USGS 7.5' Mohonk Lake; NY–NJTC Shawangunk Trails #105; Mohonk Preserve–Southern Section

Trailhead GPS Coordinates: N 41° 44' 5.5" W 74° 11' 15"

Although most of this hike follows well-graded carriage roads, with nearly imperceptible changes in grade, it starts out with a short, steep ascent on rough stone steps. The two carriage roads that are used, Undercliff and Overcliff, loop around spectacular cliffs of Shawangunk Conglomerate and offer views to the south (from Undercliff Road) as well as the north (from Overcliff Road). Both roads are part of the carriage road system that links the lands of the Mohonk Preserve, the Mohonk Mountain House, and Minnewaska State Park Preserve. Undercliff Road is particularly remarkable because of its route across the boulder rubble at the base of the Trapps. Both of these carriage roads are multiuse, and hikers can expect to encounter bicyclists along the route. You'll also have the opportunity to observe climbers on the adjacent cliffs. In winter, when there is sufficient snow cover, these carriage roads are popular with cross-country skiers and snowshoers.

HOW TO GET THERE

Take the New York State Thruway (I-87) to Exit 18 (New Paltz). After paying the toll, turn left onto NY 299 and continue west through the village of New Paltz. When you cross the bridge over the Wallkill River at the west end of the village, continue ahead on NY 299 (do not turn right toward the Mohonk Mountain House). In another 5.5 miles (from the Wallkill River bridge), NY 299 ends at a T-junction with US 44/NY 55. Turn right here and follow US 44/NY 55 for 0.5 mile

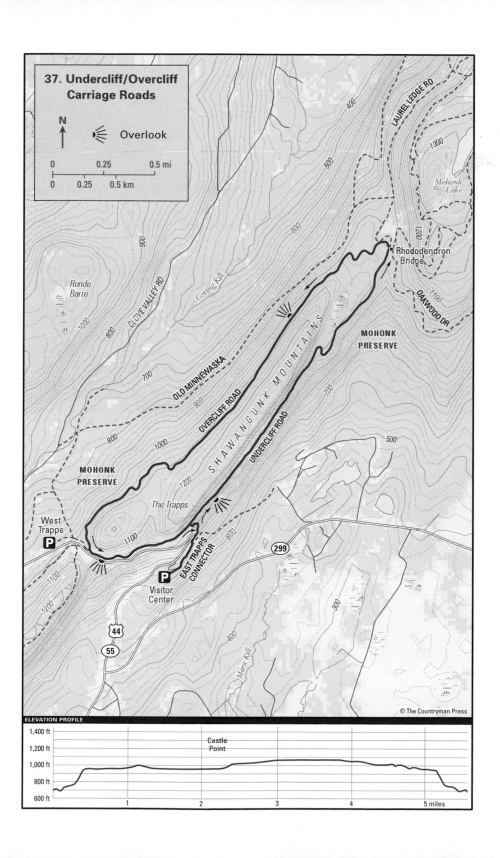

37. Undercliff/Overcliff Carriage Roads

N

Overlook

| 0 | 0.25 | 0.5 mi |
| 0 | 0.25 | 0.5 km |

LAUREL LEDGE RD

1300

Mohonk Lake

1200

400

600

800

1100

OAKWOOD DR

Rhododendron Bridge

900

Ronde Barre

Coxing Kill

1000

800

GLOVE VALLEY RD

700

OLD MINNEWASKA

900

1000

OVERCLIFF ROAD

S H A W A N G U N K   M O U N T A I N S

UNDERCLIFF ROAD

MOHONK PRESERVE

700

500

800

1200

The Trapps

MOHONK PRESERVE

1100

EAST TRAPPS CONNECTOR

600

West Trapps
P

1100

1200

P
Visitor Center

299

44

55

300

400

Mud Kill

© The Countryman Press

ELEVATION PROFILE

				Castle Point			
1,400 ft							
1,200 ft							
1,000 ft							
800 ft							
600 ft	1	2	3	4	5 miles		

North-facing view from Overcliff Road

DANIEL CHAZIN

to the Mohonk Preserve Visitors Center, on the right side of the road. Stop at the visitors center to purchase a pass ($12 per person; $55 annual pass), obtain a free map, and view the interesting exhibits. Then continue uphill on the Mohonk Preserve road (parallel to and below US 44/NY 55) to the end of a gravel parking area (beyond this point, a sign indicates that the road is private).

In the winter, the East Trapps Connector Trail, which leads from the parking area to Undercliff Road, is closed. If you find the trail closed, return to US 44/NY 55, turn right, and continue around the sharp hairpin turn. Pass beneath the Trapps Bridge (a steel overpass) and proceed for another 0.3 mile to the West Trapps Trailhead parking area of the Mohonk Preserve. From the eastern end of the parking area, follow the West Trapps Connector Trail, which leads east, parallel to US 44/NY 55. In about 0.25 mile, you'll reach the Trapps Bridge, where a stairway leads up to the Undercliff and Overcliff Roads. At the top of the stairs, turn left (do not cross the bridge), then immediately turn right at the next junction onto Undercliff Road.

Note, however, that if there is sufficient snow cover to permit cross-country skiing, these carriage roads are closed to hikers.

THE TRAIL

At the end of the gravel parking area, bear left and climb a wooden staircase, following a sign reading EAST TRAPPS CONNECTOR TRAIL, then bear right and follow a footpath

The Shawangunks

along the base of a stone wall that supports US 44/NY 55 above. Just beyond the hairpin turn in the road, the trail crosses a wooden bridge and steeply climbs 240 rock steps, passing some interesting boulders along the way. When you reach Undercliff Road, you will have climbed about 180 vertical feet—more than half of the elevation gain for the entire hike!

Turn right onto Undercliff Road, which is used not only by hikers, but also by joggers, bicyclists, and rock climbers. You may notice yellow-blazed trails that leave the carriage road to the left; these are access routes for climbers. This carriage road, completed by the Smileys in 1903, follows the cliff line. It

is amazing to think of the energy expended by the workers who built such a substantial road with only hand tools.

The cliffs on your left are world famous for their rock-climbing reputation. The Gunks were discovered as a rock-climbing area in the 1930s by Fritz Wiessner, an émigré from Germany. Climbing the cliffs remains popular to this day, and while walking you'll probably see climbers above you. Every route up the cliffs is named and given a grade indicating its degree of difficulty.

Openings in the vegetation on the right afford many views over the Wallkill Valley. Occasionally huge blocks of conglomerate overhang the road. After about 1 mile, the

Undercliff Road

DANIEL CHAZIN

Undercliff/Overcliff Carriage Roads

road enters denser woods and makes two sharp turns. In another 0.75 mile, you'll reach a complex junction of five carriage roads at the stone Rhododendron Bridge (do not cross the bridge). Laurel Ledge Road is straight ahead, but you should turn left onto Overcliff Road (marked by a sign).

Overcliff Road climbs gently through a series of curves to reach the west side of the Trapps Ridge. Along the way, it passes lichen-covered cliffs of Shawangunk Conglomerate. After leveling off, it reaches several viewpoints to the north over the Rondout Valley, with the peaks of the Catskills visible in the distance. Ronde Barre and Dickie Barre may be seen to the northwest. The vegetation along Overcliff Road is largely a mix of pitch pines and scrub oak.

About 1.5 miles from Rhododendron Bridge, the road enters denser woods and begins a gentle descent. After a series of curves, the road passes a viewpoint over the Lost City cliffs on Dickie Barre. The sounds of traffic on US 44/NY 55 below can now be heard, and Overcliff Road soon reaches the Trapps Bridge junction.

Continue ahead on Undercliff Road (do not cross the Trapps Bridge), which now descends a little more steeply, with the Trapps cliffs immediately to the left. You will almost certainly be able to observe rock climbers on these cliffs. After passing a kiosk and a small restroom building, the carriage road moves a little further away from the cliffs. A short distance beyond, you'll notice a sign for the East Trapps Connector Trail on the left side of the road. Turn right, descend the rock steps, and follow the trail back down to your car. In wet weather take care: These rock steps may be slippery.

The Mohonk Preserve has constructed several nature and sensory trails below the visitors center that would be a pleasant addition to the walk you have just completed. An interpretive brochure is available at the visitors center.

38

Bonticou Crag

Total distance: 4 miles

Walking time: 3 to 4 hours, depending on time taken for the rock scramble

Vertical rise: 800 feet

Maps: USGS 7.5' Mohonk Lake; NY–NJTC Shawangunk Trails #105; Mohonk Preserve–Northeastern Section

Trailhead GPS Coordinates: N 41° 47' 43" W 74° 07' 41"

This hike is one of the best in the Shawangunks. The route described uses parts of the Table Rocks, Crags, and Northeast Trails; sections of Bonticou and Clearwater Roads; and the Bonticou Ascent Path.

This outing includes some easy walking through a deciduous forest and has sweeping views of the Catskills plus–best of all–a challenging rock scramble on the talus of Bonticou Crag. This outcrop of white, shining Shawangunk Conglomerate rises unexpectedly like a mirage from the valley floor and can be seen in the distance from many directions.

The rock scramble is an adventure in itself but should not be tackled by young children, folks with inflexible bodies, or those who fear heights–and it certainly should not be attempted by *anyone* in wet or icy conditions. Both hands and feet will be needed to make the ascent, though the rock, by its nature, offers great handholds and grips.

HOW TO GET THERE

Take the New York State Thruway (I-87) to Exit 18 (New Paltz). After paying the toll, turn left onto NY 299 and continue west through the village of New Paltz. After crossing the bridge over the Wallkill River at the west end of the village, turn right onto Springtown Road, following signs for the Mohonk Mountain House. At the next intersection, turn left onto Mountain Rest Road and follow it for 3.3 miles to the entrance to the Mohonk Mountain House at the top of the hill. Continue ahead downhill for 1 mile and turn right onto Upper 27 Knolls Road. The Spring

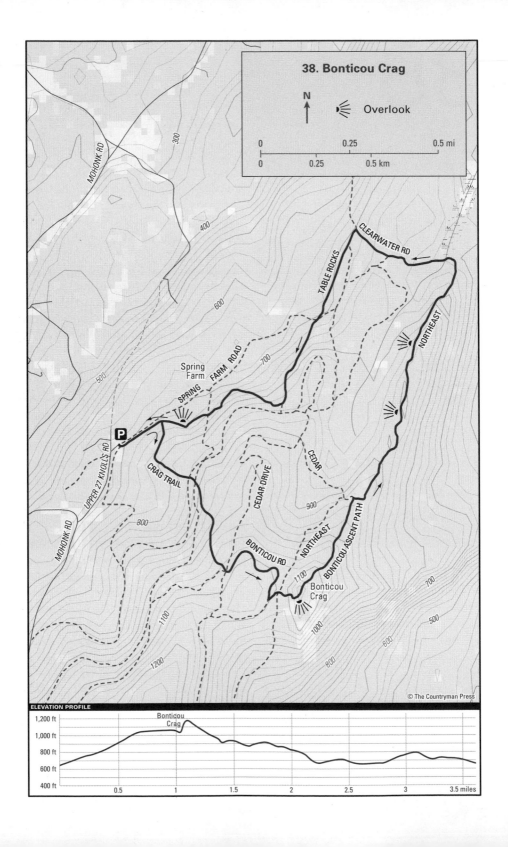

38. Bonticou Crag

N

Overlook

| 0 | 0.25 | 0.5 mi |
| 0 | 0.25 | 0.5 km |

MOHONK RD

300

400

TABLE ROCKS

CLEARWATER RD

500

600

700

Spring
Farm

SPRING FARM ROAD

NORTHEAST

P

CRAG TRAIL

UPPER 27 KNOLL'S RD

MOHONK RD

CEDAR DRIVE

CEDAR

NORTHEAST

BONTICOU ASCENT PATH

800

900

BONTICOU RD

1100

Bonticou
Crag

1000

700

500

600

800

1200

1100

© The Countryman Press

ELEVATION PROFILE

Bonticou
Crag

| 1,200 ft |
| 1,000 ft |
| 800 ft |
| 600 ft |
| 400 ft |

0.5   1   1.5   2   2.5   3   3.5 miles

Bonticou Crag

DANIEL CHAZIN

Farm parking area of the Mohonk Preserve is just ahead. A ranger is usually stationed at a kiosk to collect day-use fees ($12 per person) and distribute maps.

THE TRAIL

From the exit at the northern end of the parking area, follow a short unmarked trail uphill and turn left onto the blue-blazed Table Rocks Trail, which parallels Spring Farm Road. As the trail reaches the top of a rise, a broad panoramic view of the Catskill Mountains appears to the left. Just beyond, you'll reach a junction with the Crag Trail. The Table Rocks Trail continues straight ahead and will be your return route, but for now turn right onto the Crag Trail, which follows a row of cedar trees, continues on a wide path

across a field, and parallels an old stone wall along the left side of another field.

After about 15 minutes of uphill walking, the trail crosses two carriage roads—Cedar Drive and Spring Farm Road—in quick succession. You'll now notice some red blazes along the trail route. The Crag Trail continues to climb, rather steeply in places, reaching its terminus—about 1 mile from the start of the hike—at the intersection of Cedar Drive with Bonticou Road.

Make a broad left turn onto Bonticou Road (do not turn sharply left onto Cedar Drive, which descends rather steeply). This level carriage road soon curves to the right, with trees growing out of the thin layers of deeply tilted shale on the hillside. After the road bends to the left, then again to the

Along the Northeast Trail

DANIEL CHAZIN

right, the imposing Bonticou Crag comes into view through the trees on the left. Watch carefully for a triple-yellow blaze on the left side of the road, marking the start of the Bonticou Ascent Path. When you reach this yellow-blazed trail, turn left and follow it downhill to a junction with the blue-blazed Northeast Trail.

Now begins the fun. (For those intimidated by the sight of the steep and rocky route ahead and needing an easier route to the top of the cliff, turn left on the Northeast Trail and follow it for about 0.5 mile, bearing right when the blue blazes meet the red-blazed Cedar Trail. After a rather steep climb, turn right again when the junction with the yellow-blazed Bonticou Ascent Path is reached. This route accesses the top of the crag without having to climb the challenging rock scramble, and the hike's continuation can then be followed.)

The climb itself is only about 0.3 mile long and gains only 150 feet of elevation, but it involves a climb over large boulders and jagged ledges, and should not be undertaken lightly. It is generally considered the most difficult rock scramble in the Mohonk area. Follow the yellow blazes carefully because they indicate the easiest route. After the initial boulder is surmounted, the route winds its way up the face of the crag, first to the right and then to the left. Stunted pitch pine and paper birch survive in occasional spaces between the huge pieces of rock. Excellent views, which get better and better as you ascend, are available almost from the beginning of the scramble. On a sunny day, the startling white of the rocks, the blue of the sky, and the green of the trees below are a wonderful contrast. The last hurdle of the climb is a cleft where it might be useful to remove your packs, handing them up to your fellow hikers, before tackling the chimney itself. Once having overcome this last

obstacle, the trail becomes easy and, turning right, leads to the summit of the crag, where the views are extensive.

Walk out to the end of the ridge and admire the expansive views. The Catskill Mountains are prominent on a clear day, and the valleys of the Rondout, the Wallkill, and the Hudson can be seen. The village of New Paltz may be seen below to the southeast. The crag's summit is not that high at only 1,194 feet, but it's a fabulous place for lunch, relaxation, and contemplation of your achievement in reaching this place the difficult way.

The hard work is now over, and the remainder of the trip uses more traditional trails. Turn back toward the way you came, and, bearing right, pick up the yellow blazes of the Bonticou Ascent Path, which heads north, descending through pines and laurels to end at a junction with the blue-blazed Northeast Trail.

Turn right onto the Northeast Trail, which climbs through mountain laurel and heads north along a ridge. In about 0.3 mile, the trail shifts to the north side of the ridge and emerges on an outcrop of fractured conglomerate rock, known as the Northeast Crags, which offers a spectacular unobstructed view over the Catskill Mountains. Continuing along the ridge, the trail descends—first gradually, with many views to the left, then more steeply—to its end at Clearwater Road.

Turn left, cross a bridge over a stream, and continue through a low-lying area. As you walk, look up to the right, where, on a slight rise, you'll see the stone ruins of an old homestead, the home of the Peter Stokes family in the late 1700s. The site was subsequently bequeathed to the Mohonk Preserve by his descendants.

Continue walking on the wide Clearwater Road, climbing gradually. Bear right at a fork near the crest of the rise and begin to descend, with a stone wall on the left, then turn left at a cairn and a sign indicating a junction with the Table Rocks Trail and the Farm Road. These two trails run concurrently for a very short distance, and either route would take you back to your car. However, the Table Rocks Trail is the more interesting route.

Within a few minutes, bear right onto the Table Rocks Trail, leaving the Farm Road, which continues ahead. Soon the trail emerges into the open, with a row of cedars on the right and open fields on the left. Near the end of the fields, Farm Road briefly rejoins, but be alert for another fork and continue to follow the Table Rocks Trail, which reenters the woods, crosses a bridge, and begins a slight ascent on a footpath to a junction with the red-blazed Cedar Trail. Turn sharply right here to continue on the Table Rocks Trail. The trail now descends, passing the Slingerland Pavilion, below on the right, then levels off and crosses Spring Farm Road.

Continuing ahead, Table Rocks Trail now traverses two lovely fields. At the end of the first field, it passes through a gap in a tree hedge, and it crosses the second field diagonally to the right. Milkweed is abundant here, and another great view of the Devil's Path in the Catskills can be seen to the right of the trail, just prior to accessing the gravel path leading back to the parking lot. You should recognize this final section of the hike because you walked this way on your outgoing journey.

VI. The North Country and the Catskills

Introducing the North Country and the Catskills

"North Country" is a term usually more aptly applied to New York's great Adirondack Forest Preserve; we use the term as a catch-all for those hikes that don't quite fit any of the other sections in this book. Our north country is a large geographic expanse that includes some state parks, small semipublic preserves, and the vastness of the Catskill Forest Preserve.

These hikes provide genuine diversity: two fire towers, a point common to three states, a spectacular 500-foot-high cliff, overhanging limestone cliffs, and four of the highest peaks in the Catskills.

In this section, 6 of the 12 hikes are in the Catskills. We could write a *Fifty Hikes* book on the Catskills alone. With more than 300,000 publicly owned acres, more than 300 miles of marked hiking trails, and 35 summits over 3,500 feet, this area is truly a hiker and backpacker paradise.

Keep in mind that hiking in the Catskills is much more rugged than in areas farther south. Weather conditions are usually more inclement, so it's important to include additional clothing and extra snacks in your day pack and wear sturdy boots. At the higher elevations, snow can last well into May—even if you haven't seen any all season at home.

The Catskill Mountains are our region's most popular backpacking area. Note that neither open fires nor camping are permitted above 3,500 feet (although camping is allowed at any elevation during winter months). The New York–New Jersey Trail Conference's Catskill Trails map set is a must if you go backpacking. The maps have an outline of the camping rules on their reverse sides for easy reference. There are also more traditional state campgrounds that are available seasonally (see www.dec.ny.gov/outdoor/camping.html).

The Catskill Park is outlined with a blue line on official New York State maps, and the entire park covers over 700,000 acres. The state-owned lands in the Catskill Park, known as the Catskill Forest Preserve, are managed by the New York State Department of Environmental Conservation (see this book's introduction for contact information).

If you find yourself interested in scaling the summits of all the Catskills' 35 major peaks, you're a candidate for the Catskill 3500 Club. For more information, go to www.catskill-3500-club.org.

We hope these 12 hikes whet your appetite for the many additional offerings available "up north."

39

Black Creek Preserve

Total distance: 2.5 miles

Walking time: 1.5 hours

Vertical rise: 300 feet

*Maps: USGS 7.5' Hyde Park;
Black Creek Preserve (trail map
available online from Scenic Hudson
at www.scenichudson.org)*

*Trailhead GPS Coordinates:
N 41° 49' 11" W 73° 57' 50"*

The nonprofit organization Scenic Hudson was formed in 1963 to spearhead and co-ordinate environmental organizations to fight the plan by the Consolidated Edison Company (Con Ed) to build a stored energy facility on Storm King Mountain. The Con Ed scheme included the construction of a large reservoir in Black Rock Forest, a pumping station at the base of the mountain, and tall transmission towers crossing the Hudson River into Putnam County. The controversy continued for 17 years, until the utility company, under unrelenting pressure, dropped its plans for the project. Scenic Hudson has preserved nearly 30,000 acres in the Hudson Valley and has created or enhanced over 50 parks, including the Black Creek Preserve, Shaupeneak Ridge (Hike 40), and Indian Hill (Hike 27).

Although comparatively short, this hike has much of interest. The breeze from the Hudson and the tree canopy on a hot summer's day when energy levels are low is very welcome. Prior land use by man is evident along the way, mostly in the form of stone walls. The hike follows the yellow-blazed Black Creek Trail, the red-blazed Vernal Pool Trail, the blue-blazed Hudson River Trail, and the red-blazed Old Farm Road.

Black Creek gets its name from the dark color of its water, caused by tannic acid from hemlocks. The creek flows north for almost 20 miles from its source at Sunset Lake, passing through Chodikee Lake on its way to the Hudson River. Those seeking a longer hike in the area can combine this hike with Hike 40 (Shaupeneak Ridge)—less than 1 mile away.

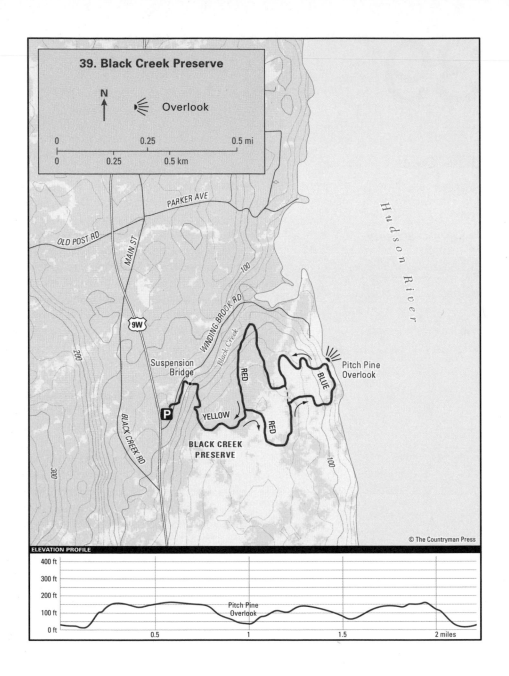

39. Black Creek Preserve

N

Overlook

0   0.25   0.5 mi
0   0.25   0.5 km

PARKER AVE

OLD POST RD

MAIN ST

Hudson River

100

9W

WINDING BROOK RD

Black Creek

200

Suspension Bridge

RED

BLUE

Pitch Pine Overlook

P

YELLOW

RED

300

BLACK CREEK RD

BLACK CREEK PRESERVE

100

© The Countryman Press

ELEVATION PROFILE

400 ft
300 ft
200 ft
100 ft
0 ft

Pitch Pine Overlook

0.5   1   1.5   2 miles

HOW TO GET THERE

From the intersection of US 9W and NY 299, proceed north on US 9W for 5.4 miles and turn right onto Winding Brook Road at a large sign reading WINDING BROOK ACRES ON THE HUDSON. Immediately bear left at the sign for the Black Creek Preserve and park in the parking area. (If coming from the north, proceed south on US 9W for 6.3 miles from the traffic light in Port Ewen, and turn left onto Winding Brook Road.)

THE TRAIL

From the kiosk at the end of the parking area, cross the road and follow the yellow-blazed Black Creek Trail, which goes under a picturesque archway and briefly parallels Black Creek. It soon turns right and crosses the creek on a 120-foot suspension bridge.

On the other side of the bridge, the Black Creek Trail climbs on switchbacks, traversing puncheons and rock steps along the way. After climbing about 160 vertical feet, you'll pass a kiosk just below the crest of the rise. The trail now bears left and levels off. It passes a vernal pool, known as Hemlock Pool, on the right (vernal pools are usually evident only in the spring), then bears left and begins a gradual descent. It crosses a small stream on a wooden footbridge and passes a kiosk with exhibits on the adjacent fenced deer exclosure.

Just beyond, a triple-yellow blaze marks the end of the Black Creek Trail at a junction with the red-blazed Vernal Pool Trail. The trail ahead will be your return route, but for now turn right and follow the sign indicating the way to the Hudson River. The red-blazed trail climbs over a small rise and passes

Pitch Pine Overlook along the Hudson River

DANIEL CHAZIN

Suspension bridge over Black Creek   DANIEL CHAZIN

several vernal pools. Soon the trail turns left and begins to parallel a stone wall. It swings through a gap in the wall, then continues to parallel the other side of the wall.

At the end of the stone wall, a triple-blue blaze marks the start of the Hudson River Trail. Turn right and follow the blue blazes downhill, with glimpses of the Hudson River through the trees. Soon you'll reach the shore of the river. You'll want to take a break here to savor the panoramic views across the river, where Mills-Norrie State Park is located. You might see an Amtrak train along the tracks on the other side of the river.

The trail continues along the river, soon reaching Pitch Pine Overlook—a jagged rock outcrop, with an attractive pitch pine

growing on the water's edge. This is another good spot to take a break.

When you're ready to continue, follow the blue blazes uphill. Note that the property to the right is private and off-limits to hikers. The Hudson River Trail climbs on switchbacks to reach a junction with the red-blazed Vernal Pool Trail. Turn right onto this red-blazed trail, which curves to the right and heads north, parallel to the river, with glimpses of the river through the trees on the right.

In 0.25 mile, the trail bends sharply left and follows the Old Farm Road (still blazed red), now heading south. After passing through an attractive hemlock grove, you'll reach a junction with the yellow-blazed Black Creek Trail. Continue ahead on the Black Creek Trail, retracing your footsteps to your car.

40

Shaupeneak Ridge

Total distance: 5.5 miles

Walking time: 4 hours

Vertical rise: 1,350 feet

Maps: USGS 7.5' Hyde Park; USGS 7.5' Rosendale; Shaupeneak Ridge (trail map available online at www.scenic hudson.org)

Trailhead GPS Coordinates: N 41° 49' 38" W 73° 58' 14"

The Shaupeneak Ridge Cooperative Recreation Area is administered jointly by Scenic Hudson, the New York State Department of Environmental Conservation (DEC), and a local sportsmen's group (the West Esopus Landowners' Association). Beginning in 1994, the property was acquired by the Scenic Hudson Land Trust, and the tract was opened to the public in 1996.

Shaupeneak Ridge is part of the Marlboro Mountains, a discontinuous ridge extending from Kingston to Marlboro along the western side of the Hudson River. The terrain is quite rugged and includes streams, a waterfall, and a pond—all of which are visited on this hike. The hike includes a number of short sharp climbs, and it begins and ends with a substantial ascent and descent on the White Trail. The hike described here follows the White, Purple, Red, and Blue Trails.

If you are looking for a longer hike, you could add the Orange or Green Trails to your hike. Both of these trails loop around the western end of the preserve and run close to the edges of interesting escarpments. Although they were constructed by mountain bike groups (and mountain bikes are allowed on the trails in this preserve), no mountain bikes were encountered on these (or other) trails during a recent visit to the preserve.

HOW TO GET THERE

From the intersection of US 9W and NY 299, proceed north on US 9W for 6 miles and turn left onto County Route 16 (Old Post Road). In 0.2 mile, you'll cross an active CSX rail line. Just beyond, turn right into

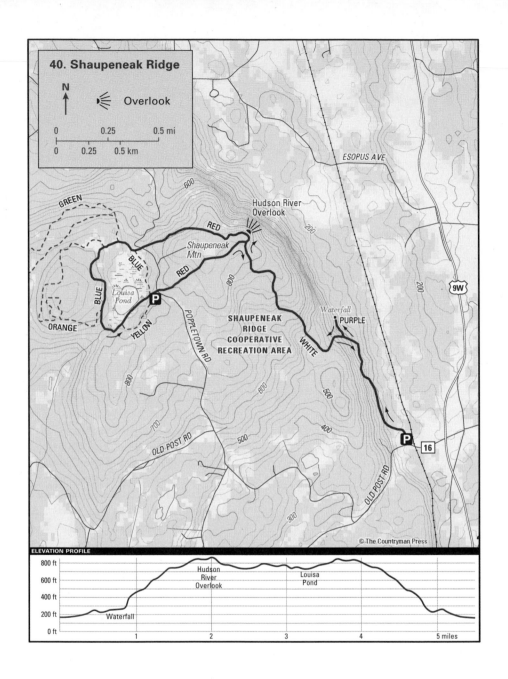

40. Shaupeneak Ridge

N

Overlook

| 0 | 0.25 | 0.5 mi |
| 0 | 0.25 | 0.5 km |

GREEN

Hudson River
Overlook

ESOPUS AVE

RED

Shaupeneak
Mtn

BLUE

RED

BLUE

Louisa
Pond

Waterfall

PURPLE

9W

ORANGE

YELLOW

SHAUPENEAK
RIDGE
COOPERATIVE
RECREATION AREA

WHITE

POPPLETOWN RD

OLD POST RD

OLD POST RD

16

© The Countryman Press

ELEVATION PROFILE

		Hudson		Louisa	
800 ft		River		Pond	
600 ft		Overlook			
400 ft					
200 ft	Waterfall				
0 ft					
	1	2	3	4	5 miles

Waterfall along the Purple Trail

DANIEL CHAZIN

the parking area for Shaupeneak Ridge. (If coming from the north, proceed south on US 9W for 5.7 miles from the traffic light in Port Ewen, and turn right onto County Route 16.)

THE TRAIL

From the kiosk at the end of the parking area, where maps are usually available, proceed uphill on the gravel path which curves to the left, then bears right and enters the woods. It runs along the base of a hill for about 0.3 mile, then begins to climb. Here the first white blazes appear. You'll be following the White Trail to the crest of the ridge.

After passing through a gap in a stone wall, the trail descends and continues along the base of the hill, but it soon bears left and begins a steady climb. A short distance up the slope, you'll notice a purple trail blaze on the right. Turn right onto the Purple Trail, which parallels a stone wall along a contour. In 500 feet, it reaches an attractive waterfall which cascades over a huge moss-covered boulder. You'll want to stop here to enjoy this special feature of the hike.

When you're ready to continue, retrace your steps to the White Trail and turn right, uphill. The White Trail snakes its way uphill alongside a cascading stream that feeds the main falls below. At the crest of the rise, the trail turns right, crosses the stream on a split-log bridge, and levels off. The trail passes a vernal pool on the right and soon resumes its steady climb.

After passing several rock outcrops on the left, the White Trail ends at a junction with the Red Trail. Bear right and continue ahead on the Red Trail, which almost immediately reaches the Hudson River Overlook—a large flat rock outcrop on the right. The castlelike building visible below served for over a century as the Mount St. Alphonsus seminary and retreat center of the Redemptorist Fathers. In 2012, the property was acquired by the Bruderhof of Rifton, New York, which has converted the building to a high school for its community. You'll want to rest here from your 600-foot climb from the waterfall and take in the panoramic views.

When you're ready to continue, proceed ahead on the Red Trail, which undulates along the ridge and eventually reaches Poppletown Road. The trail crosses the road and, just beyond, ends at a junction with the Blue Trail near the shore of Louisa Pond, visible through the trees on the left. The pond was created in a glacially carved bowl by several dams, constructed by both beavers and humans. On this side, the pond is an emergent marsh—a sensitive environmental area that should not be disturbed.

Continue ahead, following the Blue Trail in a counterclockwise direction around the pond. After paralleling the trail for a short distance, the road goes off to the right. The

View from the Hudson River Overlook

DANIEL CHAZIN

The North Country and the Catskills

Blue Trail now moves away from the pond and passes the trailhead of the Green Trail on the right. It crosses a boardwalk over a wet area and enters a hemlock grove, where the Orange Trail begins on the right.

The Blue Trail now bears right and climbs high above the pond, then descends to just above the level of the pond and begins to parallel it. It climbs again to a junction with the other end of the Orange Trail, then descends to cross the outlet of the pond on rocks just below a beaver dam. Dutchman's breeches and the white-and-lavender, round-lobed hepatica bloom here in early spring.

The Blue Trail climbs to a hemlock grove and continues along a grassy path and across puncheons to an open area, where steps on the left lead downhill to the pond. Just beyond, a wooden bench along the trail offers a broad view of the pond. Proceed ahead on a wide gravel path and pass two more benches on the left before reaching the Louisa Pond parking area, with a kiosk.

From the parking area, cross Poppletown Road and find the triple blaze that marks the start of the Red Trail. Continue ahead on the Red Trail, which climbs gently on a grassy woods road and continues on a rocky footpath to the crest of the ridge. The Red Trail descends on a wide path, crosses a boardwalk over a wet area, and continues along undulating terrain to a junction with the White Trail just before the Hudson River Overlook (which you might want to visit again before beginning the long descent back to your car). Turn right onto the White Trail and follow it downhill back to the parking area where the hike began.

A short distance south, on the east side of US 9W, is the Black Creek Preserve (Hike 39), which you might want to combine with this hike if time permits.

41

Stissing Mountain

Total distance: 4.5 to 1.7 miles

Walking time: 3 to 1.5 hours

Vertical rise: 920 feet

Maps: USGS 7.5' Pine Plains

Trailhead GPS Coordinates:
N 41° 58' 12" W 73° 40' 55"

At New York City's world-famous American Museum of Natural History is a large diorama in the popular Warburg Hall of Agriculture entitled *An October Afternoon near Stissing Mountain.* The information display reads, "This area of New York State was selected as a basis for [this] hall because it has mountains, natural lakes, forests, a variety of rock formations and both wild and cultivated land." Now you'll get to appreciate it firsthand.

Stissing Mountain's long profile so dominates the surrounding fields that the mountain appears taller than its 1,403-foot height would indicate. The fields—remnants of a glacial lake—encircle this Precambrian gneiss outcrop, enhancing its scale. A pair of trails leads to the restored fire tower on the summit ridge, making a loop walk possible. There are expansive views from the top of the fire tower, although on the way up, views are limited to openings in the forest cover.

The hike up the mountain can be combined with a delightful walk around Thompson Pond, just below the mountain. The pond is part of a kettle lake, formed—along with Stissing and Mud Ponds—by the melting of glacial blocks. The resulting bog pond, filled with grasses and cattails, is now home to many birds. From the path that winds along its shores, not only can you watch the birds, but you'll also be treated to views of Stissing Mountain across the marshes as the mountain rises steeply from the level of the lake.

The pond and 300 acres are managed as a preserve by The Nature Conservancy. The

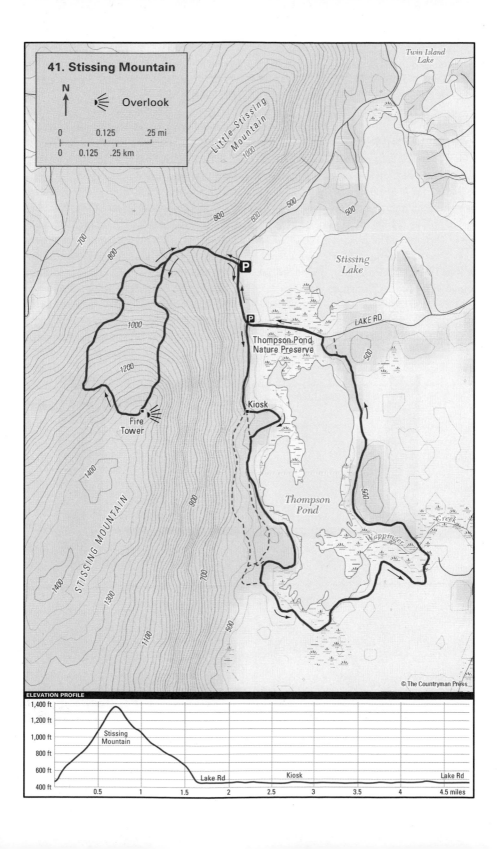

41. Stissing Mountain

N

Overlook

| 0 | 0.125 | .25 mi |
| 0 | 0.125 | .25 km |

Twin Island Lake

Little Stissing Mountain

1000

800

500

500

700

800

P

P

1000

Stissing Lake

LAKE RD

Thompson Pond Nature Preserve

500

1200

Kiosk

Fire Tower

1400

900

500

Thompson Pond

STISSING MOUNTAIN

Wappinger

Creek

1300

1100

500

500

© The Countryman Press

ELEVATION PROFILE

1,400 ft									
1,200 ft									
1,000 ft	Stissing Mountain								
800 ft									
600 ft			Lake Rd		Kiosk				Lake Rd
400 ft									
	0.5	1	1.5	2	2.5	3	3.5	4	4.5 miles

area is home to many mammals, migrating warblers, and marsh birds, plus a rich variety of plants that find their niches in areas as varied as the pond and the adjacent wooded slopes of Stissing Mountain.

HOW TO GET THERE

From the intersection of NY 82 and NY 199 in the center of Pine Plains, proceed south on NY 82 for 0.3 mile and turn right onto Lake Road (a firehouse is located at this intersection). In 1.4 miles, you will see a sign for the Thompson Pond Nature Preserve on the left, and in another 0.2 mile you will see another Thompson Pond sign on the left (at a curve in the road). Continue ahead for 0.1 mile (1.7 miles from NY 82) to a small parking turnout on the right, with a signpost for the LAKE ROAD TRAILHEAD at the parking area

and a Thompson Pond Nature Preserve sign across the road, where the trail begins.

THE TRAIL

The trails up Stissing Mountain from Lake Road are not marked, but they are quite obvious and can be easily followed. From the trailhead on the west side of Lake Road, head into the woods on a steep, rocky footpath. In about 200 feet, you'll come to a fork in the trail, where you bear left. Then, in about five minutes, you'll reach an intersection with an old woods road. Turn left onto the woods road, which soon becomes quite steep and rocky.

In another five minutes, you'll reach another fork in the trail, with a tree in the middle of the fork and many rocks piled in front of it. The right fork will be your return route,

Twin Island Lake from the Stissing Fire Tower

DANIEL CHAZIN

The North Country and the Catskills

but for now bear left and continue to follow the woods road up the mountain. Soon the grade moderates a little and the trail becomes less rocky, but a short distance beyond, the steep climb resumes. Along the way, you'll catch some views through the trees to the left of the trail.

After about half an hour of steep climbing (from the last intersection), you'll pass stone steps to the right of the trail (a remnant of the fire observer's cabin) and reach the summit ridge. Just ahead is the fire tower. There are no views from the base of the tower, but you'll want to climb the tower to take in the spectacular views.

This 90-foot-high steel fire tower was built by the Civilian Conservation Corps (CCC) in 1934. It was last used in 1973 for spotting fires. In 1986, the State of New York announced that the tower was no longer needed and would be removed. Concerned citizens formed the Friends of Stissing Landmarks (FOSL) to take over responsibility for the fire tower and keep it open for public use. In 1994, the tower was donated to FOSL, which is currently responsible for its maintenance. Unlike many other fire towers which have a locked cabin at the top, the cabin at the top of the Stissing fire tower is open to the public at all times.

From the tower, you can see the Catskills to the west. Twin Island Lake, Stissing Pond, and Thompson Pond may be seen directly below. Massachusetts is visible to the northeast and Connecticut to the east. Portions of the northern end of the Shawangunks are visible to the southwest. On the clearest days, you can see as far as Albany to the northwest.

After taking in the panoramic views, descend the tower and head south (straight ahead) along the summit ridge. In about two minutes, bear right and descend a narrow footpath, then turn left at the next intersection and descend to a woods road. Turn right onto this rocky road, which descends steeply. It might be hard to believe, but this road was used by the forest fire observer to drive up to the tower when it was in operation. After a while, the road bears right, passes rock ledges on the right, and continues to descend more gradually on a less rocky route. You'll come to a number of forks and intersections; in each case, bear right and stay on the woods road.

About half an hour after leaving the fire tower, you'll come to the fork you passed on the climb, with the tree in the middle and rocks piled up in front of it. Turn left here, now retracing your steps. At the next fork, bear right and descend the final pitch to Lake Road and your car.

OPTIONS

To add to the excursion, walk back along the road for 0.1 mile to the marked Thompson Pond Nature Preserve entrance. Thompson Pond was designated a National Natural Landmark in 1973. Managed by The Nature Conservancy, Thompson Pond is, according to the conservancy's website, "an excellent example of a calcareous (or limy) wetland that abounds with a variety of wildlife . . . 387 plant species, 162 bird species and 27 mammal species." The 2.5-mile-long yellow-blazed trail that loops around the pond is mostly flat, with some minor ups and downs—a welcome contrast to the steep climb and descent of Stissing Mountain, which looms in the background for much of the hike around the pond.

A yellow-blazed woods road leads you south into the sanctuary, and in 0.3 mile from the start, you'll reach a kiosk with a trail map. Turn left here onto a blue-blazed trail, which loops around to the east, with views of the pond. In 0.2 mile, you'll reach the end of this blue-blazed trail. Turn left onto the

Thompson Pond from the Stissing Fire Tower   DANIEL CHAZIN

yellow-blazed trail, which soon enters a hemlock grove. A short distance ahead, another blue-blazed trail forks to the right, but you should continue ahead on the yellow-blazed trail, which narrows to a footpath and runs close to the shore of the pond. You'll pass several stone benches that honor individuals who were instrumental in establishing this preserve.

Toward the south end of a peninsula jutting into the lake, the yellow-blazed trail bears right, away from the pond. It crosses a stone wall by a huge oak tree, bears left, and runs along a field, with views of Stissing Mountain to the right. The trail now begins to loop around the southern end of Thompson Pond, soon passing another field on the

right, with more views of Stissing Mountain in the background. It then heads downhill and crosses a large wetland on a boardwalk. Soon the trail loops around and passes an active livestock farm on the right. Just beyond, it crosses the headwaters of Wappinger Creek on a wooden bridge.

The trail now heads back closer to the pond. Looking across the pond, you can see Stissing Mountain, with the fire tower that you just climbed clearly visible on the right. The trail again parallels a field to the right, then bears left and returns to Lake Road. Turn left and follow Lake Road for 0.2 mile to the trailhead of the yellow-blazed trail, then continue along the road for another 0.1 mile to the parking turnout where you left your car.

42

Ashokan High Point

Total distance: 9 miles
Walking time: 6 hours
Vertical rise: 2,167 feet
Maps: USGS 7.5' West Shokan; NY–NJTC Catskill Trails #143
Trailhead GPS Coordinates: N 41° 56' 09" W 74° 19' 41"

Ashokan High Point (3,080 feet) is not one of the highest mountains in the Catskill Park, but the climb to the summit involves an elevation gain of about 2,000 feet–significantly greater than the elevation gained when climbing many of the higher peaks. The first part of the hike follows the swiftly flowing Kanape Brook. The vistas from the many viewpoints are stunning, and in fall, when the blueberry bushes turn bright crimson, the colors are stupendous.

This "lollipop-loop" hike, located within the Sundown Wild Forest, follows the red blazes of the Ashokan High Point Trail. As of this writing, trail markers are often sparse, but the footpath is usually fairly obvious, and blazes are present at all important junctions.

The Sundown Wild Forest forms the south and southeasterly border of the Catskill Park. At one time the area was heavily forested with very tall hemlocks, which prevented light from reaching the forest floor. Consequently, it appeared that the sun was always setting, hence the name "Sundown." It is believed that Kanape Brook was named after one of the first farmers in the area, John Jones Canape, and that the road you follow up the mountain took its name from another early farmer named Orson Avery.

This area has experienced more large fires than any other part of the Catskills. As far back as 1891, fires were started on the southeast slopes of Ashokan High Point and on the banks of Kanape Brook by local berry pickers. These fires ensured that the blueberry bushes would be sturdy and the crop abundant. Repeated burns typically created

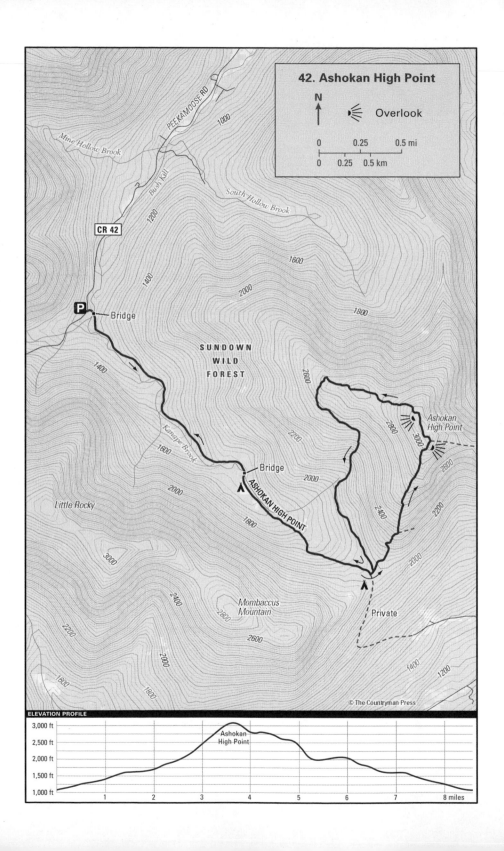

42. Ashokan High Point

N

☀ Overlook

| 0 | 0.25 | 0.5 mi |
| 0 | 0.25 | 0.5 km |

PEEKAMOOSE RD

1000

Mine Hollow Brook

South Hollow Brook

Bush Kill

1200

CR 42

1600

1400

2000

1800

P — Bridge

1400

SUNDOWN
WILD
FOREST

2600

2800

3000

Ashokan
High Point

2600

Kanape Brook

2200

2400

2200

1600

Bridge

ASHOKAN HIGH POINT

2000

2000

Little Rocky

2000

1800

3000

2400

Mombaccus
Mountain

2800

2600

Private

2200

2000

1800

1400

1200

1600

1800

2000

© The Countryman Press

ELEVATION PROFILE

Ashokan
High Point

3,000 ft

2,500 ft

2,000 ft

1,500 ft

1,000 ft

1   2   3   4   5   6   7   8 miles

View from Ashokan High Point

DANIELA WAGSTAFF

the pitch pine–oak heath tracts found on the rocky summit.

HOW TO GET THERE

Take the New York State Thruway (I-87) to Exit 19 (Kingston). Proceed west on NY 28 for 16 miles to Boiceville, and turn left onto NY 28A, which immediately crosses Esopus Creek. (Note: Do not turn left at the first intersection of NY 28 with NY 28A in West Hurley.) Proceed 2.9 miles to Olive, turn right onto County Route 42 (Peekamoose Road), and continue for 4 miles to the Kanape Brook parking area (with a kiosk and an outhouse), on the right side of the road.

THE TRAIL

Follow the entrance road to the parking area back to Peekamoose Road, cross the road, and turn left. In 200 feet, you'll notice a red New York State Department of Environmental Conservation (DEC) disc on a tree to the right. You'll be following the red-blazed Ashokan High Point Trail for the entire hike (you'll also see along the route occasional yellow discs that indicate that the first part of the hike follows a designated cross-country ski trail).

Turn right and walk down to a wooden bridge over the Bush Kill, just below its confluence with Kanape Brook. This 60-foot-long bridge was built by the DEC in 2012 to replace a previous bridge that was washed away by Hurricane Irene in August 2011. A short distance beyond, you'll come to a trail register (please sign).

The trail now begins to follow the old Freeman Avery Road along Kanape Brook, with the road high on the hillside above the brook for most of the way. This road was constructed in the 19th century as a route over the mountain linking Peekamoose Road with Upper Samsonville Road. It was improved by the Civilian Conservation Corps (CCC) in the 1930s and is still in very good condition, now serving as an attractive route for hikers and skiers (in winter). Soon you'll notice a culvert built from bluestone slabs. This culvert dates back to the original construction of the road (most other stone culverts along the road have been replaced with metal pipes).

After about 1 mile, the road becomes narrower for a while, and mountain laurel begins to appear. At 1.3 miles, you'll notice on the left an interesting stone-walled spring. After passing through dense mountain laurel thickets, the trail curves to the right, descends a little, and crosses Kanape Brook on a wooden bridge at 1.6 miles. Just beyond, there is a campsite on the right. Although it is located close to the stream, camping here is permitted because it has been officially designated as a campsite by the DEC. You may note an apple tree growing alongside the campsite—possibly a survivor of John Canape's apple orchard.

The trail now levels off and continues through groves of Norway spruce and hemlock. After crossing a tributary stream on a wooden footbridge, it resumes its gentle climb. Then, about 1 mile from the crossing of Kanape Brook, you'll pass through an attractive forest of mountain laurel, hemlock, and white pine and reach a trail junction in an open area marked by a wooden sign (the elevation here is about 2,100 feet). Straight ahead, the road passes another designated campsite and crosses into private property (closed to the public). The campsite, which has a large fire ring, is a good place to rest (note the interesting cable stretched between two trees). When you're ready to continue, return to the junction and head north

View of Catskills from open area with fire ring

DANIELA WAGSTAFF

The North Country and the Catskills

on the trail, following the wooden trail sign and the red DEC discs.

In 150 feet, you'll notice a trail, also blazed red, that goes off to the left. This trail will be your return route, but for now, continue straight ahead. The trail proceeds through stands of mountain laurel, following an old road that has largely narrowed to a footpath. You'll notice many stone waterbars along the way.

At first, the trail ascends gradually, but the ascent quickly steepens. You'll be climbing about 1,000 feet in elevation in little over 1 mile. Along the way, a woods road goes down to the right and an unmarked trail continues ahead as the main trail turns left. In each case, bear left and continue to follow the red blazes.

At about 2,600 feet in elevation, you'll notice rock ledges directly in front of you. Here the character of the trail changes. The trail climbs five separate rock ledges with the aid of rock steps and traverses relatively level sections between the ledges. Between the fourth and fifth ledges you'll notice an interesting overhanging rock on the left that could provide shelter in inclement weather.

After climbing one more short ledge, you'll reach the summit of Ashokan High Point (3,080 feet), 3.8 miles from the start. The view from the summit has grown in somewhat, but if the sky is clear, you'll be able to take in a panoramic southeast-facing view, with the Sky Top Tower at the Mohonk Mountain House in the Shawangunks visible in the distance. Two benchmarks, Samson I and Samson II, are embedded in the rock. Graffiti dating back to the late 1800s is carved into the rock. An unmarked herd path leads down to Little High Point, which offers even broader views, but this path may be difficult to follow and is not recommended.

After resting from your climb, turn left and follow the red-blazed trail, which heads northwest. Along the way, you'll pass a fairly large water-filled hole. This pool is called "the tidal pool" by locals because legend claims that the level of the water changes as tides rise and fall in the Hudson River. Soon you'll reach a large open area, with a large fire ring with rock-slab seating in the center. This spot affords a broad panorama to the northwest over the Burroughs Range. Some maps name this spot as Hoopole Mountain, derived from the hoop-making industry. The best hoops were made from hickory and ash trees, which appeared after the hemlocks were felled for their bark to be used in tanning. If you follow herd paths to the east, you can get limited views of the Ashokan Reservoir through the trees.

The trail now makes a sharp left-hand turn and begins to head downhill through an open deciduous forest. Soon the trail levels off and climbs over a rise. It then bears left and begins to head southeast through mountain laurel along a relatively level section. At an elevation of 2,500 feet, the trail bears right and begins a very steep descent over an old road covered with loose rocks. Use extreme care as you descend this trail section. At the base of the descent, the trail turns left, levels off, and soon begins a gradual ascent of about 150 vertical feet to return to the start of the loop.

Turn right, and walk the short distance to the junction with Freeman Avery Road, where you will recognize the trail sign you passed earlier. Turn right again, and retrace your footsteps, following the old road back to your car.

43

Table Mountain

Total distance: 8 miles

Walking time: 5 hours

Vertical rise: 2,088 feet

Maps: USGS 7.5' Claryville; USGS 7.5' Peekamoose Mountain; NY–NJTC Catskill Trails #143

Trailhead GPS Coordinates: N 41° 57' 56" W 74° 27' 8.5"

The hike described uses parts of Phoenicia–East Branch (yellow) and Peekamoose-Table (blue) Trails and heads to the summit of Table Mountain for an out-and-back trip. At 3,847 feet, Table Mountain is the 11th highest in the Catskills and is easy to spot from a distance because of its "tabletop" appearance. On its way north from the George Washington Bridge to the Mohawk River, the Long Path follows the entire length of the Peekamoose-Table Trail. The hike crosses the valley of the East Branch of the Neversink River and proceeds through stands of evergreens and hardwoods. The climb, although steady, is interrupted a few times by short descents.

HOW TO GET THERE

The route to the trailhead is accessed from the village of Claryville in Sullivan County, which is situated at the junction of County Route 19 and County Route 157, and may be approached from several directions. From Claryville, proceed northeast on Denning Road (County Route 19) for 8 miles until the road ends at the Denning parking area. A sawmill once operated in this locality. While driving, you will pass the Straus Center on the right-hand side. This building is thought to be the oldest in the town of Denning and is now used year-round by the Frost Valley YMCA. Just before the parking area, look for an attractive structure and gardens in Japanese style. This house, called "Grey Lodge" after the rough-sawn chestnut used in its construction, and its gardens were created in 1903 by Alexander Tison, a professor of

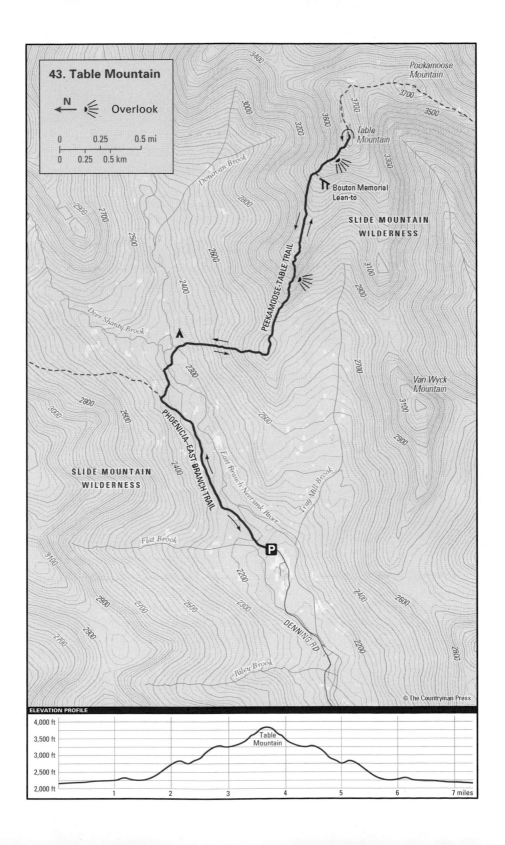

43. Table Mountain

N ← 🔆 Overlook

| 0 | 0.25 | 0.5 mi |
| 0 | 0.25 | 0.5 km |

Peekamoose
Mountain

Table
Mountain

Bouton Memorial
Lean-to

SLIDE MOUNTAIN
WILDERNESS

Donovan Brook

PEEKAMOOSE-TABLE TRAIL

Deer Shanty Brook

Van Wyck
Mountain

SLIDE MOUNTAIN
WILDERNESS

PHOENICIA-EAST BRANCH TRAIL

East Branch Neversink River

Fray Mill Brook

Flat Brook

P

DENNING RD

Riley Brook

© The Countryman Press

ELEVATION PROFILE

Table
Mountain

| | 1 | 2 | 3 | 4 | 5 | 6 | 7 miles |

Hikers crossing bridge over East Branch of the Neversink River

DANIEL CHAZIN

law at the University of Tokyo and the first president of the Japan Society in New York City. Watch for the many deer that frequent the sides of Denning Road.

As you drive, you may notice yellow trail markers on telephone poles along the road. These markers are reminders of the time when the official end of the Phoenicia–East Branch Trail was in Claryville. Older trails laid out during the 1920s and 1930s often began at a town, but these road walks are no longer considered part of the marked hiking trails.

A kiosk is located at the trailhead, with a register box where you should sign in (and out on your return).

THE TRAIL

Walk around the yellow-painted gate, and follow the yellow New York State Department of Environmental Conservation (DEC) discs of the Phoenicia–East Branch Trail as it climbs slowly on a wide woods road. The trail follows the route of the old turnpike to Woodland Valley via Winnisook, which was built between 1880 and 1892. This route was not particularly popular because of its roughness and the high pass at about 3,000 feet, which in winter was often closed by snow.

In about 1 mile, after crossing a wooden bridge, turn right onto the blue-blazed Peekamoose-Table Trail and head downhill on a footpath. You'll pass the site of the former Denning Lean-to, which was removed because it was too close to a major stream and replaced by a new lean-to further up the mountain. In 0.3 mile from the trail junction, you'll cross substantial bridges over Deer Shanty Brook and the East Branch of the Neversink River. For many years, these stream crossings were quite problematic. Makeshift log bridges were installed, only to be washed away by spring or fall floods. At

times, the crossings were dangerous or impassable. Finally the DEC constructed two substantial bridges high above the stream, one of which has steel beams. The bridges were damaged during Hurricane Irene in August 2011, but they have been repaired by the DEC, and the stream crossings are now easily negotiated in all conditions.

On the other side of the bridge, the trail begins to climb, at first through a hemlock grove and then through hardwoods. In a short distance, a yellow sign points to a campsite on the left. This large campsite is one of the most attractive in the Catskills, and you might want to consider staying there if you're planning an overnight trip. In springtime, the ground is carpeted with trout lilies and other wildflowers. Expect to find occasional short descents on the way up. The square-shaped rock to the right of the first drop has been named "Sugar-Cube Rock."

At about the 3,180-foot elevation, a short side trail on the right leads to a spectacular viewpoint from the edge of a cliff. The view is to the south and southwest across the Catskill Divide, with Van Wyck Mountain predominating. The summit of Table Mountain can also be seen.

About 2 miles from the start of the Peekamoose-Table Trail, look for a piped spring to the north (left) of the trail. This water source is not dependable as it dries up periodically in dry weather.

The short side trail to the Bouton Memorial Lean-to is 0.1 mile farther up the Peekamoose-Table Trail. You'll want to take a break here before climbing the remaining—and a little more strenuous—0.2 mile to the summit. The lean-to was built in 1999 by volunteers, together with DEC staff, and was named in memory of Frank Bouton, a longtime member of the Adirondack Mountain Club's Ramapo Chapter and a dedicated trail maintainer of the Curtis-Ormsbee Trail.

Panoramic view just below the summit of Table Mountain   DANIEL CHAZIN

The remaining climb is short but steep. Soon you'll pass the 3,500-foot sign. Just below the summit, a short side trail to the right leads to another panoramic viewpoint. The nearly level summit is dressed with small balsam fir, making a charming tunnel for the walker—particularly beautiful in winter when snow decorates the branches. The actual summit is located at the western end of the flat ridge, just before a slight turn in the trail to the right. At one time, there was a canister atop Table Mountain (it was the only trailed peak with a canister), but the canister was removed in 1990. The bracket that once attached the canister to the tree remains, however, so the location of the former canister can still be ascertained. There are no views from the summit.

The trail continues toward Peekamoose Mountain, but the summit of Table Mountain is the turnaround point for this hike. Retrace your footsteps back to your car.

44

Hunter Mountain

Total distance: 8 miles

Walking time: 6 hours

Vertical rise: 2,000 feet

Maps: USGS 7.5' Hunter; USGS 7.5' Lexington; NY–NJTC Catskill Trails #141

Trailhead GPS Coordinates: N 42° 11' 06" W 74° 16' 20"

Hunter Mountain is the second highest mountain in the Catskills (4,040 feet). It is one of only five Catskill peaks with a fire tower on its summit. This hike climbs the mountain on a woods road, formerly known as the Jones Gap Turnpike, built in 1880. For many years, this road was used by forest fire observers to access the tower. The descent is on the more rugged Devil's Path. Together with the Hunter Mountain Trail, these trails form an attractive loop. The route of the hike passes two lean-tos, so it's possible to do this hike as an overnight trip. But it also can be completed as a day trip—just allow enough time to be sure that you'll get back to your car before dark.

HOW TO GET THERE

Take the New York State Thruway (I-87) to Exit 19 (Kingston) and proceed west on NY 28 for about 28 miles to its junction with NY 42 in Shandaken. Proceed north on NY 42 for 7.4 miles to the hamlet of West Kill, then turn right and follow Spruceton Road (County Route 6) for 6.7 miles, past a dead end sign, to a large parking area for Hunter Mountain on the left side of the road.

THE TRAIL

From the parking area, proceed north on the blue-blazed Spruceton Trail, which follows a wide woods road. Soon you'll pass a trail register (please sign). In 0.5 mile, the trail crosses Hunter Brook on a wide wooden bridge, turns sharply right, and begins a gradual ascent of a shoulder of Hunter Mountain.

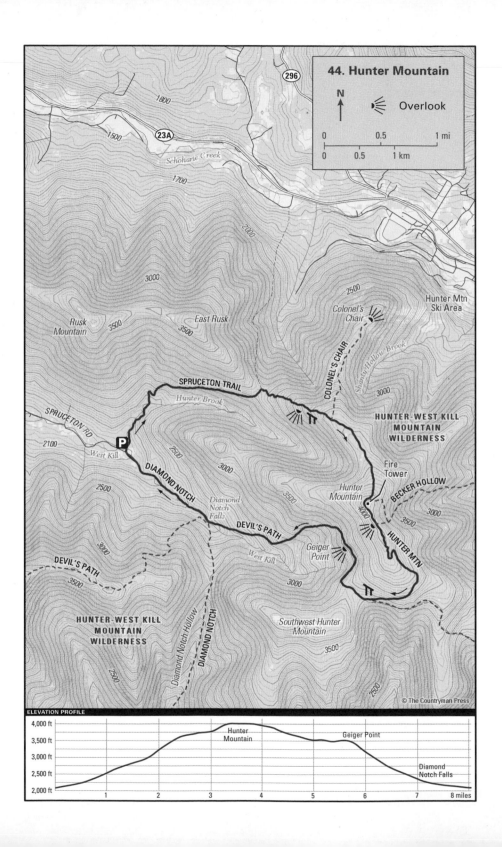

44. Hunter Mountain

N

Overlook

0   0.5   1 mi

0   0.5   1 km

296

23A

1800

1500

1700

Schoharie Creek

2000

3000

Rusk
Mountain

East Rusk

3500

3500

2500

Hunter Mtn
Ski Area

Colonel's
Chair

SPRUCETON TRAIL

Hunter Brook

COLONEL'S CHAIR

3000

Shanty Hollow Brook

HUNTER-WEST KILL
MOUNTAIN
WILDERNESS

SPRUCETON RD

2100

P

West Kill

DIAMOND NOTCH

2500

3000

2500

*Diamond
Notch
Falls*

3000

Fire
Tower

Hunter
Mountain

BECKER HOLLOW

4000

3500

3000

DEVIL'S PATH

West Kill

Geiger
Point

HUNTER MTN

DEVIL'S PATH

3500

DIAMOND NOTCH HOLLOW

DIAMOND NOTCH

HUNTER-WEST KILL
MOUNTAIN
WILDERNESS

2500

3000

Southwest Hunter
Mountain

3500

2500

© The Countryman Press

ELEVATION PROFILE

4,000 ft

3,500 ft

3,000 ft

2,500 ft

2,000 ft

Hunter
Mountain

Geiger Point

Diamond
Notch Falls

1   2   3   4   5   6   7   8 miles

After 1.7 miles of gentle uphill walking, the trail reaches a junction at a height of land, marked by a sign. The wide road continues ahead, descending to the town of Hunter, but you should turn right and follow the blue blazes, which ascend more steeply on a much rougher road. This is the steepest part of the hike. In another 0.5 mile, a sign on the trail points the way to a spring. Be particularly careful to purify the water, as this spring is sometimes used by horses.

A short distance beyond, you'll reach a sign pointing to a lean-to. Even if you're doing a day hike, you'll want to follow the yellow-blazed side trail for 500 feet to the John Robb Lean-to and a panoramic viewpoint just beyond. The lean-to was built in 2011 to replace one that burned down several years earlier. The volunteers carefully scouted out the area to find the best location for a new lean-to, and they succeeded in finding a perfect location, just below elevation 3,500 feet, with great views. You've now climbed 1,400 vertical feet from the parking area, and you'll want to take a break at this magnificent spot.

When you're ready to continue, return to the blue-blazed Spruceton Trail and turn right, resuming your uphill climb. Soon you'll reach a junction with the yellow-blazed Colonel's Chair Trail, which begins on the left and leads to the top of the chairlifts at the Hunter Mountain Ski Area. Continue ahead, following the blue blazes. The trail now levels off for a while. After some more moderate climbing, it reaches a large clearing at the summit of the mountain, with the fire tower and a fire observer's cabin. You've hiked 3.4 miles and climbed nearly 2,000 vertical feet to reach this point.

The Hunter Mountain fire tower was the first of 23 fire lookout towers built by New York State in the Catskills. It is the highest fire tower still standing in the state and the second highest in the entire Northeast, and

Hunter Mountain Fire Tower   DANIEL CHAZIN

it is listed in both the National Historic Lookout Register and the National Register of Historic Places.

The first fire tower on Hunter Mountain was a 40-foot-high wooden structure built in 1909. The current 60-foot-high tower, built of steel, was erected in 1917. The steel for the tower was hauled up the Spruceton Trail by teams of horses. Originally the tower was located about 0.3 mile further south, but in 1953 it was moved to the summit of the mountain, its current location. It was officially closed by the state in 1989, but through the efforts of volunteers, funds were raised to rehabilitate the tower, and it was formally reopened to the public in 2000.

Sunset from the John Robb Lean-to   DANIEL CHAZIN

On weekends in the summer, the tower is staffed by volunteers.

You'll want to climb the fire tower, which affords excellent views in all directions. The mountains of the Blackhead Range may be seen to the northeast, and Indian Head, Twin, Sugarloaf, and Plateau Mountains are visible to the southeast. You can see the ski trails on Hunter Mountain to the north.

After taking in the view, continue ahead on the blue-blazed trail, which proceeds through a dense spruce-fir forest. In 0.3 mile, you'll reach a trail junction at the former location of the fire tower. Here a side trail goes off to the right, leading for about 300 feet to a rock ledge with a panoramic west-facing view. The short side trip to this viewpoint is well worth it!

When you're ready to continue, return to the junction, turn right, and follow the yellow-blazed Hunter Mountain Trail, which descends gently for 1.4 miles, making two sharp turns along the way. It ends at a junction with the red-blazed Devil's Path, also marked by a sign. Continue straight ahead at this junction, and in about 250 feet, you'll reach the Devil's Acre Lean-to, just to the right of the trail. This was the site of a logging camp in the early part of the 20th century (the area was logged by the Fenwick Lumber Company between 1903 and 1917), and remnants of machinery from the logging operations are still visible in the area.

Continue ahead on the red-blazed trail, immediately crossing a stream. The trail soon curves to the right and follows a relatively level path. In 0.5 mile, a short side trail to the left leads to a rock ledge, known as Geiger Point, with excellent views over Diamond Notch below and Southwest Hunter Mountain to the left. Use extreme caution, as there is a very sharp drop from this ledge.

Return to the Devil's Path and turn left. Soon the trail bends to the left and begins to descend. For the next 1.5 miles, you'll be headed steadily downhill, with several rather rough sections. At the base of the descent, you'll cross a stream and arrive at a trail junction in an open, grassy area. Here, the Devil's Path turns left and crosses the West Kill, but you should continue straight ahead, now following the blue-blazed Diamond Notch Trail. You'll pass the attractive Diamond Notch Falls to the left and parallel the cascading West Kill.

In 0.7 mile, you'll pass a trail register and reach a cable barrier at the end of Spruceton Road. Continue ahead along the drivable road for 0.25 mile to the Hunter Mountain parking area, where you began the hike, on the right.

45

Slide Mountain

Total distance: 6.8 miles
Walking time: 5 hours
Vertical rise: 1,800 feet
Maps: USGS 7.5' Shandaken; USGS 7.5' Peekamoose Mountain; NY–NJTC Catskill Trails #143
Trailhead GPS Coordinates: N 42° 00' 31.5" W 74° 25' 39"

At 4,180 feet in elevation, Slide Mountain is the highest peak in the Catskill Mountains. The name was taken from a landslide in 1819, and a proposal was made once to change the name to something more suitable for the Catskills' highest peak.

Walking to the summit of Slide Mountain is very popular, and on fine days the summit can become crowded, so an early start is advised. Ascending by foot to the summit of the highest mountain in the Catskills is most rewarding and leaves the hiker with a great feeling of accomplishment. The view from the somewhat rounded top is becoming more limited as the trees grow in, but many other vistas can be seen on the way. It has been claimed that all the other Catskill Mountains higher than 3,500 feet can be seen from viewpoints on or near Slide Mountain's summit.

This hike uses part of the Phoenicia–East Branch Trail, ascends on the Curtis-Ormsbee Trail, and returns on the Wittenberg-Cornell-Slide Trail, also known as the Burroughs Range Trail.

HOW TO GET THERE

Take the New York State Thruway (I-87) to Exit 19 (Kingston), and head west on NY 28 for approximately 30 miles to the small town of Big Indian. Turn left and proceed south onto County Route 47 (Slide Mountain Road) for about 6 miles to a hairpin turn in the road, then continue for another 2 miles, past the Winnisook Club, to a parking area for Slide Mountain, marked by a wooden sign, on the left side of the road.

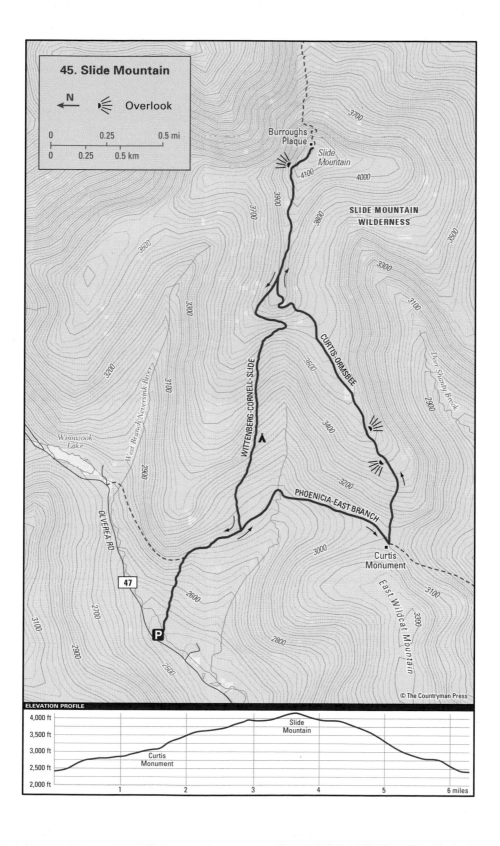

45. Slide Mountain

N ←   ⋘ Overlook

| 0 | 0.25 | 0.5 mi |
| 0 | 0.25 | 0.5 km |

Burroughs Plaque

Slide Mountain

SLIDE MOUNTAIN WILDERNESS

CURTIS-ORMSBEE

WITTENBERG-CORNELL-SLIDE

PHOENICIA-EAST BRANCH

West Branch Neversink River

Winnisook Lake

Deer Shanty Brook

Curtis Monument

East Wildcat Mountain

OLIVEREA RD

47

P

© The Countryman Press

ELEVATION PROFILE

4,000 ft					Slide			
3,500 ft					Mountain			
3,000 ft			Curtis					
2,500 ft			Monument					
2,000 ft								
	1	2	3	4	5	6 miles		

At the summit of Slide Mountain

TOM BALCERSKI

Please sign in the register (and sign out when you return). Signing in not only helps to monitor trail use but also could be useful should you need help while on the trail.

THE TRAIL

From the parking area, proceed east on the yellow-blazed Phoenicia–East Branch Trail, which crosses the West Branch of the Neversink River on rocks, and then climbs on a rocky footpath, reaching an old woods road in 0.4 mile. Follow the yellow-blazed trail as it turns right and runs along the level woods road. In another 0.3 mile, after passing a spring to the left, you will reach a junction with the red-blazed Wittenberg-Cornell-Slide Trail, marked by wooden New York State Department of Environmental

Conservation (DEC) signs. This red-blazed trail will be your return road, but for now, continue ahead along the old road, following the yellow markers. The road briefly narrows to a footpath and then descends to cross a stream on a wooden bridge.

About 1.5 miles from the start, you'll reach another junction—this one, with the blue-blazed Curtis-Ormsbee Trail. This trail was named after two well-known hikers—"Father" Bill Curtis, a sportswriter and an official of the Fresh Air Club of New York, and Allen Ormsbee—who both perished in a snowstorm on Mount Washington, New Hampshire, in June 1900 on their way to an Appalachian Mountain Club meeting at the summit (a stone monument at the junction commemorates this tragic event). Turn left here and follow the blue blazes of the Curtis-Ormsbee Trail.

The trail climbs to the top of a large rock and then continues to ascend. After a short, steep section, it reaches a viewpoint to the north from a rock outcrop on the left side of the trail. Just beyond, you'll pass the DEC sign that marks elevation 3,500 feet, above which camping and fires are not permitted.

In another 0.2 mile, in a flat area, a yellow-blazed side trail on the right leads about 200 feet to an outstanding south-facing viewpoint. Directly ahead is the unmistakable flat top of Table Mountain; Van Wyck Mountain is to the right, and Lone Mountain and the smaller bumps of Rocky and Balsam Cap Mountains are to the left. Below is the valley

of Deer Shanty Brook and, over the ridge behind, the valley of the East Branch of the Neversink.

When you're ready to continue, backtrack to the main trail and turn right, continuing to follow the blue blazes. Proceed upward through one of the loveliest parts of the hike as the trail heads through a quiet and peaceful stand of balsam fir until the junction with the Wittenberg-Cornell-Slide Trail is reached. Your target is very close now, with only 0.65 mile of gentle walking to the summit. Turn right and follow the red trail, which once served as the road to a fire tower on the summit, as it proceeds on a relatively level path along the summit ridge. In about 0.5 mile, you'll reach an excellent

Table Mountain from the Curtis-Ormsbee Trail

DANIEL CHAZIN

Slide Mountain

viewpoint to the left of the trail. Particularly impressive is the view of Panther Mountain and Giant Ledge, apparently only a stone's throw down to the left. Wittenberg and Cornell Mountains are below and beyond, Hunter Mountain and the Devil's Path are to the right, and the Blackhead Range is on the horizon. The Ashokan Reservoir is also visible from this viewpoint.

Continue ahead and you'll soon reach the actual summit (elevation 4,180 feet), marked by the remains of the foundation of the former fire tower. There are no views from here, but just beyond, you'll come to a large rock ledge which overlooks Cornell and Wittenberg Mountains to the east. Beyond these peaks is the 12-mile-long Ashokan Reservoir. Completed in 1915, the reservoir displaced several hamlets and farms from the Esopus Valley and was the first in a series of reservoirs built in the Catskills to supply New York City with water. The water is gravity fed via underground tunnels to supply the populated city far to the south.

Just below the summit slab is a plaque erected by the Winnisook Club in 1923, commemorating John Burroughs's work.

Slide Mountain was one of Burroughs's favorite places. He visited many times, and one of his most widely read essays is entitled *In the Heart of the Catskill Mountains.* This famous writer, who died in 1921 at the age of 84, had a multifaceted career. A farmer's son, he taught school in his youth and became a journalist in New York City, a treasury clerk in Washington, D.C., as well as a bank examiner.

When you are ready to leave this high point, walk back to the junction with the Curtis-Ormsbee Trail, but now go straight ahead on the red-blazed Wittenberg-Cornell-Slide Trail, which soon bends sharply to the left and then to the right. After these two sharp turns, the trail continues down the mountain on a wide but very rocky path. This route offers no views and is much less interesting than the Curtis-Ormsbee Trail that you used to climb the mountain, but it is also shorter and faster. When, after 1.5 miles, you reach the junction with the Phoenicia–East Branch Trail where you were earlier in the hike, turn right and retrace your footsteps back to your car, taking care not to miss the left turn from the woods road.

46

Huckleberry Point

Total distance: 4.8 miles

Walking time: 3 hours

Vertical rise: 1,250 feet

Maps: USGS 7.5' Kaaterskill; NY–NJTC Catskill Trails #141

Trailhead GPS Coordinates:
N 42° 07' 59" W 74° 04' 54.5"

This hike is mostly in the Kaaterskill Wild Forest area of the Catskill Forest Preserve, though the trail begins on private land, and for relatively little effort, it gives the hiker a true feel of the Catskill Mountains. In the early 19th century, places such as Plattekill Clove were used as subjects by artists of the Hudson River School, founded by Thomas Cole. The Huckleberry Point Trail passes through hardwoods, mountain laurel, and pitch pine, goes by old walls and foundations, crosses a delightful stream, and finally leads to a fabulous viewpoint where turkey vultures often soar on the thermal updrafts.

HOW TO GET THERE

Take the New York State Thruway (I-87) to Exit 20 (Saugerties). After the toll booths, turn left onto NY 212/NY 32, and continue straight ahead at the next intersection to stay on NY 212. In 2.3 miles, turn right onto County Route 35 (Blue Mountain Road). In another 1.5 miles, turn left to continue on County Route 35, now designated as West Saugerties Road. Continue ahead on West Saugerties Road when it becomes County Route 33 and then Platte Clove Road, which climbs through Platte Clove on a steep, narrow road. Just beyond the crest of the rise, turn right at a trailhead parking sign and proceed to the parking area (about 150 feet up a gravel road).

Note: The section of Platte Clove Road that climbs steeply from West Saugerties is closed in the winter (from November 1 to April 15). During this period, the trailhead should be accessed via NY 23A. Take Thruway Exit 20 and turn left after the toll

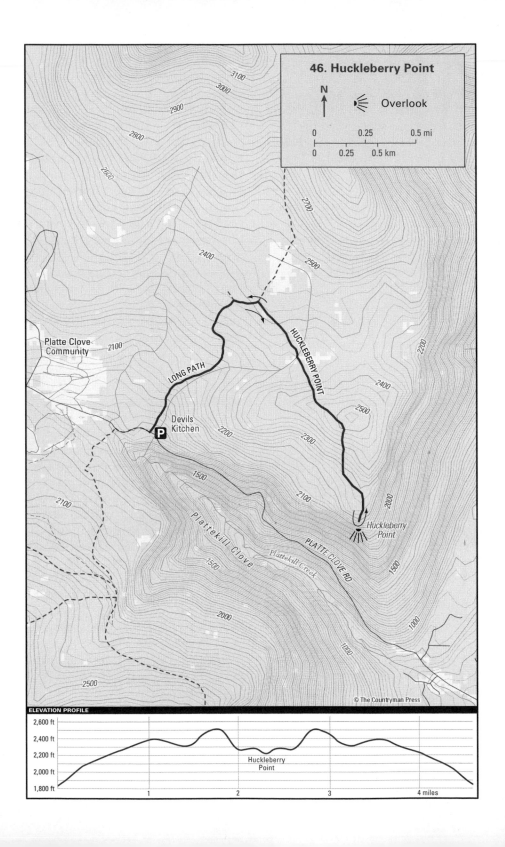

46. Huckleberry Point

N

Overlook

0   0.25   0.5 mi

0   0.25   0.5 km

3100
3000
2900
2800
2600
2700
2500
2400
2200
2400
2500
2300
2100
2000
2100
2000
2500
1500
1500
1000
1000
1500

Platte Clove
Community

LONG PATH

HUCKLEBERRY POINT

Devils
Kitchen

P

Plattekill Clove

Plattekill Creek

PLATTE CLOVE RD

Huckleberry
Point

© The Countryman Press

ELEVATION PROFILE

2,600 ft
2,400 ft
2,200 ft
2,000 ft
1,800 ft

Huckleberry
Point

1   2   3   4 miles

booths onto NY 212/NY 32, but after crossing over the Thruway, turn right onto NY 32. In 6 miles, where NY 32 bears right, continue straight ahead onto NY 32A. In 1.9 miles, when NY 32A ends, turn left onto NY 23A and follow it up Kaaterskill Clove and through the village of Haines Falls. At the traffic light in the next village, Tannersville, turn left onto Depot Road and continue ahead on Spruce Street (County Route 16). When Spruce Street ends at a T-junction, turn left onto Platte Clove Road and continue for 4.9 miles to the trailhead parking area, on the left side of the road.

THE TRAIL

Leave the parking area at the gate, and begin walking uphill on Steenberg Road, a steep and rocky road which is the route of the Long Path. The trail is marked by blue New York State Department of Environmental Conservation (DEC) discs, snowmobile trail markers, and the aqua blazes of the Long Path. Be aware that, particularly in hunting season when the gate is opened, you may encounter ATVs. Bear right at a junction at 0.7 mile and again at another junction 0.25 mile beyond.

View from Huckleberry Point

DAN BALOGH

Huckleberry Point

View from Huckleberry Point
DAN BALOGH

About 500 feet beyond the second junction, turn right onto the yellow-blazed Huckleberry Point Trail, which descends slightly to cross Mossy Brook. Crossing this stream is usually not a problem, but it might be difficult if the water is high.

Notice the stone walls, piles of rocks, and old foundations—remnants from the early settlement of the area. Occasionally you may also spot some old tin lid markers that were used by the Nature Friends, who first blazed the trail, to mark the route.

Once across Mossy Brook, the Huckleberry Point Trail levels off, but it soon begins to climb through hemlocks, which eventually give way to mountain laurel, and finally to pitch pine. It reaches the high point of the hike (2,500 feet), then begins to descend rather steeply toward Huckleberry Point, on ledges high above Platte Clove.

These steep ledges afford a broad panorama, with Overlook, Plattekill, Indian Head, and Twin Mountains visible to the south and west. To the southeast, you can see the tower on Sky Top at the Mohonk Mountain House in the Shawangunks. Take time to enjoy this stunning spot before retracing your footsteps to your car.

47

Windham High Peak

Total distance: 6.8 miles

Walking time: 5 hours

Vertical rise: 1,900 feet

Maps: USGS 7.5' Ashland; NY–NJTC Catskill Trails #141

Trailhead GPS Coordinates: N 42° 18' 47" W 74° 11' 25"

The hike to Windham High Peak at the northern end of the Escarpment Trail is a delightful one. The terrain is varied, and the climb is steady and relatively easy. A sense of history can be felt while walking past meadows and old stone walls. Sections of the trail pass through groves of Norway spruce, and there are panoramic views from the summit ridge, both to the north and to the south. Windham was once a site for the Catskill tanneries that supplied most of the saddles used in the Civil War. South American hides were shipped for processing into leather, and the bark from hemlock trees was used to tan the hides.

HOW TO GET THERE

Take the New York State Thruway (I-87) to Exit 21 (Catskill, Cairo). Turn left at the end of the ramp onto Main Street, then turn right onto NY 23 West. Continue on NY 23 West for about 19 miles to Windham. About 1 mile after a sign indicating that you are entering the Catskill Park, turn right at Cross Road and then immediately turn left into the trailhead parking lot.

THE TRAIL

You will be following the Escarpment Trail, blazed with blue New York State Department of Environmental Conservation (DEC) disks, for the entire hike. This trail is also the route of the Long Path, and you may see Long Path logo markers at junctions along the way. The trail begins on the southeast side of NY 23 (opposite the parking lot). Cross the road at the mileage sign for the Escarpment

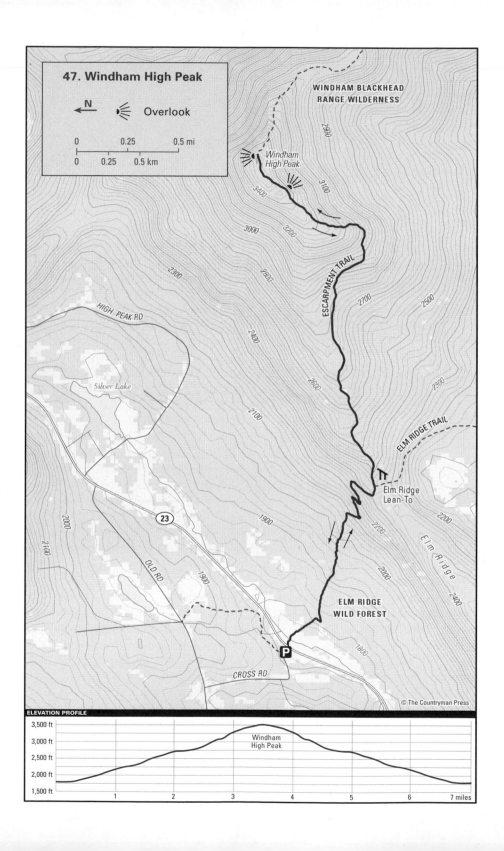

47. Windham High Peak

← N 🔆 Overlook

0	0.25	0.5 mi
0	0.25	0.5 km

WINDHAM BLACKHEAD
RANGE WILDERNESS

2900

Windham
High Peak

3400

3100

3000

3200

ESCARPMENT TRAIL

2300

2800

2700

2500

2400

2600

HIGH PEAK RD

Silver Lake

2100

ELM RIDGE TRAIL

2300

Elm Ridge
Lean-To

2000

1900

23

2200

Elm Ridge

2200

OLD RD

1900

2000

ELM RIDGE
WILD FOREST

2400

2100

P

1800

CROSS RD

© The Countryman Press

ELEVATION PROFILE

Windham
High Peak

| 3,500 ft |
| 3,000 ft |
| 2,500 ft |
| 2,000 ft |
| 1,500 ft |

1   2   3   4   5   6   7 miles

Blackhead Range from Windham High Peak DANIEL CHAZIN

Trail, cross the bridge, and continue on a flat, grassy trail for 0.2 mile to the register. Please sign in (and out on your return).

After about 1 mile of climbing, you'll reach a junction with the yellow-blazed Elm Ridge Trail. Bear left at the junction to continue on the Escarpment Trail, soon passing the Elm Ridge Lean-to on the right.

About 2 miles from the start, the first in a series of stands of Norway spruce is reached. The large and tangled roots of these trees are exposed, and the ground is often wet. Puncheons have been built in places to aid the hiker, but care must be taken when walking on the roots because they are slippery when wet. These dark and gloomy sections give a primeval feeling to your walk, and the silence beneath the trees

can almost be touched. Between the two sections of Norway spruce, the trail opens out into a tranquil meadow.

The following section is quite different. The trees become thinner and the trail more rugged. After climbing a little more, the trail levels off for a short stretch. It soon resumes a gradual climb, with views to the right through the trees over the Blackhead Range. About 2.7 miles into the hike, the trail turns sharply left and begins to climb quite steeply. This section is the steepest of the entire climb. After gaining about 200 feet in elevation, the grade moderates.

You'll know that you're near the summit when you see a sign marking the 3,500-foot elevation on a tree to the left of the trail. A short distance beyond, a side trail to the

North-facing view from Windham High Peak

DANIEL CHAZIN

right leads to a panoramic viewpoint over the Blackhead Range from a rock ledge. You'll want to pause here to rest from the climb and admire the view.

Continue ahead on the Escarpment Trail, which climbs a little to the actual summit. At 3,524 feet, Windham High Peak is the second lowest of the Catskill peaks over 3,500 feet in elevation, but it offers a view that is among the very best of all of the peaks. Proceed ahead a short distance beyond the summit, descending a little, and you'll soon notice an open rock ledge on the left. Since Windham High Peak is the most northerly of all the Catskill 3,500 peaks, on a clear day you can see across the Schoharie and Mohawk Valleys to Albany, with the southern Adirondacks visible beyond.

After taking in the view, retrace your steps on the Escarpment Trail down to the junction with the Elm Ridge Trail. Bear right at the junction, and follow the Escarpment Trail back to the parking area where the hike began.

48

South Taconic Trail

Total distance: 12 miles

Walking time: 8 hours

Vertical rise: 1,600 feet

Maps: USGS 7.5' Copake (NY/MA); USGS 7.5' Bash Bish Falls; NY–NJTC South Taconic Trails

Trailhead GPS Coordinates: N 42° 05' 09" W 73° 27' 42.5"

Forming the border between New York State and Massachusetts and Connecticut is a sentinel line of hills. A 15-mile range trail follows the crest, paralleling the border. This most eastern of New York's great trails is a relative newcomer, built between 1972 and 1976 by Bob Redington and Frank Cary, both residents of Connecticut. This loop hike begins in Mount Washington State Forest in Massachusetts, continues into Connecticut, and then proceeds into New York, where it joins the South Taconic Trail. Along the way, you'll pass the monument that marks the point where Massachusetts, Connecticut, and New York touch.

The Taconics are remnants of a thrust mass of mostly unmetamorphosed shales ranging from Cambrian to Middle Ordovician in age. The ancestral Taconics, products of violent upheavals known as the Taconic orogeny, eroded away; sands and gravels from the mountains were washed west into a sea whose waves deposited a thick layer of the quartz-pebble conglomerate; its later upthrust became the Shawangunks. By Late Silurian times, only the eroded vestiges of the original Taconic Mountains remained, and fine muds and limestones again accumulated in a shallow sea, forming the bed of Upper Silurian limestone near Pine Plains and beneath Stissing Mountain. From overlooks on the Taconic Ridge, this quiet plain contrasts vividly with the forces that created the mountains on which you'll walk.

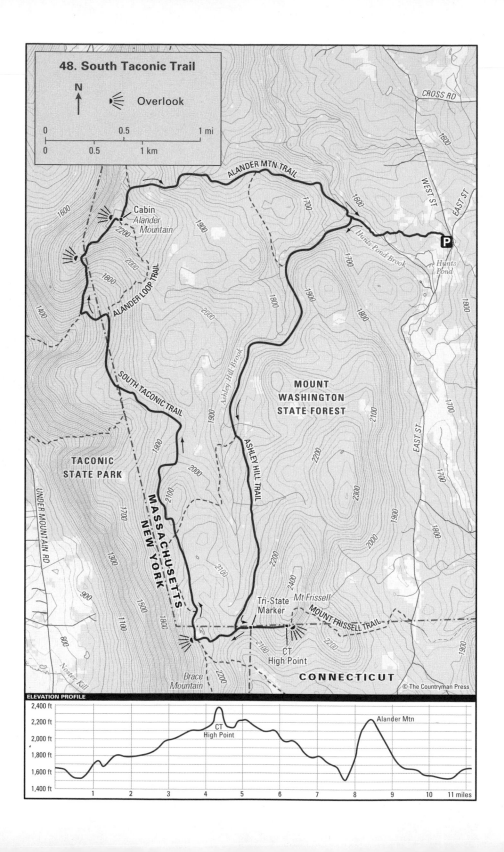

48. South Taconic Trail

N

Overlook

0   0.5   1 mi
0   0.5   1 km

CROSS RD

1600

ALANDER MTN TRAIL

1700

1600

WEST ST

EAST ST

Cabin
Alander Mountain

2200

Hunts Pond Brook

1700

P

Hunts Pond

1800

1900

ALANDER LOOP TRAIL

2000

1800

1400

1800

1900

1800

1700

1600

SOUTH TACONIC TRAIL

2000

Ashley Hill Brook

MOUNT
WASHINGTON
STATE FOREST

2100

EAST ST

1700

1700

TACONIC
STATE PARK

1900

ASHLEY HILL TRAIL

2200

2300

1900

2000

UNDER MOUNTAIN RD

1700

1300

2100

MASSACHUSETTS
NEW YORK

2000

900

1500

1100

1800

2200

2400

Tri-State
Marker

Mt Frissell

MOUNT FRISSELL TRAIL

2200

1900

800

Nester Kill

2100

CT
High Point

Brace Mountain

2200

CONNECTICUT

© The Countryman Press

ELEVATION PROFILE

2,400 ft											
2,200 ft											
2,000 ft											
1,800 ft											
1,600 ft											
1,400 ft											

CT
High Point

Alander Mtn

1   2   3   4   5   6   7   8   9   10   11 miles

HOW TO GET THERE

Take NY 22 north to NY 344 in Copake
Falls. Turn right onto NY 344 and proceed
east, entering Massachusetts (where the
road becomes Falls Road). In 3.3 miles, turn
right onto West Street. In about 1 mile, continue ahead on East Street, a gravel road.
When you again reach a paved road, make
the next right into the headquarters of Mount
Washington State Forest and continue to
the parking area.

THE TRAIL

From the kiosk near the end of the parking
area, enter the woods, following the Alander
Mountain Trail, which is not blazed at this
point. In 0.8 mile, after crossing a brook on
a footbridge, you'll come to an intersection
(marked by a sign) with the blue-blazed Ashley Hill Trail. Turn left and follow this pleasant trail for the next 3.5 miles, paralleling a
brook for much of the way. In 1 mile, proceed straight ahead where a side trail leads
right to a camping area, but be sure to turn
sharply left in 2 miles at a junction (also
marked by a sign) to continue on the Ashley
Hill Trail.

In 3.4 miles from the start of this trail,
you'll pass on the right a Massachusetts–
New York boundary monument placed in
1898. A short distance beyond, you'll reach
an intersection with the red-blazed Mount
Frissell Trail. Turn left onto this trail, which
soon begins to climb.

In a short distance, you'll pass another
boundary monument that marks the point
common to three states—Massachusetts,
New York, and Connecticut. Interestingly,
although the names of Massachusetts and
New York are inscribed on the monument,
the name of Connecticut is not. Continue
ahead, climbing a little more steeply, and in
another 0.25 mile, you'll reach the highest

Tri-state boundary marker   DANIEL CHAZIN

point in Connecticut (marked by a green
pipe and a cairn), with views south over Riga
Lake. Proceed ahead on the trail for another
200 feet, and you'll come to an even more
expansive viewpoint to the southeast.

Now retrace your steps to the junction
with the Ashley Hill Trail, and continue ahead
on the Mount Frissell Trail to its terminus at
the white-blazed South Taconic Trail. Turn
right onto the South Taconic Trail, and you'll
immediately reach a panoramic viewpoint
over New York to the west and Brace Mountain to the south. The trail continues along

South Taconic Trail

Along the South Taconic Trail

DANIEL CHAZIN

open rocks, with more views, for another 0.25 mile, then reenters the woods.

Continue ahead on the South Taconic Trail for the next 3.7 miles, proceeding ahead on the white-blazed trail at several intersections with blue- and red-blazed trails. After reaching an intersection in about 2.7 miles with the blue-blazed Alander Loop Trail, the South Taconic Trail bears left onto a footpath and descends rather steeply (on the way, rejoining the woods road). It crosses a brook at the base of the descent and soon turns right, leaving the woods road (be alert for this turn, which is easy to miss).

After steeply climbing about 600 vertical feet, the South Taconic Trail emerges on open rocks, near the New York–Massachusetts boundary, with spectacular views to the west and south. The trail continues along the ridge for another 0.5 mile until it reaches the west summit of Alander Mountain (marked by foundations of a former fire tower), with more views.

As you descend, you will see a cabin below to the left. Bear left and pass in front of the cabin, then continue ahead on the white-blazed Alander Mountain Trail. Follow this trail for about 3 miles back to the parking area where the hike began.

49

Vroman's Nose

Total distance: 1.4 miles

Walking time: 1.5 hours

Vertical rise: 500 feet

Maps: USGS 7.5' Middleburgh

Trailhead GPS Coordinates:
N 42° 35' 41" W 74° 21' 29"

Rising abruptly from the surrounding landscape, the cliffs of Vroman's Nose command a striking view across the peaceful farmlands of the Schoharie Valley. This short hike offers a splendid reward for a modest effort.

In 1712, the Dutch pioneer Adam Vroman purchased fertile land in the Schoharie Valley from Native Americans. Included in the purchase was the prominence that came to be known as Vroman's Nose. The local Iroquois called this mountain *Onistagrawa,* or Corn Mountain. Middleburgh Village began as a fort established during the American Revolution. The mountain was of greatest interest for hikers, and in 1983 local residents formed the Vroman's Nose Preservation Corporation to save the mountain from development. It will now be maintained in its "forever wild" state for all of us to enjoy.

Vroman's Nose is on the route of the Long Path, a 350-mile hiking trail that runs from the George Washington Bridge to north of John Boyd Thacher State Park (see Hike 50).

HOW TO GET THERE
Take the New York State Thruway (I-87) to Exit 21 (Catskill, Cairo), and turn left at the end of the ramp. Take the next right turn onto NY 23 West and continue for 8 miles to a fork, where you bear right onto NY 145. Follow NY 145 for about 28 miles to the village of Middleburgh. Turn left (south) onto NY 30 for 0.6 mile, then turn right onto Mill Valley Road and continue for another 0.6 mile to a parking area on the left with a sign: VROMAN'S NOSE TRAILS.

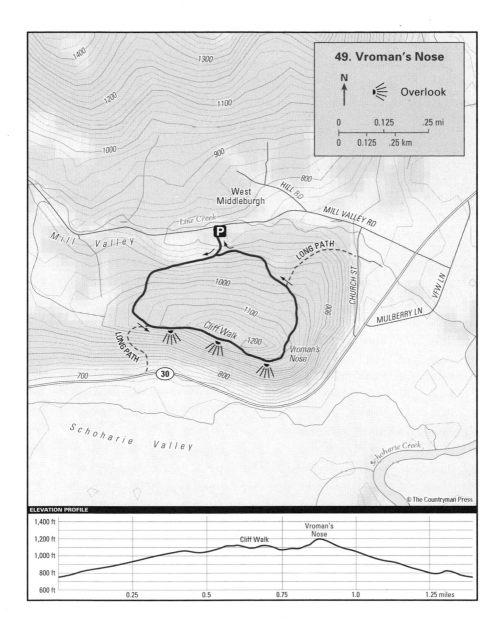

49. Vroman's Nose

N

≋ Overlook

0   0.125   .25 mi

0   0.125   .25 km

West Middleburgh

Line Creek

P

Mill Valley

HILL RD

MILL VALLEY RD

LONG PATH

CHURCH ST

VFW LN

1000

1100

Cliff Walk

1200

LONG PATH

900

MULBERRY LN

Vroman's Nose

700

30

800

Schoharie Valley

Schoharie Creek

© The Countryman Press

ELEVATION PROFILE

1,400 ft					
1,200 ft		Cliff Walk	Vroman's Nose		
1,000 ft					
800 ft					
600 ft	0.25	0.5	0.75	1.0	1.25 miles

To reach Middleburgh from the Albany area, take I-88 to Exit 23 and follow NY 30A and NY 30 south to Middleburgh; then continue as above to the trailhead.

If you wish to follow your hike on Vroman's Nose with a visit to the Indian Ladder Trail in John Boyd Thacher State Park (Hike 50), proceed north on NY 30 for about 6 miles to the historic village of Schoharie. A short distance beyond the village, turn right onto NY 443 and follow it for 14 miles to a sign for NY 157A. Turn left and continue on NY 157A

View from Vroman's Nose

DANIEL CHAZIN

and NY 157 for 4 miles to the entrance to Thacher State Park on the left (signs indicate the route to the park from NY 443).

THE TRAIL

From the parking area, proceed uphill around a gate and follow along a barbed wire fence on the right. You'll notice a yellow-blazed trail that begins on the left. This will be your return route, but for now, continue uphill on a green-blazed woods road through a hemlock grove, with a grassy field below on the right. Where the road is blocked off with branches, turn left and continue heading uphill on a footpath through a pine grove, still following the green blazes. With a private home visible on the right, the trail curves to the left and passes the trailhead of an orange-blazed trail on the left.

A short distance beyond, you'll reach a junction (marked by a trail register; please sign) where the aqua-blazed Long Path comes in from the right. Bear left and follow the aqua blazes uphill. Soon you'll come to a panoramic viewpoint over the Schoharie Valley on the right. This is the first of many viewpoints along this trail. The trail continues to climb more steeply, passing more viewpoints.

At the top of the climb, you'll reach an extensive flat rock slab at the top of a 500-foot cliff. The unobstructed views of the valley below reveal a pastoral scene of farm fields, with hills in the background. In the distance,

Village of Middleburgh from Vroman's Nose

DANIEL CHAZIN

you can see the peaks of the northern Catskills.

Aside from the great views, the top is a story in itself. You are standing on Hamilton Sandstone, rich in fossils from the mid-Devonian age. Thin sheets of this stone were once used for sidewalks in nearby cities. Just after the Civil War, local residents cleared the top of Vroman's Nose for square dancing. Some of the names you see carved in the rock date back to 1863 (unfortunately, some of the carvings are much more recent—please leave this area as you find it and do not add any of your own). Some of the dwarf red cedars along the top of the cliffs are thought to be at least 150 years old.

The Long Path continues along the summit ridge for the next 0.3 mile, running very close to the edge of the escarpment for most of the way, with more spectacular views. As it approaches the eastern end of the summit, the trail curves to the left. You can now see the Schoharie Creek meandering through the valley below, with the village of Middleburgh beyond. You also get a good view of the layers of the sandstone cliffs from this location.

When you're ready to continue, follow the aqua blazes down the mountain (they are now joined by blue blazes, marking a co-aligned trail beginning at the overlook). The first part of the descent is very steep, and extreme caution should be exercised, especially if the trail is covered with leaves. As the descent moderates, you'll pass the other end of the orange-blazed trail on the left. Continue ahead, following the aqua and blue blazes. When you reach a T-junction, turn left (following the sign to the parking lot) and proceed along the yellow-blazed trail, which continues to descend more gradually. When you reach the end of the yellow-blazed trail at the barbed wire fence, turn right and head down along the fence to the parking area where the hike began.

Especially if you're coming from a distance, you might want to combine your Vroman's Nose hike with the Indian Ladder Trail in John Boyd Thacher State Park (Hike 50). Directions to Thacher State Park from Vroman's Nose are set forth above. On the way, you'll pass through the historic village of Schoharie, where the Old Stone Fort museum (www.schohariehistory.net/OSF .htm; 518-295-7192) is well worth a visit. An informative history of the Vroman's Nose area—written by Vincent Schaefer, who conceived the idea of the Long Path—is available for purchase at the museum. Another nearby attraction worth visiting (especially if you're bringing children along) is Howe Caverns (www.howecaverns.com; 518-296-8990). To reach the caverns (open year-round) take NY 145 north from Middleburgh. In 7.5 miles, just beyond I-88, turn right onto NY 7 and follow signs to the caverns.

50

Indian Ladder Trail, John Boyd Thacher State Park

Total Distance: 1 mile

Walking time: 1 hour

Vertical rise: 200 feet

Maps: USGS 7.5' Altamont; Thacher State Park

Trailhead GPS Coordinates:
N 42° 39' 18" W 74° 01' 05"

John Boyd Thacher State Park protects some 6 miles of cliffs and rock slopes, a significant portion of the Helderberg Escarpment. The Helderbergs form a dramatic and readily recognizable ridgeline extending north from the Catskill Mountains. This hike includes a walk along the base of the cliffs, passing underneath two waterfalls. The return along the top provides views across the Mohawk and Hudson Valleys toward Albany, the Adirondacks, the Taconics, and even Vermont's Green Mountains—views that are nothing short of magnificent.

Trails throughout the park are open for hiking, biking (limited to designated trails), snowshoeing, and groomed cross-country skiing. While the described hike is very short, Thacher Park offers additional trails and many other activities to occupy your day. There is the year-round Emma Treadwell Thacher Nature Center (named for Thacher's widow), camping at nearby Thompson Lake, and many fine picnic areas—some with reservable pavilions. You may also want to combine your trip to Thacher Park with a hike on Vroman's Nose (Hike 49). Keep in mind that the Indian Ladder Trail is open seasonally, usually May 1 through November 15. You may wish to call ahead to be sure: 518-872-1237.

John Boyd Thacher (1847–1909) was known as an author, bibliophile, and public servant. As a state senator and two-time mayor of Albany (1886–88, 1896–98), he is remembered as a dedicated public-minded official. A discriminating book collector, Thacher assembled one of only two dozen

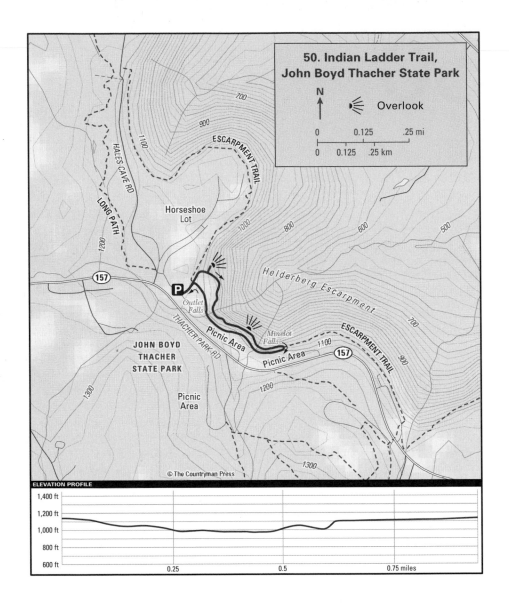

50. Indian Ladder Trail, John Boyd Thacher State Park

N

◖≋ Overlook

| 0 | 0.125 | .25 mi |
| 0 | 0.125 | .25 km |

700
900
1100
ESCARPMENT TRAIL
HALES CAVE RD
LONG PATH
1200
Horseshoe Lot
1000
800
600
500
157
Helderberg Escarpment
P
Outlet Falls
Picnic Area
Minelot Falls
Picnic Area
ESCARPMENT TRAIL
1100
700
900
157
JOHN BOYD THACHER STATE PARK
THACHER PARK RD
1300
1200
Picnic Area
1300
© The Countryman Press

ELEVATION PROFILE

| 1,400 ft |
| 1,200 ft |
| 1,000 ft |
| 800 ft |
| 600 ft |
| | 0.25 | 0.5 | 0.75 miles |

or so sets of the signatures of the signers of the Declaration of Independence, a collection now housed at the Library of Congress. As a writer, he made a meaningful contribution to our understanding of American history with his multivolume *Christopher Columbus* (1903–04) as well as several other books. In 1914, Emma Thacher, as a memorial to her husband's love for his community, gave the core 400 acres of the park to the people of New York.

___

HOW TO GET THERE

Take the New York State Thruway (I-87) to Exit 22 (Selkirk). After the toll booths, turn right onto NY 144 South and proceed for

The North Country and the Catskills

Along the Indian Ladder Trail

DANIEL CHAZIN

Overhanging rocks at Minelot Falls

DANIEL CHAZIN

a short distance to its junction with NY 396. Turn right onto NY 396, proceed for 6 miles, and continue straight onto County Route 301. In another 6 miles, you'll reach Clarksville, where County Route 301 ends at a junction with NY 433. Turn right onto NY 433, and follow it for 1.9 miles to NY 85. Turn right, and proceed on NY 85 East for 2.1 miles to NY 157. Turn left onto NY 157 and continue for 3.7 miles to the main entrance to John Boyd Thacher State Park (you will pass several picnic areas along the road, as well as an overlook, before reaching the main park entrance). There is a seasonal entrance fee. Immediately beyond the entrance booth, turn right and proceed to the Indian Ladder Trail parking lot.

To reach Thacher State Park from Albany, take I-90 to Exit 4 and proceed south on NY 85 to NY 157. Turn right onto NY 157 and proceed to the park.

THE TRAIL

The hike itself is simple and very easy to follow. It is also very popular, and you're likely to share the experience with a crowd, especially if you come on a weekend. If you arrive on a weekday in the spring or fall, though, you may have the trail to yourself.

From the parking area, follow a path to the right of a restroom building and continue down a flagstone staircase. At the base of the staircase, you'll notice another flagstone staircase that descends between two wooden fences. Continue down this staircase, which follows the route of the historic Indian Ladder.

Why the name "Indian Ladder"? Verplanck Colvin, famous to hikers as an Adirondack surveyor, was one of the first people to write about the Helderbergs. In 1869 he wrote: "What is this Indian Ladder so often mentioned? In 1710 this Helderberg region was a wilderness; nay, all westward of the Hudson River settlement was unknown. Albany was a frontier town, a trading post, a place where annuities were paid and blankets exchanged with Indians for beaver pelts. From Albany over the sand plains . . . led an Indian trail westward. Straight as the wild bee or the crow, the wild Indian made his course from the white man's settlement to his own home in the beauteous Schoharie Valley. The stem cliffs of these hills opposed his progress: his hatchet fells a tree against the stumps of the branches, which he trimmed away and formed the round of the Indian ladder."

The Indian Ladder was originally used to climb the cliffs at this location. It was removed in 1828, when the Indian Ladder Road was built. To complete this road, the cliffs were blasted away. Until about 1920, when it was abandoned, the road was used as a route to transport goods from farms in the Helderbergs to the Meadowdale train station in the valley below. Interpretive signs along the flagstone staircase provide historical information. The staircase itself seems somewhat incongruous—a modern-looking intrusion at this historic site—but the rest of the trail has a more natural appearance.

At the base of the staircase, wooden stairs lead ahead to a viewing platform, which offers a panoramic east-facing view. The main trail descends a set of metal steps and continues along the base of the cliffs on a dirt footpath. Along its 0.4-mile route, the trail crosses a wooden bridge over the outlet of an underground stream and passes under Outlet Falls. A short distance beyond, it passes under Minelot Falls, even more dramatic than Outlet Falls. Here a broad pocket has formed from the eroded limestone, and you walk beneath overhanging cliffs. If it has been wet, the falls will roar down and you'll be able to walk behind them. In dry seasons, the falls may be only a trickle. Towards the end, the trail goes under a rock formation with a clearance of only about four feet—you will have to duck to pass underneath. At the end of the cliffs, the trail climbs 71 metal, wooden and flagstone steps and returns to top of the cliffs.

Turn right and follow the wooden fence along the cliff edge, paralleling the route you followed along the base of the cliffs. You'll be afforded some more panoramic views along the way. When you reach the start of the Indian Ladder Trail, continue up the flagstone steps to the parking area where the hike began.

Glossary

"lollipop"-loop hike: Out and back on the same trails with a loop in the middle.

benchmark: A permanent metal disk at a known elevation used for surveying.

blaze: A trail marking that can be either a painted symbol on a tree or a metal or plastic marker.

bog bridges: A low boardwalk over fragile terrain that is often wet.

bushwhack: Walking off trail to reach a goal.

cairn: A pile of stones to indicate a trail junction or the route of a trail.

carriageways: Also known as carriage roads. Long-established horse and carriage routes. Most often found on old estates.

col: A pass between two peaks or a gap in a ridgeline.

erratic: Large boulder assumed to have been left by a retreating glacier and usually of a different rock type from that in its vicinity.

herd path: An unmarked footway (see bushwhack).

lean-to: A three-sided shelter used for overnight stays.

marker: A metal or plastic disk nailed to a tree to indicate the route of a trail.

puncheons: See "bog bridges."

ravine: A deep narrow cleft in the earth's surface usually caused by runoff.

saddle: A ridge between two peaks.

scree slope: A slope covered with small rocks and gravel that have broken away from the cliffs above.

stile: A structure built over a fence or wall that allows hikers to cross without having to deal with a gate.

switchback: A trail that zigzags on the side of a steep ridge, hill, or mountain, which allows for a more gradual and less strenuous ascent or descent, thus preventing erosion.

talus slope: Talus slopes are more angled than scree slopes. Talus is also larger than scree, and the rocks have sharper edges, all of which makes a talus slope far more dangerous to cross and more difficult to scramble up or down.

through-hiker: A hiker attempting to hike an entire long-distance trail from end to end in one continuous journey.

trailhead: The beginning/end of a trail.

vernal pools: Small ponds that form in the spring from winter snowmelt and that usually dry up later in the year. Breeding grounds for frogs and salamanders.

woods road: Old dirt road formerly used for farming, logging, or mining activities.

Bibliography

Adler, Cy A. *Walking the Hudson: From the Battery to Bear Mountain.* Woodstock, VT: Countryman Press, 1012.

Anderson, Scott Edward. *Walks in Nature's Empire: Exploring The Nature Conservancy's Preserves in New York State.* Woodstock, VT: Countryman Press, 1995.

Appalachian Trail Guide to New York–New Jersey, 17th edition. Harpers Ferry, WV: Appalachian Trail Conference, 2011.

Binnewies, Robert O. *Palisades: 100,000 Acres in 100 Years.* New York: Fordham University Press & Palisades Interstate Park Commission, 2001.

Buff, Sheila. *Nature Walks In and Around New York City.* Boston: Appalachian Mountain Club Books, 1996.

Burgess, Larry E. *Mohonk, Its People and Spirit: A History of One Hundred Years of Growth and Service,* revised edition. Fleischmanns, NY: Purple Mountain Press, 1993.

_____. *Daniel Smiley of Mohonk: A Naturalist's Life.* Fleischmanns, NY: Purple Mountain Press, 1997.

Chazin, Daniel. *Hike of the Week: A Year of Hikes in the New York Metro Area.* Mahwah, NJ: New York–New Jersey Trail Conference, 2013.

Clyne, Patricia Edwards. *Hudson Valley Tales and Trails.* New York: Overlook Press, reprinted 1997.

Copeland, Cynthia C., and Thomas J. Lewis. *Best Hikes with Children in the Catskills and Hudson River Valley,* 2nd edition. Seattle: Mountaineers Books, 2002.

Daniels, Jane and Walter. *Walkable Westchester.* 2nd edition. Mahwah, NJ: New York–New Jersey Trail Conference, 2014.

Dunwell, Frances. F. *Hudson River Highlands.* New York: Columbia University Press, 1992.

Fagan, Jack. *Scenes and Walks in the Northern Shawangunks,* 3rd edition. Mahwah, NJ: New York–New Jersey Trail Conference, 2006.

Fried, Marc. *Tales from the Shawangunk Mountains. A Naturalist's Musings—A Bushwhacker's Guide,* revised edition. Geneva, NY: W. F. Humphrey Press, 1981.

_____. *The Huckleberry Pickers. A Raucous History of the Shawangunk Mountains.* Hensonville, NY: Black Dome Press, 1995.

_____. *Shawangunk: Adventure, Exploration, History, and Epiphany from a Mountain Wilderness.* Gardiner, NY: M. B. Fried, 1998.

Harrison, Marina, with Lucy D. Rosenfeld. *A Walker's Guidebook: Serendipitous Outings near New York City, Including a Section for Birders.* New York: Michael Kesend Publishing, 1996.

Henry, Edward G. *Catskill Trails: A Ranger's Guide to the High Peaks. Book One: The Northern Catskills.* Hensonville, NY: Black Dome Press, 2000.

_____. *Catskill Trails: A Ranger's Guide to the High Peaks. Book Two: The Central Catskills.* Hensonville, NY: Black Dome Press, 2000.

Kick, Peter. *AMC's Best Hikes in the Catskills and Hudson Valley.* Boston: Appalachian Mountain Club Books, 2006.

_____. *Catskill Mountain Guide.* 2nd edition. Boston: Appalachian Mountain Club Books, 2009.

Kiviat, Erik. *The Northern Shawangunks: An Ecological Survey.* New Paltz, NY: Mohonk Preserve, 1988.

Kudish, Michael. *The Catskill Forest: A History.* Fleischmanns, NY: Purple Mountain Press, 2000.

Lenik, Edward J. *Iron Mine Trails.* Mahwah, NJ: New York–New Jersey Trail Conference, 1996.

Myles, William J. and Daniel Chazin. *Harriman Trails: A Guide and History,* 3rd edition. Mahwah, NJ: New York–New Jersey Trail Conference, 2010.

New York Walk Book: A Companion to the New Jersey Walk Book, 7th edition, revised. Mahwah, NJ: New York–New Jersey Trail Conference, 2005.

O'Brien, Raymond J. *American Sublime: Landscape and Scenery in the Lower Hudson Valley.* New York: Columbia University Press, 1981.

Perls, Jeffrey. *Paths along the Hudson: A Guide to Walking and Biking along the River.* Piscataway, NJ: Rutgers University Press, 1999.

_____. *Shawangunk Trails Companion.* Woodstock, VT: Countryman Press, 2003.

Quinn, George V. *The Catskills: A Winter Sports Guide.* Fleischmanns, NY: Purple Mountain Press, 2001.

Ransom, James M. *Vanishing Ironworks of the Ramapos.* Piscataway, NJ: Rutgers University Press, 1966.

Stalter, Elizabeth "Perk." *Doodletown: Hiking through History in a Vanished Hamlet on the Hudson.* Bear Mountain, N.Y.: Palisades Interstate Park Commission Press, 1996.

Turco, Peggy. *Walks and Rambles in Dutchess and Putnam Counties: A Guide to Ecology and History in Eastern Hudson Valley Parks.* Woodstock, VT: Countryman Press, 1990.

_____. *Walks and Rambles in Westchester and Fairfield Counties: A Nature Lover's Guide to 36 Parks and Sanctuaries.* Woodstock, VT: Countryman Press, 1993.

_____. *Walks and Rambles in the Western Hudson Valley: Landscape, Ecology, and Folklore in Orange and Ulster Counties.* Woodstock, VT: Countryman Press, 1996.

Van Valkenburgh, Norman J. *The Forest Preserve of New York State in the Adirondack and Catskill Mountains: A Short History,* revised edition. Fleischmanns, NY: Purple Mountain Press, 1996.

Via, Alan. *The Catskill 67: A Hiker's Guide to the Catskill 100 Highest Peaks under 3500'.* Lake George, NY: Adirondack Mountain Club, 2012.

Waterman, Laura and Guy. *Forest and Crag: A History of Hiking, Trail Blazing, and Adventure in the Northeast Mountains.* Boston: Appalachian Mountain Club, 1989.

_____. *Backwoods Ethics. Environmental Issues for Hikers and Campers,* 2nd edition. Woodstock, VT: Countryman Press, 1993.

_____. *Wilderness Ethics: Preserving the Spirit of Wildness,* 2nd edition. Woodstock, VT: Countryman Press, 1993.

_____. *A Fine Kind of Madness: Mountain Adventures Tall and True.* Seattle: Mountaineers Books, 2000.

Weinman, Steve. *A Rock with a View: Trails of the Shawangunk Mountains.* New Paltz, NY: One Black Shoe Productions, 1997.

White, Carol and David. *Catskill Day Hikes for All Seasons.* Lake George, NY: Adirondack Mountain Club, 2002.

_____. *Catskill Trails,* 4th edition. Lake George, NY: Adirondack Mountain Club, 2013.

Zuger, Sascha. *Moon New York State Handbook,* 5th edition. Emeryville, CA: Avalon Travel Publishing, 2010.

HIKING MAPS PUBLISHED BY THE NEW YORK–NEW JERSEY TRAIL CONFERENCE:

Catskill Trails, six-map set, 2013

East Hudson Trails, three-map set, 2012

Harriman/Bear Mountain Trails, two-map set, 2013

Hudson Palisades Trails, five-map set, 2012

Shawangunk Trails, three-map set, 2013

South Taconic Trails, 2014

Sterling Forest Trails, 2013

West Hudson Trails, two-map set, 2013

For latest information, see www.nynjtc.org/catalog/maps

USEFUL ROAD MAPS:

Rand McNally/New York City, Metro Area Counties, Long Island

AAA New York State